P9-DML-547

"Trotti, who flew 600 missions, lets the reader feel the energy and adrenalin pumping as he tries to outmaneuver a surface-to-air missile and bores straight down to target to pickle his bombs..."

—SPRINGFIELD MORNING UNION

"From the boredom of the Hot Pad (playing acey-deucy and waiting for the Scramble) to moments of sheer terror when a SAM missile pops out of the cloud cover... you can feel the exhilaration of no-holds-barred combat, then a deep sense of loss as a comrade's plane is shot out of the sky."

—SAN DIEGO UNION

"One can easily conjure up the whine of powerful jet engines, the press of 'Gs' and the grunts of ordnance men humping 500-pound bombs on to bulky ejector racks slung from highly swept wings... the author's descriptions of cockpit procedures, escape from... gravity, and the deadly dance of air-ground attack will awaken strong memories for those who have been there."

—MARINE CORPS GAZETTE

PHANTOM OVER VIETNAM

JOHN TROTTI
FIGHTER PILOT, USMC

BERKLEY BOOKS, NEW YORK

PHANTOM OVER VIETNAM

A Berkley Book / published by arrangement with
Presidio Press

PRINTING HISTORY
Presidio Press edition published 1984
Berkley edition / September 1985
Fourth printing / November 1986

ISBN: 0-425-10248-3

A BERKLEY BOOK ® TM 757,375
Berkley Books are published by The Berkley Publishing Group,
200 Madison Avenue, New York, NY 10016.
The name "BERKLEY" and the stylized "B" with design
are trademarks belonging to Berkley Publishing Corporation.

PRINTED IN THE UNITED STATES OF AMERICA

Contents

Preface

I began *Phantom Over Vietnam* to answer a friend's question, "What was it like to fly one of those thundering smokers in combat?" I've never talked much about the war, partly because the experience was so personal, but more because people didn't seem much interested. Even when I talked "airplanes" (as I am wont to do on most any occasion), I've tended to avoid the military aspects. The question, however, was provocative, and I found myself trying to answer it the easiest way possible, looking for some way I could haul him up (figuratively, of course) into the cockpit and take him out on a few missions. His reaction to my first attempts to have him see some of the motivations of a fighter pilot was surprising. I came to the jarring realization that to many people, that entity in the cockpit is faceless and lifeless—some sort of an automaton issued at the factory for the purpose of caring for the needs of the machine.

On deeper reflection, I began to see a reason for this. Fighter pilots make good Hollywood fare so long as John Wayne or Ronald Reagan are there to give them substance, but the truth about fighter pilots is that they come off boring in real life. After all, formulae and minutiae are the building blocks upon

which a pilot's understanding is founded, and these don't trans-
late well at the dinner table. Early on (as in other fields) a
pilot's knowledge is more a matter of breadth than depth. As
his experience accumulates, details give way to patterns of
awareness until at some point, his actions proceed directly from
intuition. The learning crutches drop away. If the neophyte
appears to have been programmed, the mature fighter pilot must
seem even more so. In fact it isn't just fighter pilots—though
perhaps it is more pronounced in them. I think this progression
is found in all pilots regardless of age, background, or sex. I
have heard it said that the distinction between military pilots
and those in civil aviation is a matter of kinesthetics. While to
some extent this is true, it must be borne in mind that there
are civilian acrobatic pilots whose physical prowess is easily
the equal of their uniformed contemporaries. To my mind, what
distinguishes the fighter pilot is his sense of purpose.

To the military aviator, flying is more than a way of life;
in a sense, it is life, growing with time increasingly central to
his existence. At first, the attempt to differentiate between the
two is upsetting, but after a while the conflict is resolved in
favor of the calling—for such it is. One is not just steeped or
inoculated, but as truly as any fanatic, reborn into a new crea-
ture with goals and priorities subtly but definably different from
those of his former self.

Without overstating the case, it is probably fair to say that
it would be hard to find a business requiring a college degree
that involves such great physical risk, and such small tangible
rewards. As a middle of the zone captain in 1965, I made
$558.00 a month base pay along with $185.00 flight pay and
another $55.00 hostile fire pay for a grand total of $798.00—
which worked out to a little less than $10,000 a year. The hours
were long—rarely less than sixteen hours a day, seven days a
week—and even when there was a respite from the seemingly
interminable round of briefings, missions, and office work,
there was nowhere to go. We lived in tents with no plumbing,
donating our subsistence allowance for the privilege of eating
red death and peanut butter. From the outside world, there was
little in the way of appreciation or respect, and even within the
body of the Marine Corps, aviators are held in something less
than high esteem. "We understand about the flight pay," the
statement goes, "we just don't know why you zoomies get base
pay." As aviators get older, they spend more and more time

pushing pencils and less behind a stick and throttle, and unless they manage to make the transition to staff life, they are likely to find themselves on the street at age forty-two on the verge of becoming farsighted. Being a fighter pilot is a form of madness, but a glorious one when you think about it. I used to marvel at the fact that they actually gave me money to do something that was so much fun.

Though the picture of a fighter pilot is that of an immature hot rodder—a speed demon looking for a place to stack his bones before they get old enough to ache—the truth lies somewhere in the statistic that fighter pilots as a class have a lower incidence of suicide than people from almost all other walks of life. Indeed an argument could be raised that the pilot's seeming disregard for his own safety is actually a celebration of life and a desire to plunge more deeply into it.

The average age of the pilots in my squadron in 1965 was thirty-one (more typically throughout the fleet it was twenty-seven), meaning that most of us would have been grounded for being too old to fly combat back in World War II. But more significantly, our expectations were different from those of our predecessors. Most were married with children. All (but one, and he was our leader and among the finest pilots to ever grace a cockpit) were college graduates who selected this kind of life from among a rather large number of options. With a few exceptions, we were not flamboyant except at happy hour or around our nonaviator contemporaries (which is expected).

The fighter pilot is about as aware of the day-to-day affairs of state as your average citizen but less concerned, as he is steeped in the tradition of the military's subservience to its civilian leaders—and happy to leave it at that. He is generally the firstborn child (I wasn't), politically conservative, family oriented, achievement oriented, and middletown. He is unconsciously iconoclastic because of his underlying realization that complacency is the implacable enemy. But his desire for the recognition of his peers is without bound.

In contrast with his civilian contemporaries, the fighter pilot is doing professionally that which before all other things he wants to do. His fascination with flight is endless. There are few other professions to which men will give their undivided attention day after day and never tire of it. When the flight schedule is through, fighter pilots draw chairs together around a table at the club and between rolls of the dice cup, talk about flying. Alone in the solace of his cigarette and coffee—the fighter pilot's breakfast—his mind is on flight. Awakened in the small hours, he turns at once to an item of technique or the peculiar demands of an upcoming mission. In almost anyone else, this obsession might be treated as a serious symptom of some deeper disorder. "Take some time off, boy," he'd be counseled, and he probably would, gaining in the process *perspective*. A fighter pilot has no perspective because if he did, he'd probably go find another line of work. There's no telling whether it is the personality that brings this into play, or whether it goes with the territory, but once a fighter pilot loses his obsession, he's ready for a desk or on his way to the grave.

Where others might liken the job of the fighter pilot to that of an eagle swooping on his prey, reality to the pilot himself comes in sobering doses of things like maintaining formation on a jitterbugging wingtip at night in the middle of a thunderstorm. It's the uncertainty of whether, when the formation light disappears, it has merely bounced in the turbulence, or whether the leader has turned, setting up a collision situation. A lot of seat cushion gets inhaled in variations of that scene and more than a few careers have been snuffed in the faith that the wingtip would show up where it belonged.

Aviation is clannish, with so many wives tales and the like that it would be impossible to sort them out—and not worth it. I have tried to tell the story from the perspectives I had at the time, not today. Thus, during my first tour, I viewed the world and the war from inside narrow blinders, questioning little except for some of the material shortages and arbitrary restrictions that kept us (I felt) from winning the war. By contrast, I had become downright cynical by the end of my second tour, returning home as what one could call "a not particularly nice person."

For those interested in scientific fact or sound technical explanations on flight in general or the Phantom in particular, there are a number of excellent books available, covering such diverse things as aerodynamics, ordnance, meteorology, etc. For my present purposes, reference to such phenomena as stability index vectors, and asymmetrical thrust are included not to add a technical dimension to the book but to suggest that behind the immediate concerns of the mission and flight itself are myriad assumptions and understandings that are the real milieu. For example, when viewed externally, a bomb bull's-eyes a target in fulfillment of a set of fixed physical principles. That's true of course, but there's more to it. A bomb bull's-eyes a target first in the imagination of the man behind the stick, and then because he is able to transmit this image through the several hundred miles of wires and hydraulic lines that link him to his twenty-five-ton air-drilling machine.

The last thing in the world that I am is a military expert, yet here and there you will find me pontificating about what we should or should not have been doing. I wrestled with this for a long time before deciding that it added a needed dimension to the story. They were my personal biases at the time, but probably not unlike those of most of my contemporaries. If you happen not to share my views, I would happily defer to yours.

Enough different things happen on nearly any flight to fill several books, and if you add to the things that *do* happen, the things you worry about that *might* happen, you could have a small anthology. Sometimes the distinctions blur with the passage of time, particularly when you remember that I, like everyone else, lived in a sort of perpetual pressure cooker—not that I dared let myself lose sleep over it at the time.

With the exception of those named in this section I have used fictitious names throughout, only because I have been unable to run to earth all the people involved. The use of the first person is not so much an attempt to personalize things (in fact I think the third person facilitates this to a greater degree), but I found myself stuck for a better way to tie events to the pilot's assumptions and responses.

There are a number of people who were in various ways instrumental in bringing this project to fruition. From the outset, my friends Patty Berg, Jim Chapman, and Ed Concha offered encouragement without which I would never have gotten the manuscript finished, much less had the temerity to send it off to a publisher. Tom Clay and Dennis Anderson's ability to transform my viewpoint into graphic form is a feat that boggles my mind. Bob Kane of Presidio Press, who was kind enough to roll the dice on a neophyte in the first place, has been generous with his time and experience, helping me overcome my natural propensity for digression. Without Presidio Press Senior Editor Joan Griffin's fortitude in the face of an almost incomprehensible manuscript, the whole thing would have been a fiasco, and even I wouldn't have known what was happening to whom, or when. The list could go on and on: Lynn Cordell is responsible for the overall graphic tone; Jan King of Desert Typesetting, for the typography; Kathleen Jaeger for the cover design, and George Hall for the cover photograph. Thank you all.

Finally, I would like you to know that some things glow so brightly in my memory that they will be there even as my life dissolves. Among them are the sudden sense of loss during our first weeks of combat, when four of my squadron mates failed to return from a raid over the North. They were classified MIA, and stored away in some distant corner of our bureaucratic maze, but they appear to me now in my mind's eye, as vividly as the morning they left the briefing tent en route to an unknown destiny.

    Capt. Al Pitt, austere and serious
    Capt. Doyle Sprick, plucky and sincere
    2nd Lt. Larry Helber, studious and precise
    CWO Dale Booze, tough, charming, and confident

Prologue

It was June 1964, and I was sitting in a stuffy classroom at Los Alamitos Naval Air Station barely listening to a flight surgeon decry the evils of self-medication. Suddenly, the door at the back of the room crashed open. A black pajama'd figure—coolie hat and rifle at the ready—stormed to the front shouting, "Yankee, you die!" It was meant to be funny, and it was. Only while it was happening, I felt shivers running up and down my backbone. I had read about Vietnam—even done some targeting studies the year before while I was going through Weapons Employment School at Norfolk—but that far-off land had no more reality to me than Antarctica. It might as well have been invented by our instructors to provide us with planning problems. Yet in that instant I was overwhelmed by the sensation that Vietnam would some day have a momentous impact on my life.

The fighting in Southeast Asia had been chronicled for over a year, but between the official denial of a policy other than advisory and the more earthshaking developments (the Cuban crisis, Kennedy's assassination, the space program, and continuous clashes with the Russians), Vietnam was a backwater— or so it had seemed to me until that moment. From then on, I watched the developments more carefully, noting how the newspapers and, to a lesser extent, television began paying greater and greater attention to Vietnam. By January of 1965, when it became obvious that we were going to be involved in a shooting war, I began serious lobbying to get into a Phantom squadron. It wasn't jingoism that prompted me (at least I don't think so). It was more a desire to test myself and the skills that had been honed over the five years since I had entered the Naval Air Training Command, a snot-nosed second lieutenant in quest of a shiny set of golden wings. I had always known I would be a fighter pilot, this sure knowledge shaping my view of myself and the world around me to such an extent that it wasn't until I actually flew in combat that I realized how skewed many of my preconceptions were.

My first flight had been at the controls of a Link trainer, an electrohydraulic box that lurched and tilted and spun around in response to the control manipulations of its erstwhile operator. To say that the trainer simulated anything else in the world—let alone the flight of an airplane—is hyperbole without bound, but for a boy of six, it was unbridled joy. There was a War Bond drive on, and at the corner of Fairfax and Beverly Boulevard in Los Angeles, some enterprising souls had pitched a tent and loaded it up with all kinds of war trophies. For the price of a $25 War Bond ($18.75 in those days) you could go inside the tent and see a dented midget Japanese submarine, the aileron from a Zero fighter plane, a samurai sword, flags with writing drenched in guaranteed real 100 percent Japanese blood and—wonder of all wonders—a Link trainer. For another $25 War Bond you could (gulp, pant) fly it. I was hooked, and it never crossed my mind that I would be anything but a fighter pilot living in a state of eternal bliss, shooting down "yellow perils" from the Land of the Rising Sun in a world that never grew old. It was a glorious time to grow up: everything was black and white; you knew who the good and bad guys were and what they wore and what they flew; and every once in a while, soldiers or sailors or Marines came by to dinner en route to that mystical place referred to in hushed tones as "overseas." The war ended, first in Europe and finally in the Pacific, leaving me with a sense of loss. No more were the skies of limitless blue crisscrossed with Mustangs and Lightnings, Havocs and Marauders, trailing behind them such a glorious collection of sounds that the gods themselves must have reveled with my same ecstasy. The seed had been sown, though, and I claimed the destiny of slashing across a war-torn sky in a gleaming fighter, questing for a glory brighter than all the lights on Hollywood Boulevard during the premiere of a John Wayne spectacular. An inaccurate vision—but not altogether unlike the one I took to Vietnam.

I received orders to Marine Fighter/Attack Squadron 314 (VMFA-314) at El Toro Marine Corps Air Station in early July 1964. Just back from a tour in the Far East, the squadron was in the process of reforming. Its members had been together nearly three years, ever since they had first received and operationalized the Marine Corps' initial batch of Phantoms. Typically, squadrons formed and froze their rosters a year prior to a scheduled deployment, remaining intact until their return, which allowed them to go overseas in the highest state of readiness possible. I was one of the first arrivals of the new brood; most of the present members were preparing to leave for new assignments. I had barely finished checking into the base when 314 was refrozen with virtually the same roster it had had from the first. It looked as if I might be out on the sidewalk. Fortunately, I convinced the commanding officer that my background in attack aircraft might be useful should we be sent to Vietnam. What I didn't mention was that my stateside checkout in the Phantom had consisted of exactly six flights. Before I had finished even the ground school courses, it was August 1965 and we were on our way overseas. Instead of flying our planes across the Pacific, we watched them hoisted aboard the *Valley Forge,* a straight-decked aircraft carrier used for antisubmarine work. It was humiliating to be ferried to Japan, but at least I had time to study the aircraft and its systems.

We dropped anchor off Iwakuni, Japan, in the middle of a typhoon, and with winds of better than seventy knots lashing the waters of Japan's Inland Sea into fifteen-foot swells, the airplanes were snaked from the carrier onto awaiting barges by a floating crane, which bobbed and surged like a cork. It was an intricate ballet scored by a wizened old man who timed his actions perfectly. For all the risk of catastrophe, the only casualty was a skinned radome when a maverick wave slewed the crane nearly 90 degrees, allowing the nose of the plane to rub against the side of the carrier.

The base was still in the grip of the storm's trailing edge

when training began in earnest. I flew far more than my share of the hops because of my inexperience in the airplane. For the same reason, I got the nod when we were directed to send an airplane to Vietnam to replace one that had flown into Monkey Mountain at the mouth of Da Nang Harbor. It was a three-stage journey with intermediate stops at Naha Naval Air Station, Okinawa, and Cubi Point NAS, Philippines, taking in all the better part of eight hours flight time. I expected to have to beg and plead with the resident squadron to give me a flight or two, but they were only too happy to put me on the schedule. For the first couple of missions, I was all over the sky looking for AA, MiGs, and SAMs, but after that I settled down and grooved into what was happening. After three days and six missions, I returned to Japan expecting a little adulation for the "cold-blooded, steely-eyed combat veteran." What I got instead was bitterness from other squadron members because the newest pilot in the squadron was the first to fly in combat. It was several weeks before some of them got over it.

September dragged by, then October. After a wild missile-shoot in Okinawa in which we destroyed every target drone in the Western Pacific, we again found ourselves sitting on our thumbs up in Japan flying training missions, augmented by an occasional intercept of a Russian reconnaissance plane over the Sea of Japan. We were beginning to become testy because it seemed patently obvious to us that the shooting was sure to stop any moment, and we weren't going to have played a part in it. We were VMFA-314, we told ourselves, the Marine Corps' premier Phantom squadron and bearer of a proud heritage. Now, after the ignominy of being carted overseas on the deck of an antiquated boat, we were forced to twiddle our thumbs a thousand miles from where the action was, competent, it seemed, only to provide replacement aircraft to the shooters.

Another Phantom squadron then arrived at the base by barge, along with aircrews from a third whose aircraft would arrive in like manner. Both units had been hastily scraped together, and unlike ours, their experience levels varied all over the block. There was clearly a problem; and just as clearly, a solution—as unpalatable as it seemed to us at the time. The rosters of the three squadrons were thrown into a pot during the first week of November, and while I remained in 314, we all came to learn something valuable about the magic of numbers and names.

The squadron is the heart of military aviation. From the outside, it looks like a fraternity, but it's more. In a sense, speciation starts with the branch of the service, where one dons the mantle of Marine (or soldier, or seaman, or airman), and from there to the subset of zoomy or grunt. Continuing on, one belongs to an air wing (division), air group (regiment), and finally squadron. While this equates organizationally to a battalion, there is no comparison in terms of bond. More than alma mater, it is alma omnia. One's squadron leaves a stamp more indelible than that of an Eton or Harvard. It is the repository of all knowledge, lore, fable, rumor, and misinformation relating not merely to the aircraft and mission at hand, but to the world of military aviation in general. It is the culture bearer in a world that leaves few tracks, the leaven that makes each outfit a discrete entity. You might look at a squadron and say "Those guys are what make VMFA-314 what it is," but you'd have it backwards. The truth is that VMFA-314 makes those guys what they are . . . in the mold of what VMFA-314 has always been. It doesn't matter whether you talk about squadrons, regiments, armies, ships, or even corporations, there are winners and losers, and rarely do they change their stripes . . . and then only temporarily. Thus it was for us. When the great new deal came to pass there was a lot of howling, particularly when the sacrosanct stick-scope team was broken up, but quickly things fell back into place so that when we were tapped to go into country, we were a cohesive unit, bearing all the credentials that got our predecessors rated "Black Knights."

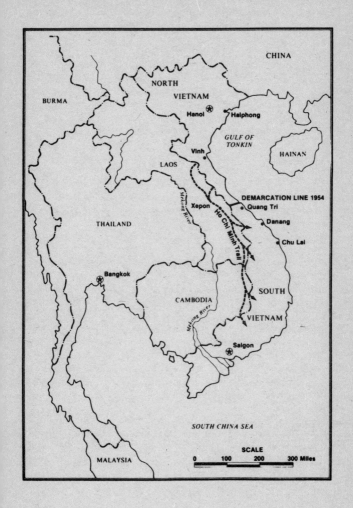

— 1 —

—— Wings of Thunder ——

On the third day of 1966 we island-hopped from Japan to Da Nang via Okinawa and the Philippines to relieve the previous Phantom squadron onsite. As one of our birds touched down, one of theirs departed, and as the last engine clanked to a stop, an almost unbearable silence descended on the flight line. My immediate impression (as it had been during my first trip into country two months earlier) was of how heavy the air felt— as if it were a semisolid made of water vapor and construction dust with jet fumes acting as a catalyst for the glop. Somewhere out there a war was going on—a fact confirmed by the sporadic thuddings from the 155mm-howitzer battery east of the field— but for the moment we weren't part of it, so most of us spent our first few hours wandering around poking our heads into the tents and sheds that served as maintenance spaces, wondering what came next. The proud warriors had arrived in their menacing chariots with a fanfare worthy of an Alexander, yet in less than the time it takes to tell, the exhilaration was gone, leaving in its wake an uncertainty that was to continue even when things had settled into a more or less steady routine.

In midafternoon, the flight crews gathered in the operations tent for the first of a series of interminable briefings on the

Rules of Engagement, which were (and would forever remain)
in constant flux. The briefing tent was so hot and stuffy, even
with the sides raised, that no one heeded the urge to smoke
except for the briefing officer—a sanguine lieutenant colonel
from the First Marine Air Wing (Forward) staff who used his
pudgy cigar as a pointer. As bad as it was, the stench of his
stogie couldn't cover the smell of latrine and jet fuel that settled
over everything in a noxious pall. Among the subjects covered
were clearing authorities, flight leader responsibilities, free drop
zones, route packages, and off-limit targets. On and on he
droned, oblivious to our discomfort—a condition all the more
painful for our acclimation in the cool Japanese autumn. While
we sweltered in the canvas sauna, the bulk of our troops arrived
in C-130 transports from Clark Air Force Base (Philippines),
and before dark, all of our planes were up and ready for flight,
configured with bomb racks and live missiles. It was well after
dark when the last presentation was over, and it was then we
found that the baggage hadn't arrived on the transports. As it
turned out, we were to be without a change of clothes for three
more days—not a big deal except as a harbinger of things to
come.

Despite the build-up, Da Nang looked like any rinky-dink
municipal airport in the Far East, with only the addition of
concertina strung on both sides of the chain-link perimeter fence
to suggest another facet to its character. Here and there, tents
were pitched among the mud-sided Vietnamese buildings, while
on and off the airport, lines of traffic seesawed back and forth,
tooting frantically at the pedicabs and carts that blocked their
way. Gooney Birds (DC-3s) and Curtiss Condors maintained
a constant parade in front of the passenger terminal, which was
filled to overflowing with pajama-clad civilians, while ARVN
soldiers strutted among the crowd dressed in khaki fatigues
three sizes too big. The casual disorderliness lent the base its
unique aura—a sort of Bob and Bing Road to Nowhere pre-
posterousness—but there is something in the military makeup
that can't stand that. One by one, the buildings yielded to the
purposeful attack of bulldozers and graders, intent on devouring
everything in sight to make way for the labyrinth of orderly
red-earthed cells filled with orderly blocks of strong-back tents
such as those of our squadron compound. Only the headquarters
area retained its charm, and that was blunted by the knowledge
that in the low-roofed barracks area, the flower of the French

Foreign Legion officer corps fell to the knives of midnight assassins.

Equipment and supplies streamed onto the base in an endless flow by air and sea, while spit-shined troops in heavy stateside utilities blocked the flight line awaiting transportation to their newly formed units. Some milled about, smoking, among stacks of white mattress-bag-like sacks, unaware that they were treading hallowed ground. Some horsed around until the heat got the better of them. But mostly they paced back and forth, eager to get on with the job they had been trained to do before it was too late and the Cong and NVA had a bellyfull and laid down their arms.

The squadron area consisted of some fifty-odd strong-back tents that housed the 350 officers and men who made up the fully complemented F-4 squadron (actually the table of organization called for 231, but we needed the extra hands to cover such nonoperational pursuits as mess duty, guard duty, and the like). Along the perimeter, several rows of concertina were strung (to keep us in), with a guarded gate facing the main service road. We called it Dogpatch, but it was far worse. The inspired placement of the six latrines ensured that one of them was always upwind no matter where you were, and at that time there was but one shower in the whole compound, served by a Lister bag suspended in an A-frame. Once a day, Wing would send over a water buffalo and everyone would get in line. The drill was to tug the rope to wet yourself and then move out of the way while you soaped and scrubbed, all the while praying that there was enough water to rinse off. There were always those who got stuck, so by the second day, most of us had written home for glycerine soap on the premise that it was somehow less harmful to the skin if left on.

Because it was my duty to write the flight schedule for the next day, I was the last one to show up at the tent that first evening, so I had to settle for the corner farthest away from the entrance, but it turned out to have the best ventilation, so I came out ahead. We were billeted by flights, eight to a tent—nine in ours to accommodate the flight surgeon—with barely enough room for our cots and wall lockers, which stood back-to-back in the center of the raised wooden floor. The officers' living area consisted of eight strong-back pyramid tents arranged so as to face onto a thirty-by-sixty-foot quadrangle headed by the commanding officer's tent. An electrical generator chugged away at the opposite end, feeding power to our living area and the office spaces behind us. One high-intensity light lit the central area, but it was hardly enough to cast a shadow; and there was a single fixture hanging in the center of each tent, but if you wanted to read, you needed a flashlight. There were several electrical outlets in the tent, but it made little difference as the system's capacity was woefully inadequate. About the only appliance we kept going was an electric coffeepot which was used for making hot water for tea and shaving. Drinking (and shaving) water came from a water buffalo parked next to the CO's tent, while the nearest latrine was fifty feet away by the fence next to the mess hall tent. When the wind was from the north, the chow hall lost a lot of business. Without our gear, there was nothing to do but turn in, and though I had already flown several missions back in September, I had difficulty getting to sleep. Perhaps it was a reaction to the tension of the others, or perhaps the novelty of the cot and mildewed mosquito netting were a bit at fault, but I tossed and turned until it was time for my first brief.

It was a helicopter escort flight, providing air cover for a pod of choppers taking supplies into a remote base at the base of a dazzling outcropping known as the "Rockpile." We stayed on station for over an hour while the shuttle was in progress, and when our on-station time came to an end with not so much as a hint of enemy activity, we were shifted to a Marine air tactical control unit (MATCU) that was in the process of setting up a ground-based radar bombing control system. TPQ bombing (as the procedure was called) allows a ground-based radar controller to vector aircraft to a computer-generated release point, from which, if the solution is accurate, the bombs will strike in the vicinity of a preestablished target. The idea—which was to allow us to deliver ordnance at night and in bad weather—was good, but there were so many variables with which the system had to account that accuracy was severely hampered. The MATCU was just setting up shop, so we drilled around the pattern several times while the controller fiddled and fumed. Each time, the system broke lock-on just as we approached the drop point. Between commands to vary our headings or altitudes he kept up a running commentary of his woes, but finally, everything hung together, and with a whoop, he instructed us to drop. There was silence for several minutes while we awaited the outcome of the strike, and finally, in an uncertain tone he asked if indeed we had dropped. When we replied in the affirmative, he said something to the effect of "Oh, well, ain't nobody up that way but gooners, no how." Mission accomplished.

My next mission, coming late that same night, was a little more strenuous. It was a BARCAP mission (barrier combat air patrol) providing on-station air defense for the fleet at Yankee Station. I was selected to lead it because I had flown on two BARCAPs during my brief stay in September. I quickly learned why my hosts were so generous with the missions . . . BAR-CAPs were a bore. The drill was to launch from Da Nang in time to take on fuel from an orbiting tanker and arrive on station off Haiphong Harbor ready for action. My wingman and I took off a little after 2000 (8 p.m.) in order to make a 2130 time on target (TOT). We were in the clear all the way up, so the rendezvous and air refuelling plug-ins were routine. Typically, the mission involved two and a half hours en route and another hour and a half on station, but I was warned that because of aircraft availability problems, my relief might be a little late.

BARCAP configuration generally consisted of a 600-gallon centerline fuel tank and four Sparrow and four Sidewinder missiles. The roughly 15,000-pounds of fuel translated to any of several options: if there was no activity other than drilling around the orbit point, we could stay on station for up to two hours before heading for the barn; if we had to respond to an incoming aircraft, our stay time would be cut in half; if the intruder turned out to be hostile, forcing us to use afterburner, ten minutes would be our limit if we hoped to make it back to base. The presence of the tanker changed all that, as every forty-five minutes, the flight would return to the tanker to top off, resetting the clock to zero again.

On this particular night, things went smoothly until it came time for our relief. Nobody showed up. As it turned out, they were not merely late, they didn't arrive at all, subjecting us to an additional ninety minutes and two extra refuellings in the process. It was past eleven at night, and I could hardly stay awake. When the time came for the subsequent relief, only one plane showed up, so I detached my wingman for home and continued to drone around. The situation was beginning to become dangerous. I almost overshot my approach to the tanker, and after finding myself going into microsleep in the midst of refuelling, I told my RIO to keep up a running dialogue if he didn't want to go for a swim. Finally, after another hour spent fighting the nearly overwhelming urge to take a catnap— by now nearly six hours into the flight—my relief came and I headed home worn out and in a foul mood. It was after three-thirty when I rolled into the bag.

For the first week or so, all of the missions had memorable aspects, but gradually things fell into a routine, and soon they began to overlap one another. Right from the start, a kind of speciation took place, with some of us taking over the majority of the night flying duties. I'd always liked night flying—even the bombing in the mountains—finding that I attuned myself to the airplane to a far greater degree than in the day, so even though the risks were higher (some claim that there is no lift in the night air), it suited me fine . . . at first. It was on my sixteenth straight night Steel Tiger against Xepon (pronounced Tchepone, with the tongue against the upper teeth) that things took a turn for the worse. Steel Tigers were night raids into southern Laos to interdict traffic on the Ho Chi Minh Trail. (Both the Steel Tigers and the Barrel Roll missions against the Pathet Lao in northern Laos were classified, as was the fact that U.S. pilots were flying Royal Laotion T-28s in bombing strikes against the People's Liberation Force, which was to Laos what the NVA was to South Vietnam.) Xepon, a major crossroads through which an inordinate amount of supplies for use by the NVA and Cong in South Vietnam were staged, was a flak trap because the target was in a valley whose flanks dictated our bombing runs. We were stuck with a run-in heading of 260 or 080 degrees, so all they had to do was put up a box of flak on our in-run. We had no choice but to fly through it, so it was a numbers game. My guess is that already more than a dozen aircraft had been bagged there, and that number was to multiply over the years. The worst part for us was that our planes fairly glowed in the dark. The undersides were painted white, so when we rolled in above any kind of illumination, we were the brightest light source in the sky.

On February first, we arrived over Xepon at two-thirty in the morning—a four-plane flight armed with twelve 500-pound bombs apiece. We had departed Da Nang in a driving rainstorm with no assurance that the weather would improve enough for us to return there to land—a routine but nonetheless nettlesome situation. But when we cleared the angry deck of clouds, we were greeted by a fairytale night—a world studded with visual

jewels of such beauty that for a moment I lost all thought of
the task at hand. The weather was clear in Laos, where flickering fires—remnants of previous raids—created the powerful
illusion of a world turned upside down. The moonless sky was
ablaze with stars, and in successive bouts of vertigo, I saw
them as the lights of a faraway city, the misconception accen-
tuated by the reflection of the instrument lights above the canopy bow. From time to time, a searing flash of lightning erased
the black, presenting with stark radiance a row of boiling thunderheads towering like sentinels above the jutting Assam. Mag-
ically, the crossroads leapt into view, an arc-lit tableau crafted
in the cozy detail of a miniature railroad scene. It was a glorious
mirage—one of such stunning clarity that I was almost beguiled
into forgetting that this was the most heavily defended point
on the Ho Chi Minh Trail. A sudden flare farther off to the
west jerked me into the present. We were less than three minutes
from the target, and it was time to make sure one last time that
my R10 knew exactly what I expected of him.

"OK, Terry, keep in mind that the target elevation is 670
feet, so we'll be rolling in at seventy-five hundred, and releasing at thirty-five, bottoming out at fifteen. I want 30 degrees
of dive and 450 knots at release, so keep me posted." I'd already
briefed him on this before, but there were several factors that
gave promise of an interesting evening. To begin with, this was
Terry's first combat mission with the squadron, as he had only
reported in on the previous afternoon. Review of his logbook
and training records revealed that he had received almost no
air-to-ground weapons delivery training—none at all at night
or in bad weather. In literal fact, he had no business being out
on a Steel Tiger mission at all (not to mention one at night),
but it was his mouth that had earned him the opportunity. Terry
had managed to alienate almost everyone in the squadron in
the thirty hours since his arrival, so no one challenged me for
writing him in for the flight when my scheduled RIO was
grounded for a blocked Eustachian tube.

Because of his inexperience, I had sat him down an hour
before the scheduled brief time to go over in great detail how
the mission would probably go; what he could expect from me;
and what I expected from him. It was a mistake. Every time
I tried to emphasize a point, he dismissed it with an I-already-
know-all-of-this-stuff gesture of impatience. His response to
the lead RIO's offer to go back over the communications brief-

ing was even more indicative of his attitude problem. "I got all of this today at the orientation briefing. I don't need to be told again." You could have cut the atmosphere with a machete, things were so tense in the tent.

Normally, the RIO's job was to operate the air-to-air weapons system, the heart of the Phantom and the initial reason for its existence. In Vietnam, the majority of our missions had little or nothing to do with air-to-air combat. Only select Air Force and Navy squadrons were assigned strictly fighter missions which, though fun for the crews, rarely proved to be productive. In the attack role, the RIO took on the responsibility of backstopping the pilot in things like navigation, switch settings, altitudes and airspeeds during attack, and lookout to and from the target area. For this, the RIOs got their base pay, flight pay, ejection seat activating handles, and a total lack of control over the aircraft. What motivated them to get up each day, don flight gear, and climb into the rear seat is a mystery. To me it is like jumping onto the back of a motorcycle with anyone who happens to have one. . . . you have to be awfully brave or certifiably nuts.

Most of the old salts began as enlisted radar operators whose career pattern took them from all-weather fighters to ground radar facilities, to electronic countermeasures duty, and back again to fighters. Just before we rotated into Vietnam, all RIOs became officers, either by commission or warrant; and the new breed had college degrees, had been through Officer Candidate School (OCS), and many (as was the case with Terry) had entered the program as flight students. In the proper form of all traditional single-seat fighter jocks, I was skeptical of the value of RIOs at first, believing fuel to be a better use of the space, but after my first few night bombing missions in the mountains, I became a cautious believer. They relieved a large part of the load, allowing the pilot to focus his attention outside the cockpit. Because the pilot could concentrate on the task at hand, not only were the results consistently better, the odds of staying out of the trees were greater as well.

Compared to the violence of the thunderstorms, Laos seemed tame, but it was an illusion. Farther to the west, a stream of tracers slithered up the sky like a visual stream of Morse code, arcing away to erupt in a train of sparkles. It was a Lilliputian display when viewed from a distance, but head-on, it was a different matter. There, you could feel the glowing tentacles of iron searching for your innards, and your bowels contracted involuntarily.

"Spooky Two-Four, Manual Four-Five with four Fox-Fours overhead at base plus twelve." Ed Knight, the flight leader for the mission, checked in with the tactical air control airborne (TACA), giving him our altitude in code. I was his wingman, flying the number two slot.

"Roger, Manual, we're at base plus seven, northwest of the target. Make your runs heading two-six-zero with a left pull. We've got movers half a click to the north, heading for the crossroads. We're out of flares, but you can use the two fires southeast of the crossroads as a reference. On your run-in, they're seven-thirty for five hundred and a thousand meters each. You're cleared in hot."

The pilot's thought process during a strike is anything but a smooth orderly flow along logical lines. It's a "pop . . . pop . . . pop" sort of affair, in which you pick out seemingly random stimuli from among perhaps thirty or forty factors, each vying for attention.

Check the gunsight setting for 105 mils . . . OK . . . pipper's a little too bright . . . there . . . loosen up on the turn a little to give Ed more clearance.

We descended to pattern altitude (7,000 feet above the ground) in a wide left turn to the downwind, looking to keep the target just ahead of the wing crank.

"Manual Forty-Five Dash One's in." A lightning flash silhouetted Ed's plane against the sky, freezing him in an instant in time and space before releasing him again for his deadly role.

Ten seconds before roll-in . . . look out, ace, here come the tracers. Hold the nose up! Look at those mothers . . . two thick streams that look like railroad tracks. OH, HELL! ED'S HIT! He's a sheet of flames! Where are the chutes? No chutes . . . I'm through the ninety . . . roll it up and pull the nose through. Still no chutes!

Then I was at the roll-in point, poised at the brink. "Dash Two's in." My own voice repeated through my headset had a distinctly foreign ring to it.

"Ok, Terry, keep me honest." It was important from then on that he kept me abreast of our altitude and airspeed until we were climbing away from the target.

"Six thousand . . . uh . . ."

*There's the crossroads . . . I'm a little shallow . . . let it scooch
out to the right a little . . . they're shooting—*

"Five thou . . . aahhh . . . oh, my God!"

*The hills are coming up . . . the tracers're sitting dead still
. . . talk to me, Terry—say something to let me know you're
still back there . . . the tracers . . . coming up on wings level—*

"Talk to me, dammit! What's my altitude?"

"Oh, my God!"

*The tracers . . . look at them boogie . . . they're splitting off
to the side . . . I've got to be at release by now . . . the hills are
a blur . . . almost there . . . standby . . . n-n-NOW!*

"OH, MY GA-AWD! . . . OHH!"

There was nothing more than a light thump to mark the
ejection of a pair of low-drag 500-pound bombs as they were
kicked off onto their own to add to the madness of this multicolored fireworks display. Tracers, which but a moment before
rode ruler-straight tracks seemingly anchored to the cockpit
floor, now sheared away aft and to the right. At the instant of
release the pipper was spiked on the northerly arm of the crossroads, 200 mils to the right of the intersection. The night was
ripped by another colossal flash, then plunged again into a
deeper darkness.

*Stick back! We're way below the tops of the hills! Give it
more pull. There's the truck . . . nose coming through the horizon . . . stars . . . relax the pull . . . easy . . . damn! The truck
was farther off to the right . . . bend it back to the left.*

"Dash Two off. The truck's a good hundred meters right of
my hit." Terry's breathing came over the ICS in rasps. He had
been hyperventilating so badly I was afraid that he'd pass out.

"Terry? TERRY! Get it under control!" Gradually, his
breathing became more even.

Back again at altitude there was time to handle the housekeeping chores. Temperatures and pressures were where they
belonged. Fuel transfer from the internal wings was still in
progress. No caution lights had lit, and except for an occasional
bang of a valve cycling, all seemed well. There was nothing
to be done for Ed and his RIO but to listen up on the emergency
frequency and pray that if they were still alive, they would
remain hidden until the morning when the choppers could get
in and pull them out. What remained for us was dodging the
flak monster and staying out of the weeds, which brought my
attention back to Terry. "Well, I wouldn't worry about it too

much, hotstuff, we've still got five more runs to work on your technique."

A pair of flashes confirmed the completion of Dash Three's first run, and mentally I fixed Four's position in his run. Terry began his litany in preparation for our next run. Again we rounded to the north to intercept the inbound heading, and in a distant flash I caught a glimpse of Four as he hauled steeply off the target.

"Dash Four is off. No drop. Nice going, Dash Two, only next time why don't you have your scope switch to *guard* and let the rest of the world in on his prayers?" Terry's humility quotient soared from zero to ninety-nine point nine in less than five seconds. It was bad enough that he had panicked for my benefit, but worse than that, he had keyed the mike button to the radio rather than the intercom, transmitting his gibberish over the air for everyone on the frequency to hear. (Guard is the emergency frequency 243.0 megahertz, which is constantly monitored or guarded by all military aircraft in the event that an aircraft in distress needs help, or, as was even more the case in Vietnam, a downed aviator was calling for rescue on his personal emergency radio.)

Thus it was a chastened person who read off altitudes and airspeeds for the rest of the runs, coming up to veteran speed in the process. I was prepared to forget the incident, and I figured that with the loss of Ed and Rick, the others would too, but it was out of our hands. Word of the fiasco had preceded us, and draped in toilet paper on the debriefing tent were the words "WELCOME HOME OMIGOD FLIGHT."

It wasn't until the next morning that we found out that Ed and Rick had been able to eject safely and had been rescued and flown to Thailand. Ed got two days of rest courtesy of the Air Force before coming home to the mud and mildew. Rick was less (or was it more) fortunate with two broken legs and collarbones, which was a one-way ticket back to the States.

Both were lucky. Rick tangled with some trees on the way down, falling the last forty feet totally out of control. When he came to, he found himself wrapped up in his parachute shroud unable to move. All around him there were people running and shouting, cranking off occasional shots into the underbrush. The commotion subsided towards dawn and he spent the next several hours trying to maneuver the emergency radio out of his g-suit pocket.

Ed came down in a clearing and after ditching his parachute, he took off down a trail away from where he thought he had sighted a village. The next thing he knew, he was in the middle of a settlement with a pack of dogs yapping at his heels. He led them out of the village and into a thicket, where one by one, they dropped off until at last he was alone. He walked for a while, catching his breath until he came to another trail and took off again at a lope. He ran for what seemed like an eternity, pausing every once in a while to listen. All at once he was back in the same settlement again, with the dogs, and this time several of the villagers, in hot pursuit. Again he got away from them as he tripped and plunged through the tangled underbrush. It was like a bad dream that you can't seem to shake. Finally, unable to go any farther, he threw himself into the thickest cover he could find. The night was deadly quiet and even a twig-snap sounded like an artillery barrage. He decided to wait for morning before turning on his emergency radio.

By half past six, the sky lightened sufficiently to allow him to make out larger shapes. By seven he could see people moving up the trail from the village below. They passed within thirty feet, but he was certain that with the thickness of the brush, they could not see him. Presently, he heard voices from behind and turning carefully to see what was going on, he found that he had plunged so deeply into the brambles that he was fully visible on the other side. Carefully he made his way back into the brush.

At seven-fifteen, Ed decided to give his radio a try, and no sooner had he turned it on than he was greeted by a familiar voice. It was Rick talking to a rescue helicopter that had come out to take a look for them. Rick was unable to move or even mark his position, but as luck had it, one of the crew members spotted his chute almost as soon as the chopper came into the area. The pilot took one swing to look for ground fire before breaking into a hover over Rick's position. One of the crew members rappelled down the line, stuffed Rick into the sling and with an Italian salute, disappeared into the trees to await pickup at a later time. When the chopper lifted up, Ed popped a flare and dashed out into the clearing, where a group of farmers stared at him for several seconds before returning to their chores. The chopper roared onto the scene trailing its forest penetrator, breaking stride just long enough for Ed to clip on before it bounded away to the west. It was a near thing, and we had a large bash on his return.

For a while we were the only Marine fixed-wing squadron on the base, sharing most of the air-to-air Hot Pad and flak-suppression missions with a pair of Air Force squadrons flying F-102s and F-100s. There were relatively few "troops in contact" calls during that time, most of the activity occurring in conjunction with operations involving Marines sent ashore in regimental strength or less, from assault ships lying offshore out of sight of the watchful enemy. Unfortunately, these sweeps were rarely successful because, despite the stealth with which the ships could put troops into position, the operations themselves had to be cleared with Saigon beforehand, meaning that the enemy had quite likely received adequate warning. What Saigon didn't leak, our own press correspondents did; but it didn't seem critical at the time. Getting the show on the road was bound to be fraught with problems.

February saw the resumption of strikes into the North, and what was immediately apparent was that the enemy had used the layoff period for increasing their air defenses. It seemed to us that just about the time we'd pretty well beat down the SAMs and AA, there would be a moratorium, after which they'd come back stronger than before. Typically, losses would be high for the first few days and then begin to taper off until we could roam around the North in relative safety. Then we'd go through the whole sequence again. To a certain extent, it was a matter of their coming up with new wrinkles that we'd have to sort out and develop tactics to combat, but there was a noticeable difference in the types and amounts of ordnance slung into the sky to oppose us.

March 1966 was the month when everything changed, though it started routinely enough with the mounting of Operation UTAH against an NVA Main Force headquarters at Sonchau just north of Quang Ngai, eighty miles south of the air base. For once we achieved a modicum of surprise and things went well for the first few days. Then in rapid succession, events occurred in I Corps that were to influence deeply the future conduct of the war. That they happened away from Saigon where the majority of the press was located tended to limit the attention given them at the time, but their eventual effect on how we chose to prosecute the war was profound.

On March 10, the Special Forces camp at Ashau was overrun

by a regiment of North Vietnamese regulars (though we didn't know their identity at the time). I was given to saying that the Hot Pad phone had a little extra stridency to its ring when something really serious was up, and it was that way when Ashau was hit. The attack started early in the day, and even as the first two sections of airplanes were getting airborne, the decision to cancel regular launches and configure the birds for close air support had been reached. Crews were shuttled directly to the flight line, where a hasty briefing was conducted. Even though the weather at Ashau was horrible—ceiling and visibility less than 500 feet—Wing wanted us to keep four aircraft overhead at all times in case the clouds lifted. The entire operation, from original attack until the base was completely abandoned, took less than three days, during which time I made a total of ten flights into the area, six on the first day alone. The weather was so poor that four times I brought ordnance back (normally we would have TPQ'd the stuff or jettisoned it over the water, but the idea was to turn the birds around as quickly as possible, so we landed with full racks). Seven aircraft sustained battle damage—three from ground fire and four from fragments of the aircrafts' own bombs—and during all that time, I doubt that we launched a truly telling strike. The weather and terrain combined to make ours a bitter and impossible task.

By coincidence, on the same day the battle for Ashau began, Nguyen Cao Ky fired General Thi, commander of the northern provinces of South Vietnam and the leading Buddhist figure in the Vietnamese Army. He was replaced by General Chuan, who immediately stated his opposition to Ky and his Saigon regime. A series of labor strikes in Da Nang and Hue threatened to tear the country apart at the seams, causing Ky to respond by sending 1,500 of his crack troops and his vaunted Tiger Squadron of A-1 Skyraiders to Da Nang to restore order, relieving General Chuan with Lt. Gen Ton Thant Dinh at the same time. It was too late, as Chuan had already deployed his troops to defend the city of Da Nang against Ky, going so far as to train his weapons on the air base. Up to that point, it was an internal affair.

The VNAF parked their A-1 Skyraiders (Spads) on the flight line next to ours. When General Chuan got wind of what Ky was up to, he sent a battalion of infantry reinforced by armor over the Hai Van Pass to occupy positions outside the air base perimeter fencing, training his guns on Ky's Skyraiders. Even the Cong decided to take a grandstand seat for this one. Our own uneasiness lay in the fact that our flight line lay directly between Chuan's tanks and Ky's A-1s.

Nothing moved for a full day, and while we continued to fly our assigned missions, we were briefed that we might have to intercede between the two Vietnamese units—on whose side we weren't told. Early in the afternoon of the third day, a flight of A-1s fired up and taxied for takeoff. As they were taking the runway, our Hot Pad was told to scramble and escort the A-1s to prevent them from bombing General Chuan's tanks. It was a zoo. Everyone who was not flying or working on the airplanes was out by the taxiway watching to see what would happen next. Crowds of Vietnamese had gathered throughout the day and were waiting patiently outside the gate to see what new fun and games their bozo leaders had in store. Things were pretty tense for the troops buttoned up inside the tanks, and there was a better than even chance our whole flight line was about to turn into a junkyard.

In a classic blunder, the lead A-1 poured the coal to the 3,000 horsepower R-4360 and smartly trundled off into the dirt between the runway and taxiway, executing an ignominious ground loop. When he paddled through a full 360-degree turn, reemerging from the weeds with a vengeance to continue his takeoff, it was an anticlimax. Our troops were rolling in laughter on the apron; the arming crewmen at the end of the runway were jumping up and down, waving and hooting at the rest of the flight of Spads, who must have been a little unnerved by their leader's performance. Above all, I thought, imagine Ky's mortification at this Mack Sennett in plain view of God and the world. Unfortunately, our turn was still to come.

Escorting the A-1s was anything but humorous. We were told to prevent them from getting to a point from which they could start a bombing run against the tanks, but that was more easily said than done. There was no question about slowing down to the Spad's speed and riding herd, so it became a game of chicken with us playing a dangerous version of "cut them off at the pass" with an aircraft that cost easily five times as much as theirs and was likely to come off the worse for it in the event of a midair collision. After a while, the VNAF landed, and everyone pretended that this was all a matter of fun and games.

Late that afternoon, a balding Marine Corps staff type major from III MAF arrived in all his puffery at our Hot Pad van (an airconditioned forty-foot trailer that, inhabited by our five-minute alert crews, smelled like a used jockstrap). He briefed the duty officer that if the VNAF fired up and attempted to taxi, we were to block the taxiways by any means at our disposal to prevent them from taking off. It was the kind of order one gets in the heat of battle to meet an immediate crisis but is rescinded as soon as a more permanent solution to the problem can be found. The trouble was that they had either forgotten about the order up at III MAF or run out of ideas. In any event, at 0600 the next morning, the VNAF did fire up, and Lieutenant Silas, the fourth duty officer since the order was issued, dispatched the maintenance trucks to blockade the taxiway.

The Vietnamese taxied up to the trucks, gunning their engines and brandishing their fists, but it was all to no avail. Finally they shut down on the taxiway, where they sat. It was an impasse with repercussions no one had anticipated. With the taxiway blocked by trucks and airplanes, nothing could move, not even the Hot Pad birds. For all intents and purposes, the base was out of business. Da Nang was an Air Force base on which the Marine Corps was merely a guest tenant, yet here was the Marine Corps clearly operating in support of General Chuan against Ky, who was supported by the U.S. Air Force. It was an interesting bit of sideplay, and long before the last propeller came to a stop, telephones were ringing in puzzle palaces all over Vietnam.

Perhaps if the loss of Ashau and the internecine debacle of Da Nang had not occurred in close proximity, things might have gone differently. Perhaps if the United States had closed ranks behind the Ky government in the middle of the crisis, everyone's confidence would not have been shaken. Unfortunately, from that time on, the tenuous ties between ourselves and the Vietnamese were broken. We didn't trust a government that appeared ready to fly apart at any moment, and they mistrusted our motives and sincerity. In successive stages we escalated the bombing of the North in a vain attempt to break the will of the Hanoi regime, while drawing our forces back into coastal enclaves and attempting to turn more and more of the fighting over to the South Vietnamese. But those were problems of a different order of magnitude. We had our own.

The squadron we relieved had lost but one plane and crew in a four-month stint, and that because it plowed into Monkey

Mountain trying to sneak back to the field VFR (visual flight rules) under the clouds. For reasons that were not immediately apparent, we fared far worse. We had barely finished unpacking before four of our most experienced people disappeared over North Vietnam. By the end of our first month, two more of our brand-new Phantoms had bitten the dust. In three months, nine Phantoms were all that remained of our original batch of eighteen, and many of them bore the scars of battle. There were questions raised as to why we lost so many airplanes so quickly, particularly since after the first few months we went a long time without taking so much as a hit. Most people ascribed it to the luck of the draw, but it wasn't. In the beginning, the Vietnamese were apt to dive for cover when they saw us coming, but after a while it became apparent to them that this made relatively little difference in their survival—either they were going to get creamed or not—so they might just as well stay at their guns and keep firing. We happened to get caught in the cusp, allowing prior experience to lull us into a false sense of security. We spent too much time in our runs and we paid for our complacency. On those of us who were still around, the months had left their mark, but our tactics and skills were honed to a fine edge indeed.

— 2 —
Kick the Tires

The moist breeze coming off the South China Sea muted the crescendoing whine of a jet engine start cart, while indistinct figures carrying light wands scurried like fireflies amid invisible airplanes. There had always been something about the smell of jet exhaust that quickened my pulse, and once again I was drawn into the magic of the flight line by that softening of focus that always anticipates the first launch of the day.

It was the last week in April 1966 and our target was at Vinh, a provincial capital halfway from the DMZ to Hanoi, 140 miles north of the DMZ in the panhandle region of North Vietnam. It was a primary staging point for the shipment of men and materiel westward to the Mu Gia or Ban Karai passes, where the Ho Chi Minh trail exited North Vietnam into Laos. Vinh's defenses had undergone a rapid upgrading in previous weeks, indicating that increased activity along the Trail was either contemplated for the near future or was under way. Two months before, we had been surprised when a flight took 57mm antiaircraft fire in the area. A week later, intelligence reported a SAM installation. In that morning's briefing, we were told that there were now four SAM rings and a new search radar, so something was going on. Until recently, the panhandle had not been as dangerous as the Red River delta, but that seemed to be changing. Now, Dong Hoi, fifty miles to the south, had a SAM ring, and the week before, one of our flights was chased by 57mm antiaircraft fire just north of the DMZ.

Our job was to neutralize the air defenses at the marshalling yards northeast of Vinh for a flight of four Air Force 105s coming in from their base in Thailand. This was my third trip to Vinh that month, and each time it had been to pin down the guns while an Air Force or Navy flight took out the real target. At first, the role of spear carrier rankled, but I had mellowed in the realization that while I'd seen plenty of guns, I had yet to spot vehicles or materiel at the staging site.

"The Thunderchiefs will be on target at precisely zero-seven zero-five, so you should be into your runs two minutes earlier." The briefer was a puffy Air Force major from Korat, Thailand, in to coordinate the attack and prepare for the possible divert for damaged aircraft.

"Don't get brave up there; just get on and off target in a hurry and out feet wet [over the ocean] at the coast so you don't get in the way. All there is up there is a lousy dirt field that some photo interpreter thinks might be being used for staging materiel for the trip south. Personally, I think that he's full of it, but that's not my problem." He looked for a moment as if he wished to pursue the subject a little further, before deciding differently. "Anyway, there's no target worth getting your ass shot full of buckshot, and I sure as hell don't want to be the one that has to explain to Seventh Air Force why another damned Marine got dinked doing flak suppression."

"Why don't you get the Thuds to hit the guns and give us a crack at the lousy dirt field?" my wingman asked, but it was a dead issue as far as the Seventh Air Force was concerned. Shooters were shooters and spear carriers were spear carriers and that's the way it was going to be.

The weather in the target area was marginal, but that was typical for the time of the year. At least we would have an ELINT (electronic intelligence) bird with us—a Whale—whose job it was to keep the SAMs and radar-controlled 57mm and 87mm antiaircraft fire off our tails. Of the bunch, the 57mm fire was the spookiest. Even on a clear day, you might not know that it was coming until you were in the midst of a bunch of grayish-brown smudges with pigtails. It amazed me how accurately the stuff could sneak up from behind—when you saw it rippling off at your altitude, it was a gut-grabber. It had been a long time since I'd flown straight and level over the North. You developed the "five-second twitch," where you made fairly abrupt and random changes in altitude and airspeed on an almost continuous basis. About every third jink, it was a good idea to reef the plane far enough around to take a good look at where you'd been.

SAMs were easier to spot, at least where you could see the ground, because their launch was a memorable event—even from 15,000 feet. If you could see the missile coming, you could outmaneuver it, but that didn't mean that you were home free. Where there was one missile with your name on it, there could well be two—or more—so while you were slapping yourself on the back for avoiding one "telephone pole," another one might stop your clock. SAMs were much more dangerous on a mission like this one, where we'd be cruising to the target over a cloud deck. The route of flight was designed to keep us away from the known sites, but there were plenty of pilots who'd been tagged by missiles that "couldn't have been there."

"Willie" the Whale was the venerable F-3D (later F-10) Douglas Skynight, an aircraft that came and went unnoticed between Korea and the Vietnamese war. It was designed as a night fighter carrying a crew of two and lots of radar gear. Time would have passed it by, but the need for airborne electronic intelligence and countermeasures gave Willie a new lease on life. Crammed to the teeth with electronic goodies, it was able to ferret out and jam enemy radar sites, degrading North Vietnamese antiaircraft gun and missile capabilities over a fairly large area at one time. Even where it couldn't jam the missile system, it could give warning of the system's presence, and often it could tell by the radar pulse whether or not a missile was in the air.

If all went according to plan, flight time for this mission would be less than two hours, and though that may not seem like very much, it was actually a long flight. It's a matter of prime time, where length is only partly a function of the number of minutes spent airborne. To begin with, the total time involvement for the mission was not exactly trivial. With the vagaries in the weather and transportation, our briefing commenced at 0415, an hour and forty-five minutes before takeoff and nearly three hours before our target time. Assuming that everything went according to plan, we would return for an eight o'clock landing, but it would be past nine before we got through with the debriefing, making it a five-hour turnaround.

A more valid measurement of this particular flight's length was the large number of discrete activities that had to be accomplished, and the need for being in the right place at the right time. After takeoff, our two aircraft were to proceed up the coast to rendezvous with a KC-130F tanker to take on 5,000 pounds (something in excess of 700 gallons) of fuel. Departing the tanker at the ARCP (air refuelling completion point), we would then cross the coastline slightly north of the DMZ, where we would join with our Whale for the flight into the target area. Coordinating with the F-105 flight, we would set ourselves up to arrive on target two minutes ahead of the Thuds, returning home over the water to make an instrument approach to landing. Any one of these milestones presented a number of opportunities for delay or change of plan. What was significant here was not "how hard" this all would be, or "how smart" I had to be in order to handle things, but rather how adaptable I would be in responding to a constantly changing situation. That is a matter of nurture, not nature. There are several attributes that the fighter pilot needs to bring with him when he signs up in the first place, chief among which are an unconcious but highly developed sense of time, the ability to concentrate his attention on the job at hand, and the desire to live forever. The importance of this last cannot be overstated, because without it, he might well stop inventing new options when the obvious ones dry up.

This was a priority mission, which meant that if either of our airplanes went down for some unforeseen maintenance problem—a likelihood of one in four at home and one in eight or nine in Vietnam where mission requirements obliged us to press on with aircraft we would not have taken on a training flight —there would be another airplane ready and waiting, but the switch would involve a minimum of ten minutes' delay in launch.

As it stood, the tanker was supposed to be at the southern end of his racetrack pattern, ready to turn to his outbound leg at 0620, the time that we should be reaching his station. The pattern was designed for us to use his outbound turn to facilitate rendezvous, putting us in position to plug in as he rolled wings-level heading northwest. If this went according to plan, we

should have completed our refuelling prior to the time that the
tanker had to turn back to the southeast to stay below the DMZ.
A late takeoff would almost certainly break down the timing
of the refuelling segment, compounding the problem and pushing an even greater delay into the next stage. At some point,
the decision might have to be made to bypass the tanker and
press on to the rendezvous with the Whale or even directly to
the target regardless of the increased risks involved. It wasn't
like, "I'll stop at a pay phone and let them know that we'll be
a little late." That things rarely went as planned was how it
was. Every change to the baseline mission introduced a new
set of givens that involved costs and choices . . . and only rarely
"opportunities." As long as you had reasonable options, you
were OK, but at some point you ran up against the irreducible
and that's where you earned your flight pay.

Suiting up for flight was no mean feat in itself. The first
layer of clothes was the flight suit, a tiger-striped camouflaged
jumper, made of a heavy worsted material to stand up to the
jungle, but hotter by far than the traditional cotton summer
flight suits they replaced. We received them when we arrived
in Vietnam, and for a day or two they fit just fine. Once we
had shed all of our excess weight, they hung on us like tents,
making us look like school kids playing "big people." The
visual aspect may have been humorous, but the comfort factor
wasn't. The tucks and folds inside the outer garments became
almost unbearable on long flights.

Next came the g-suit which is an inflatable girdle covering
the abdomen, thighs, and calves. It is laced tightly to begin
with, so that when the suit inflates, blood is prevented from
moving from the torso into the abdomen and legs. In jet aircraft,
engine compressor bleed-air is directed to the suit by the g-suit
controller any time the unit senses an acceleration on the airframe in excess of a predetermined amount. In the Phantom,
this was 2.5 g's (two and one-half times the force of gravity).
The greater the acceleration, the greater the volume of air that
is directed to the suit, so that at 8 g's, the effect can be quite
startling. By keeping the blood from being forced to the bottom
of the body, the g-effects—notably blackout, where the brain
doesn't receive enough blood to process optic inputs—can be
delayed considerably. Though the onset of blackout varies from
person to person, 5 to 6 g's are generally enough to humble
most unaided bodies. By tensing the abdomen and with the aid

of a g-suit, pilots are able to withstand in excess of 8 g's for considerably long periods of time. If you're properly prepared for high-g maneuvering, the onset of blackout is rarely rapid. Rather it is a progressive affair where peripheral sight and color degrade in an ever-constricting brown tunnel, until all is darkness. Held still longer, unconsciousness can follow, which is nature's way of saying "leggo the stick, dummy."

Over the g-suit is the torso harness which is designed to spread the loads from the four seat-attachment fittings over a large area of the body through a maze of crisscrossed straps connecting the various parts of the corset. During flight, it keeps you snugly pinned to the seat so you don't go sloshing around the cockpit during maneuvers, but its real purpose is to spread the load of parachute-opening shock following ejection. Attached to the outside are flashlights, D-rings, pistol restraint and flotation ring. It's reminiscent of a lady's corset, and were it not for the bristling hardware, it would be very Victorian. Properly snugged down, it keeps you bent slightly forward at the waist.

Our outermost garment was a survival vest that looped over the shoulders, providing a haven for another twenty pounds of gear, most of which would separate at ejection or at the deployment of the parachute. In all, it was a load, and thus configured, one did not march or walk or even plod. Movement was more of a rolling plunge.

Following suit-up, the last stop before the flight line was the line shack, where the pilots went through the yellow sheets to check the squawks from earlier flights and sign for the aircraft. The yellow sheets weren't yellow and hadn't been for quite some time, but tradition is a big thing in aviation. Some day, some admiral (perhaps one not yet into the fleet) might look at the form and ask "Why the hell do they call it a yellow sheet?" and no one will know. It will become a "white sheet" or "Aircraft System Evaluation and Flight Time Sheet," and that will be that.

My aircraft for the mission was Victor Whiskey Eight, a steady performer despite the network of patches and zinc chromate blotches adorning her aft fuselage and stabilator. These were a grim reminder of the bomb fragment damage during the battle for the Ashau Valley fire support base six weeks earlier. Eight had been lucky. One of our planes was a write-off, three others ate bomb fragments, while another three took

hits from the 23mm guns dug in on the flanks of the valley, which lay twenty-eight miles southwest of Hue, astride one of the major infiltration routes from North Vietnam. The worst part was that it had all been for naught as the base had to be abandoned.

The Phantom is a rugged airplane despite the complexity and sophistication of its systems. They were to our Douglas A-4 Skyhawks and F-4D Skyrays what those were to propeller-driven aircraft of World War Two. The Phantom was designed to take two men, several missiles, and an enormous radar and fire control system into the stratosphere at supersonic speeds to intercept incoming raiders at long range, or range out large distances to provide air superiority even over enemy territory. When it was introduced into service, the Phantom was the world's greatest tactical toy, filled with all kinds of "gee charlie whiz bangs" guaranteed to make any fighter pilot go into a state of terminal ecstasy. On the other hand, there were those who secretly doubted our ability to maintain them, and at first these fears seemed to have been all too well founded. The airplane had the potential for becoming a flying nightmare. The thousands of feet of plumbing, miles of electrical wiring, hundreds of servos and actuators made the Phantom an unparalleled challenge to the men who were tasked to maintain her. As experience with the machine grew and its more troublesome systems were refined, the maintenance effort rose to the level that the maintenance hours for each flight hour statistic moved into somewhat the same order of magnitude as that of the less complex F-8s and A-4s.

Looking at some of these airplanes after seven months of combat, I had a hard time recognizing them as the same shiny fighters that had come from the factory—the ones in which we made paint-blistering mach-2 runs during the acceptance flights. Now, with the dirt and grease and dents and tears, most of the birds would be lucky to hit a thousand knots, much less the 1,300 of their youth. Anyone seriously inspecting Victor Whiskey Eight would have had to ground her for major repair. She was dirty and tired with fuel and hydraulic fluid seeping from half a dozen places. Just behind the starboard main gear, an access panel was completely gone; there was galvanic corrosion in the vicinity of the tailhook attach fitting; the inner port main landing gear door had a gash where a servicing cart had run into it; and the port main tire had a flat spot with metal cord showing. Except for the tire, Eight had been that way for a long time, so there was no need to look for these things unless you had some sort of masochistic bent. If you planned on flying with these discrepancies anyway, you might just as well ignore them. Better just to make sure that the bombs were properly rigged and hung, that the accumulator pressures were where they belonged, and that the ejection seats were installed correctly.

A Ford tractor—one of two purchased with squadron coffee-mess funds from the local Ford dealer because our zoomy aircraft tow carts wouldn't stay together in that environment—waddled down the line on its mud tires, towing an aircraft start cart already whistling away at rated thrust. It was bad enough to use farm tractors for moving support equipment around, but ten times worse towing a 50,000-pound aircraft. If one ever had to stop quickly, the tractor's inferior weight and small footprint wouldn't be up to the task. In fact it was not uncommon to see a tractor held totally off the ground after a stop, when the aircraft it was towing settled back on its haunches. Worse yet was the plight of our ordnance crews, who had to hand-load bombs because the special purpose machines kept breaking down. There were these nifty gadgets designed to load an entire rack full of bombs at one time, but we couldn't keep a single one running. As a result, the ordnance people had to shove pipes into the fuse wells at either end of the bombs to act as handles to allow one group of men to muscle the bomb lugs up into the rack latches while another tightened the sway braces that snugged the bombs to the rack. Not only was this ordeal time-consuming, it was wasteful of people. Already, more than a dozen ordnance men had been placed on light duty because of back strains and there seemed to be no end in sight.

I finished my preflight inspection just as the last of the 500 pound bombs was being rousted onto the centerline rack. Jerry Wright, my RIO for the mission, rounded the wing and stared with horror at the bad tire. Calling the plane captain over, he began to complain, unmindful of the fact that the squadron had started the day with only six spares—enough to last us half a day if we were lucky. Maybe we'd get some new ones on the Marlog Flight from Okinawa that noon, but if we didn't, we'd have to rob tires from our down aircraft until we ran out of those too. It was what's known as the "breaks of Naval Air." Several months before, we had been going to North Vietnam with a lousy pair of World War II vintage, 270-pound, high-drag bombs, because the supply system couldn't keep up with the demand for the new low-drags. Tires, hydraulic pumps and drop tanks were the current panic, and though these would eventually come into adequate supply, by then we were sure to have turned up another critical shortage—a fact of life.

Climbing into the Phantom's front cockpit is a challenge. In the first place our flight gear had gotten out of hand. With all the junk and paraphernalia packed into the profusion of pockets that infested our tiers of garments, we were prepared to cope with any situation imaginable. Aside from the obvious things like a canteen of water, a flashlight, maps, and code books, I carried two emergency transmitters (experience had shown that they didn't work half the time), a 38-caliber pistol, 250 feet of rappelling line (some of the trees were taller than that), flares, knives, a saw, compass, fishing gear, a pound of rice, a spoon (for keeping the elephants away), morphine, gold coins, first aid pack, a book on survival, matches, shark repellent, whistle, signalling mirror, sewing kit, water purification tablets, and as the climax of a list that included perhaps seventy other items, two prophylactics (just in case, I suppose).

The cockpit is large compared to other tactical aircraft, and being a little runt, I felt adrift. It was not a bit like the friendly little cockpit of the A-4, which fits you like a glove. There's a plane you strap *on*, not *into*. This one was made for monsters. Still, that didn't seem to make a lot of difference when it came to climbing aboard. One problem for me was that the footholds are fairly far aft in the cockpit area, adjacent to the canopy hinge. As a result, front cockpit entry is an acrobatic maneuver, particularly if you want to avoid stepping on the seat cushion while missing the myriad handles and switches that protrude from every bulkhead and panel. Worse still for me was when the last person to fly the airplane had been one of our behemoths. Because of my size, I flew with the seat all the way up and the rudder pedals all the way aft. Tom Wilson, who flew Eight on its previous hop and who was six feet three, left the cockpit set up exactly the opposite, so after I snugged into the seat, I was faced with a full minute of cranking on a balky handle to bring the rudder pedals back to where my feet could reach them and even then I wasn't home free. I had to wait for external electrical power before I could raise the seat high enough to see out. People always worry about the major ca-

tastrophes such as fire or flameout or runaway trim, but my
secret terror was that the *seat* might run away to its lowest
position, leaving me stranded eyeball to eyeball with the stick
grip and forced to eject because I couldn't see out.

For me, finding a comfortable position was impossible.
There are those who swear that the designer was a sadist, others
who say that since the seat was designed by the British it was
made to accommodate Limey frames, but the truth is that if
things were too comfortable, there would be a danger of the
pilot falling asleep on a long hop. The way the seat is configured, you are almost forced to fall forward into the shoulder
straps. It takes an act of will to nestle into the molded seatback,
parachute pack, and headrest.

Strap-in is a matter of attaching four quick-release fittings
to the hip and shoulder rings on the torso harness, and then
threading a line through the eyelets of the leg restraint straps
buckled to each leg below the knee. The purpose of the leg
restraints is to draw the legs tightly against the seat during
ejection so that they will clear the dash panel and canopy bow
and hold them there until time for seat separation and parachute
deployment. Once firmly buckled in with the oxygen mask,
helmet and G-suit plugged in, movement other than fore and
aft is cumbersome at best.

Eight's cockpit smelled of sweat, mildew, hydraulic fluid
and burnt wiring and as always (it seemed) there was a pair of
pliers left by one of the maintenance people beneath the seat
just out of my reach. Adrift articles of this sort present no
problem as long as the plane is maneuvered under positive g-
loads. Only if the airplane were unloaded—flown at less than
one positive g—would the pliers present a danger, either by
rising up and striking the pilot or migrating to someplace where
they might jam a control. As I fastened my leg restraints, I
went over the various switch positions to make sure that when
electrical power was put to the airplane, nothing exciting would
happen. The week before, the fuel dump valve switch on one
of our planes had been inadvertently placed in the open position
while there was no power to activate the valves, so that when
power *was* applied, the valve cycled, dumping fuel all over
the flight line. The dump valves are located far aft on the wings,
well out of the pilot's line of sight, so by the time that the
plane captain got the pilot's attention, more than a hundred
gallons of JP-5 had been dumped on the ground. It was a mess,

and even after a fire truck hosed the area clean, the ramp was slippery and, in the blazing heat, extremely uncomfortable to be around.

The start cart next to the airplane began its tortuous climb to full power. Powered by a small jet engine, it provides both electrical power and the large volume of impingement air needed to activate the numerous electrical components and spin the engines for start. Selecting the external position on the electrical power panel brings the cockpit instantly to life. Bathed in a red glow from half a dozen hooded floodlights, the instruments spin and dance frenetically, finally steadying as their gyros come up to speed, while along the left side of the instrument panel two rows of amber lights on the *telelight panel* tell the status of various systems throughout the aircraft. Finally, completing the first section of my prestart checklist, and after noting the position of the inlet ramps and speed brakes, I was at long last ready to raise the seat to the top of its travel, which allowed me to fix my final position by reference to the gunsight image projected onto the combining glass atop the glare shield directly in my line of sight.

From this point on, the prestart check is a matter of monitoring warning lights and circuits and is, as such, mercifully simple. Still, this is the time to accomplish a lot of the little housekeeping tasks such as selecting radio and navigation frequencies, checking the gunsight, setting the clock and homing the racks. These could wait until later, but once the engines are running, the aircraft is going through six gallons of fuel a minute sitting in the chocks at idle—an amount sufficient to take the airplane two miles at cruise—so I always figured that it was better to waste the start cart's fuel rather than mine.

Though there is nothing difficult about firing up the Phantom, it is still a step-by-step procedure designed not only to get the engines running, but to allow the pilot to test the flight control systems as well. Air is selected to the left engine and as PC-1 (power control system-1) hydraulic pressure is developed for the flight controls, the control stick is pulled full aft to cycle the stabilator. This ensures that there is full longitudinal control authority with the left engine's hydraulic system alone. All of the main flight controls are served by two separate hydraulic systems, either of which can provide full authority throughout the entire flight envelope. Each system has its own pump, reservoir, pressure and return plumbing and actuating cylinder. During this check, the pilot is watching to see that the stabilator (the horizontal "flying tail" assembly providing nose-up and -down control) deflects fully to the nose-up stop and that the PC-1 system pressure stabilizes at 3,000 psi. There is a little judgment involved regarding how far the pressure drops off and how long it takes for the pressure to come up, as well as how the stick feels, but the check is quickly accomplished and when complete, start air is directed to the right engine for a similar check and engine start.

The needle unsticks and the RPM indication increases quickly to 10 percent, at which time the ignition button on the inboard edge of the right throttle is depressed and held. Simultaneously, the throttle itself is moved forward, then inboard around the idle detent. The first indication of light-off is a jump in exhaust gas temperature (EGT) accompanied by a more rapid increase in rpm. After light-off, you release the ignition button, and as the engine spools up to idle, the temperatures and pressures seesaw back and forth, ducts and ramps and auxiliary air doors open and close as if with minds of their own. Without consciously looking at all of the lights and gauges, you can pretty much tell the condition of the various systems. It is a matter of sound and feel and timing that give the clues. In combat, where you accept minor problems in the aircraft as a way of life, you come quickly to intuitive grips with the airplane and the health of its various parts. For instance, the slight buzz coming through Eight's airframe indicated to me that something deep in its innards was beginning to give up the ghost. I remember thinking at the time that it was the thrust bearings in the right engine, and that within perhaps 100 hours (should Eight last that long) the engine would have to be replaced. I was wrong—it was something in the accessory-drive section—but at least I was aware of it.

With the right engine at idle, I selected internal electrical power and repeated the same procedure for the left engine. With both engines started, and while the plane captains removed the air start hose and electrical umbilical from their receptacles, buttoning up the bottom of the aircraft in the process, I completed my cockpit duties and prepared for the pretaxi checks.

Internal electrical power is supplied by a pair of 10-KVA alternators mounted on either engine, each capable of handling the total aircraft electrical requirement. Because of the complexity and sophistication of the aircraft radar and fire-control systems, alternator frequency output is critical. Frequency is strictly a function of alternator speed (rpm) and is maintained by means of a constant speed drive (CSD)—a kind of automatic transmission bolted to the engine that reduces engine speed to the rpm for the correct frequency. When both engines are running, electrical output from the alternators is married through the bus tie relay. If there is a mismatch in the frequencies, this relay will not close and the two alternators will independently distribute power to selected buses. Normally, this is not a problem, but if either of the alternators subsequently fails with the bus tie relay open, electrical power to certain buses will be lost, with a commensurate loss in fighting potential.

The lead plane captain moved out front, signalling me to spread and lock my wings, and after the warning flags (beer cans) had disappeared, he had me drop flaps, speed brakes, and tailhook and cycle the stick full aft and to the left. To aid in low-speed lateral control, the Phantom uses both ailerons and flaperons. Positioning the stick to the left simultaneously raises a spoiler on the left wing, decreasing its lift, while increasing lift on the right wing by lowering its aileron. The combined actions make for crisper roll response. Finally, when all the pressures and indications confirmed the completion of these operations, I popped out the refuelling probe and finally the ram air turbine (RAT)—an emergency source of electrical and hydraulic power that is deployed by stored pneumatic pressure and is driven by the airstream.

My plane captain for the flight was Cpl. Carl Rodgers, nineteen years old, of south Texas. Compact and muscular, he was known to be something of a hell raiser at the club, but he was strictly business on the flight line. He joined the Marines right out of high school along with half of his graduating class. They went out and got drunk together on grad night and made a pact. Though some backed out in the cold light of morning, Rodgers didn't. He'd done well in the year and a half since he joined, taking correspondence courses in electronics, and he'd put in for avionics school at the end of the tour. If he got it, he'd probably reenlist for another tour and there was a good chance that from there he'd make it a career.

Of all the squadron maintenance functions, the plane captain's job is the hardest, requiring judgment and attention to detail. We tend to put our youngest and least experienced troops

on the flight line, yet they come into more direct contact with
the flight crews than do the troops from any of the other shops.
If something is not right with the plane, they bear the brunt of
the aircrew's frustration even when they're in no way to blame.
Their job is to turn the aircraft around from its previous flight,
seeing to the refuelling, servicing, drag-chute repacking and
general airworthiness. Often it is the plane captain who finds
a dangerous condition during his preflight and it is he who
must assess whether a problem is within limits or whether the
flight should be aborted. These are heavy responsibilities, and
ones not totally appreciated by many aircrew members.

Corporal Rodgers' assistants monitored the actuation of the
various systems, checking for full operation and leaks before
signalling their satisfaction with a thumbs-up. On Rodgers'
signal, I placed the stick full forward and to the right, simultaneously retracting speed brakes, flaps, tailhook and refuelling
probe. Again, the operations were monitored and their condition acknowledged.

The cockpit lights were noticeably paler as daylight approached and I could make out Rodgers' face as he awaited
my signal to pull the chocks and direct my taxi out of the line.
My wingman's lights came on, indicating that he was almost
ready to go.

"Asp Two up." That was Mike James, my wingman for the
mission. Asp was my personal flight call sign, so that whenever
I led a hop, it was used in intraflight communications. Other
people had more colorful calls such as Fokker and Deadbug
and Skidrow, but I chose mine because it was short and because
I had just seen the movie Cleopatra, which shows just how
inane all of this can be.

"Button Two." The headphones came alive with pops and
clicks as Jerry selected the new radio channel, which the control
box translated to a specific UHF frequency. The radio has
twenty preset frequencies, an emergency frequency Guard receiver, and a manual selector that permits access to any of the
several hundred discrete frequencies that comprise the UHF
spectrum.

"Da Nang Ground, Boilerplate One taxi for two. Request
blocktimes zero-zero, four-zero, and four-four."

Boilerplate One was the flight's tactical call sign that had
been assigned to this particular mission. It was our identifier
to all other agencies, and as we were a two-plane flight, Boil-

erplate One was composed of Boilerplate One Dash One and
Boilerplate One Dash Two. The blocktimes were our lost communications recovery times for the flight, and were given in
Greenwich mean time (also called GMT or Zulu time) instead
of local time to create confusion. GMT makes sense in situations where flights transit different time zones, but there launch
and recovery were in the same place, so it was merely some
extra workload. In any event, were we to lose radios, we would
be automatically cleared to commence a penetration through
the clouds at 7:40 and 7:44 local time, and all traffic would
be routed out of the way.

Aircraft radio communications are terse to the point of being
almost unintelligible to the uninitiated. One of the most difficult
things for student pilots is to make heads or tails of the staccato
bunch of gibberish that rattles out of the radio. If that weren't
bad enough, simultaneous transmissions produce a loud squeal
blocking out both messages, adding to the chaos and congesting
the airwaves still further. As a result, pilots try to make their
messages as brief as possible, and nothing is more painful than
listening to a bunch of citizens-band hotdogs with their "ten-
four, old buddy" garbage.

Jerking my thumbs aft past my ears, I gave Rodgers the
"pull chocks" sign, and at his signal added thrust to glide
smoothly out of the line. A light tap on the brakes ensured that
they were working before the aircraft built momentum for the
turn onto the taxiway. There were several factors here. First,
if the brakes failed to work, there would be time to shut the
engines down before the aircraft crunched into the planes parked
across the flight line. Second, you wanted to be moving fast
enough to make the turn with the throttles at idle because excess
thrust would cause the tires to scrub, and third, because as it
exited at over a hundred miles an hour, the exhaust blast could
cause injury or damage farther back on the flight line.

"Boilerplate One cleared runway three-five, winds zero-
four-five at one-five, gusting two-two. Altimeter two-niner point
eight-nine. Blocktimes zero-zero, four-zero, and four-four confirmed."

It takes a fair amount of throttle to get the Phantom moving,
but once rolling, even with a full load, it taxis along briskly
at idle thrust. Here I had to temper my desire to get airborne
on time with the necessity of protecting the bad tire. We were
running half a minute late, but we could make it up. It may

seem petty to worry about so small an increment of time, but in much the same way that a businessman looks at time in terms of money, a fighter pilot looks at time in terms of fuel or, more to the point, alternatives of action. In order to make up the half-minute in the air, I would have to increase my speed en route to the tanker by roughly fifteen knots, for which I would pay a penalty of 200 pounds of fuel. Not much you might say, but that same amount of fuel is good for twenty miles of range at the other end of the flight, which could prove to be significant.

Jerry was involved with his BIT (built in test) checks on the radar and weapons system, but even a glance at BIT Two told me that our air-to-air capability was nil. It could have been that there was moisture in the radar and that it might cook out after takeoff, but I doubted it. What it came down to was spare parts, reliable test equipment, decent working conditions and strong technical supervision—categories that were at that moment, less than optimal.

Flying is full of checklists, the single most important of which is the takeoff check, requiring teamwork between the pilot and RIO. Much of it can be accomplished on the taxi-out, particularly those parts involving switch positions, compass and navigation settings, and auxiliary equipment selection. It is a time to review immediate action emergency procedures and go over the flight profile for the first minute or so of flight when cockpit duties require a good deal of attention.

Most people seem to regard landing as the most hazardous portion of a flight. Certainly it requires concentration, but by the time the flight is into the landing phase, the pilot is (or at least should be) ahead of the airplane. Not so during takeoff, where the pilot's mind is playing catch-up. Everything is moving at once. Instrument indications are in flux; the aircraft is transiting its most critical boundaries; sensory inputs to the pilot are often jumbled and confused; and in the first few moments of flight the opportunities for error are increased fivefold above those found in cruise. The crew is "along for the ride" for some amount of time subsequent to the decision to commit to flight. (Without a doubt, the most dangerous regime in all of flight is the night catapult-shot off an aircraft carrier, where the first hint that you have of an emergency is probably your last sensation at the instant that the aircraft slaps the water.)

After the aircraft is established comfortably in its climb

configuration, the workload diminishes and there is time to take stock of things. But until then, so many things are changing so rapidly that it is wise to have the cockpit cleanup and departure procedures established firmly in mind, so they can be handled automatically.

Just before the head of the runway was the arming area where our racks were connected and the missiles plugged in. We pointed our noses in pretty much the same direction that we were heading on the taxiway, angled slightly towards the coast towards a clear area, just in case there was stray voltage on the pigtails. Asp Two was parked on my right between me and the runway, so that as I pulled out, I passed in front of him to keep from hitting him with my jet blast. Even though it was swept twice daily, the taxiway was littered with debris, and it wouldn't take much to FOD (foreign object damage) one of his engines.

"Asp, button three."

"Asp Two up."

"Boilerplate One ready for takeoff."

"Boilerplate One flight cleared for takeoff. Maintain runway heading. Contact departure control on button four when safely airborne."

It was just starting to rain again as we wheeled onto the runway. This presented no particular problem except to our forward visibility, which was bad enough to begin with. Until the advent of HUDs (heads-up displays) in the mid-seventies, there wasn't a fighter in the world with good forward visibility characteristics. Typically the windshield braces and canopy bows abounded with such add-ons as mirrors, angle of attack indexer, outside air temperature gauge, wet compass, compass correction card, airspeed correction card, etc. On the glare shield above the instrument panel, there was a gunsight and its setting mechanisms, which intruded on perhaps 40 percent of the forward field of view. On a scale of one to ten, I would give the Phantom a three (about the same as a Pantera with a set of fuzzy dice), compared to a six to the A-4 and an eight point five for the Grumman A-6 Intruder. It was of little consolation then to know that the designers of the next generation of fighters realized that good visibility was more important than an extra tenth of a mach number or ten miles of radar range.

Prior to its engine run-ups, the Phantom might seem to be just another airplane, but as each J-79 in turn is jam accelerated

from idle to 100 percent (roughly 10,200 rpm) you begin to
sense how extraordinary it really is. In earlier airplanes, ram-
ming the throttle home rarely met with anything but the sluggish
engine acceleration exhibited by most jets. In fact, any over-
zealous use of the throttle was likely to induce a chuff-back or
even a flameout. By contrast, the J-79's response is so superb
that there is virtually no lag. The engine with its variable inlet
guide-vanes and complex system of sensors and controls ac-
counts for most of this, but the inlet design of an airframe is
a funny thing. It is anything but an exact science, particularly
where supersonic flight is to be part of the envelope. Designing
inlets that permit all the extremes of performance—instant
throttle response from sea level to 60,000 feet; zero airspeed
to above mach 2; straight-and-level 1-g flight to the pulled-to-
the-limit-of-corkscrewing-madness air combat maneuvering
regime—requires more than mere knowledge or skill. It takes
inspiration and luck.

My run-ups were normal and after one final check of my
instruments and indicators, I turned my attention to Mike's
airplane, watching as his flaps came down, their full transition
confirmed by a puff of steam from water trapped in the boundary layer control ducts. Hot air is bled from the engines, routed
through ducts running just behind the wing leading edges and
exhausted into the space between the leading edge flaps and
the wings. By adding energy into the airstream—the so called
boundary layer of air that tends to stagnate under slow speed
conditions—the lifting capacity of the wing is increased so
enormously that the Phantom is able to slow to 135 knots for
landing aboard an aircraft carrier. (Military aviation uses the
convention of the knot, which is a speed equivalent to one
nautical mile per hour. The nautical mile, which is 6,076 feet
in length as opposed to the 5,280 foot statute mile, is more
useful in navigation in that it equals one minute of one degree
of latitude. The Phantom's 135-knot approach speed works out
to 155 miles per hour in your Nash Rambler.)

As Mike's head came up out of the cockpit he simultaneously
signalled his status with a thumbs-up. This kind of cavalier
treatment bothered me, because one of the supposed advantages
of section flying is mutual support, which in this context suggested that he look my airplane over for obvious discrepancies
such as improper configuration, major leaks, fire or the like.
It was a minor thing, but it showed a lack of discipline that

was then more prevalent among Phantom pilots than (for example) the A-4 community. Perhaps this was a reflection of the training cycle back in the States, where Phantom squadrons often launched single aircraft to run their air-to-air missile training exercises alone against other types of aircraft with which they would rendezvous (or perhaps merely intercept) at a later time.

It was time to go, and I threw the throttles forward to their military (nonafterburning) stops. As the engines accelerated through 80 percent rpm, at which point I released the wheel brakes, the airplane began to gather momentum. At its present weight (nearly 53,000 pounds), the airplane's acceleration was something less than startling. After six seconds in basic engine, and at an airspeed of perhaps forty knots (the airspeed indicator needle doesn't bother to come off the peg until fifty or sixty knots), I selected afterburners by moving the throttles outboard and then forward to the stops. The response was immediate and vastly more satisfying as the thrust jumped from 20,000 to 34,000 pounds. Runway markers began to gallop by as the airspeed needle rose from the peg and wound quickly past the century mark. With the stick held full aft, the nose gear began to extend at 125 knots and unstuck with a little shimmy at 140. I established a 12-degree nose-high attitude to allow the airplane to fly itself off, easing forward on the stick as the airplane approached its proper climbing stance. One moment the main wheels were thumping and thudding along the runway, rocking the airplane from side to side, and the next there was a chilling smoothness as the Phantom clawed into its element. The airspeed was passing 185 as I began the transition to climb configuration.

Gear retraction takes less than three seconds, but the sequence of events is no less intricate than a ballet. It begins with selection of the gear handle to the up position. In military airplanes, the gear handle is a hefty chunk of metal that pilots are taught to move with a vengeance, as if the force itself were important to the success of the operation. (It's a deeply ingrained habit to slam the handle to the stops, and every time I fly a civilian airplane I have to stop and think lest I tear the puny little selector off at the stump.)

What the pilot sees in the cockpit while the gear are in transition is a red light in the handle itself and unsafe "barber poles" in the position indicator windows. When the gear are fully retracted and all doors closed, the light goes out and the word *up* appears in each of the windows. It doesn't seem that complicated, but underneath the aircraft it's a different matter.

So tightly interwoven are the various actions that at real speed they tend to appear haphazard. The inner doors of the main landing gear open while the internal gear-locking mechanisms unlatch. The sidebrace support knuckles break, allowing the retract cylinders to draw the gear inboard into the wells. As the struts come up, the oleos are mechanically compressed to provide clearance in the wells, while simultaneously the spinning wheels are snubbed to a stop. Up front, the nose gear is centered and rotated aft into its well. All three gear engage and cock over-center up-lock mechanisms, and the gear doors slam shut, completing the sequence. For all of this, the pilot feels but the slightest pull on the nose.

No sooner had the light in the gear handle gone out than the speed swept through 200 knots and it was time to bring the flaps up. This sequence, while less intricate than that of the landing gear, holds potential hazards of its own. Mechanically, things are pretty much straightforward. The leading and trailing edge flaps are drawn up rails hydraulically, and direct linkages close the BLC control valves, shutting off compressor bleed-air to the boundary layer control ducts. All well and good, but if for some reason a BLC control valve doesn't close, the result is swift, detrimental and occasionally spectacular. The ducts are nested among bundles of wires and a profusion of fuel and hydraulic lines. With the flaps up, hot compressor air can't escape, nor is there airflow to take away the heat. The likelihood of a wing fire under such conditions is high—so high in fact that the mere suspicion of a BLC malfunction is to be treated as if it were confirmed and met with the immediate response of relowering the flaps, returning to land as soon as possible, or in the jargon of the day, ASAP.

With the gear and flaps up, the Phantom—even heavily laden with bombs and fuel tanks—responded like a powerful cat loosed from its bonds, and the airspeed vaulted swiftly. At best, the Phantom is a noisy airplane full of thumps and whistles, shimmies and unsynched vibrations, groans and wheezes, all punctuated by occasional bangs. Fuel transfer valves rack back and forth and the three separate hydraulic systems are continually in action. The pneumatic system is constantly building and discharging pressure, while the engines, with their myriad pumps and accessories, whirr and buzz in a cacophony of mismatched sounds. Underlying all is the rush of slipstream ripping and tearing at the profusion of carbuncles, protuberances and discontinuities that make the combat-laden Phantom the aerodynamic anomaly that it is. Now, reaching 300 knots, I secured the afterburners and rotated to climb attitude. Behind me, Mike, who had delayed his takeoff for thirty seconds, confirmed his status.

"Asp Two airborne, button four."

— 3 —

— Heading for the Pub —

With the nose now 5 degrees above the horizon and the power reduced to 95 percent rpm, the rate of climb indicator held steady at 2,000 feet per minute. It would be ten minutes and roughly seventy miles before we would level off at our initial cruising altitude of 21,500 feet. It was now time to check the gauges, the time to settle in, attuning myself to the noises and motions that distinguished Victor Whiskey Eight from others on the flight line; a time to get thoroughly read into the instruments before boring into the bottom of the overcast. It was time to turn my attention from the task of becoming airborne to that of performing the mission.

"Departure control, Boilerplate One flight airborne at zero-one, blocktimes zero-zero, four-zero, and four-four."

"Roger, Boilerplate. Radar contact. Your wingman is one mile in trail. Report VFR on top."

The weather guessers had set the tops of the lower level at 14,500 feet, with an upper deck based at 27,000, tops to 41,000. That was pretty much typical for the time of the year, and we should have begun to run out from under the high clouds on the other side of the DMZ and see the ground somewhat south of Vinh. The altimeter had just rolled through 15,000 feet as

42

we scratched through the ragged tops into clear air. The upper deck was pewter-colored, textured with lines of ribs, but far out over the water to the east there was a swath of blue.

"Boilerplate One Dash Two is on top at fifteen-two. Tallyho Dash One."

Tallyho is a throwback to our Limey cousins and their old-school customs of the Second World War. It signified the sighting of the quarry in a hunt and was thus dashingly apropos. It remains a part of military aviation because of its colorful heritage, but not purely so. It happens that its propagation on the radio is highly distinctive, particularly when contrasted with its opposite, "no joy." Phraseology is far from being an exact science, but it is of critical importance in aviation, where misinterpretation of the spoken word can bring about disaster, or worse still, acute embarrassment.

Over the years controllers and aviators have developed standard phrases covering the entire spectrum of flying activities so that individual words need not be understood in order for communication to take place. Moreover, even simple words may convey a body of implicit understandings to those of a particular discipline. The word *break* to a transport pilot might connote a shift in recipient for a particular transmission, whereas a fighter pilot hearing *break* will immediately pump up a bucket of adrenaline in preparation for bringing his aircraft into a nosedown, hard as possible, last-ditch emergency turn to evade imminent danger.

"Roger, Boilerplate One Dash Two; we show you in a half-mile trail. You're cleared to Panama."

"Thank you, Departure. Dash Two come starboard twenty. Switch button five."

Our immediate concern was to get joined up and established in combat spread as expeditiously as possible—no trivial matter despite the fact that rendezvous was a part of virtually every flight. Mike was 2,000 feet below me at my four-thirty position on our base heading to the tanker of 350 degrees magnetic at the prebriefed airspeed of 310 knots. While he had been climbing at full power, I'd reduced thrust to 95 percent to allow him to work off the altitude differential. If he wished, he could go to a higher airspeed to join, but doing so could pose problems. Closure is a matter of angle-off and airspeed differential, and at jet airspeeds and distances, the rates can be insidiously high.

Often, if you wait until you are able to judge the relative motion visually, you are into a situation where only a last-ditch maneuver has any chance of salvaging things—and even that might not hack it. This illustrates a point that deserves emphasis: in contrast with its piston-engined cousin, a jet requires far more anticipation, particularly if it is to be flown anywhere near the boundaries of its envelope. At high altitudes and airspeeds, small changes in attitude can lead to unbelievably large excursions in the aircraft's rate of climb or descent, accompanied by changes in the aircraft's flight characteristics and maneuvering potential. Often the changes are too small to show on the gyro instruments, appearing on the pressure-sensitive gauges long after they have taken place. Where the margin for error is small, the pilot must stay way ahead of the airplane, making corrections because he knows he *must*, not in response to a perceived problem.

"Panama, Boilerplate One is fifty nautical on the zero-zero-five Da Nang TACAN out of angels one-eight, climbing for base plus seven."

"Radar contact, Boilerplate One. Negative traffic in your vicinity. The tanker bears three-five-zero for forty-six. Remain this frequency until advised."

It was preferable both from the standpoint of fuel usage and final positioning that Mike's rate of closure be primarily a function of angle-off rather than airspeed. Under the best of circumstances, the wingman will burn roughly 5 percent more fuel than the leader in the process of maintaining position, so it is important not to add to the imbalance. By turning him away, I forced him further forward on the rendezvous bearing, and as he drove up to my three-thirty position (relative to the direction in which my nose was pointing), I turned into him 40 degrees, setting up a *hot* crossing angle in which he (were he to do nothing to change things) would pass in front of me. In response, he was forced to turn back to the left (into me) to avoid overreaching me, increasing his angle-off still further, while creating a closure of over a hundred knots. At this rate, he was able to work off the half-mile trail in less than a minute.

Mike slid up the rendezvous bearing, closing rapidly. Cutting behind my tail at less than a 1,000 feet, he assumed the base course while I maintained my heading, waiting until he appeared in my seven-thirty position. Judging the relationship of the two aircraft, I rolled back to the base course in time to place him directly abeam on my port side, sliding out to the combat spread position where the aircraft were separated by 6,000 to 10,000 feet, a distance dictated by several factors having to do with turning performance, visibility, and the nature of the presumed threat.

Combat formations are, if anything, more difficult to maintain properly because the immense distances involved allow differential velocities to occur before anyone in the flight becomes aware of the situation. It is easy enough to say that it is the wingmen's responsibility to maintain position on the leader, but clearly it is not that simple. The leader who doesn't make little adjustments to help his wingmen out is going to find himself in a state of continual frustration.

The worst situation occurs when the wingman sits *sucked* where, because he is behind bearing, he is in a poor position to clear the leader's tail from a threat requiring the leader to turn away from the section. Moreover, in lying aft of the leader's abeam position, he cuts down on the distance behind his own tail that the leader can see. Good formation work takes planning and virtually total concentration.

Present-day section tactics (in the doctrinaire sense at least) date from World War II, when they were developed and employed to offset the initial superiority of the enemy fighter planes. The essence of section tactics is the concept of *mutual support*, in which the security of one element rests in the hands of the other. It was my job to keep Mike's aircraft clear of danger, not his, and if he were to come under attack, I would: (1) issue maneuvering instructions as necessary, (2) move to "sandwich" the intruder, and (3) shoot the intruder down if possible. In the present context, the danger area included not merely Mike's tail, but the ground underneath, from which a surface-to-air missile (SAM) attack might occur. In like manner, Mike was responsible for protecting me, though as a matter of curiosity, I would check my own tail occasionally.

Air combat maneuvering is the pinnacle of flying performance. It combines every basic flying skill at the level of maximum performance, where the wages of error or indecision are possible death, and worse still, the ignominy of defeat. Though dogfighting appears to be quick and dirty, it isn't. Even the successful completion of a stealthy slicing attack requires skills that are sown by intrepidity and nourished by repetition. The imagination and concentration that allow the fighter pilot to maneuver confidently in the three-dimensional arena describing the world of the dogfight are the product of hard work and attention to detail. They go to confer a badge that is as visible to other pilots as any insignia a pilot might wear on his uniform.

The first commandment in dogfighting is to see the enemy—before he sees you if possible, but certainly before he reaches a firing position. Historically, the vast majority of the kills have come by stealth, where the first warning the victim has is the sound of his aircraft buckling in a fusillade of cannon fire.

With the Phantom in Vietnam, if you saw the enemy before he got "in the saddle," and if you didn't lose your head, the odds were that you could maneuver to keep the attacker from reaching a tracking solution—even against the vaunted (but now out-dated) MiG-21. Granted, there is not much that you can do against a forward-quadrant attack by an enemy equipped with a missile with an all-aspect capability such as the Sparrow, but luckily the North Vietnamese didn't have anything of that caliber or we'd have been in deep kimchee. As it was, they were stuck with a tail-on attack, so the key was to keep them from achieving a position within the lethal range and g-envelopes for their weaponry—guns or a heat-seeker missile that was a carbon copy of our original Sidewinder. A guns attack had to be pressed to within 500 feet, whereas the range of the missile could be as much as a mile, depending on altitude and closing rate. Suffice it to say that once the missile seeker-head has locked on within the missile's range and g-limits, it is almost impossible to escape no matter how hard you maneuver, so it is mandatory that you begin evasive tactics as soon as possible.

Next in importance is increasing your aircraft's energy to a higher level than that of your adversary. Not only does this provide a margin of performance, but it allows you more options as the engagement continues. In a dogfight, you might be waxing your opponent's tail and just about to blow him out of the sky, but lose when another aircraft jumps you while you are concentrating on the first enemy. If you have an energy advantage (aka "positive delta mach") you may be able to disengage and get away. Without it, you're the one who's sandwiched, and against two opponents, your goose is likely on its way to the table.

The third mandate is that you think offensively. Even while you are on the defensive, you must be thinking ahead to how you are going to neutralize the situation and wrest the advantage. Then it's a matter of taking the attack to him. With the Phantom, this means getting the attacker onto your turf. The MiG-21 has a lot of good qualities, chief among which is its small frontal area, making it hard to spot. On the positive side of the ledger (ours), it has some very exploitable weaknesses. The 21 is in its element at high mach above 25,000 feet, but get him down to 10,000 and the Phantom with its tremendous thrust-to-weight advantage will eat him up. At 8,000 feet, a clean Phantom (one without racks, rails or tanks) is able to maintain altitude while reefed into an 8-g turn. Put a MiG-21 into a high angle of attack situation and it becomes a bucking bronco that can only be pointed rather than aimed. Inlet design deficiencies in the MiG-21 limit its airspeed to 570 knots indicated, while the Phantom can go on up to 750 (in Vietnam, only the F-105 was faster), allowing us to gain energy and separation at the same time.

Rule four is that you don't get locked into a fight unless you have enough fuel to finish it. The Phantom was designed as an air superiority fighter rather than as an interceptor, meaning that it is supposed to be able to range out and fight over a distant battlefield. Even so, doing battle over North Vietnam imposed a rather severe restriction on our options. Often, the North Vietnamese pilots were within minutes of their landing fields, while we had more than an hour to get to ours. There would be scant pleasure in knocking a MiG down and having to eject on the way home for lack of fuel.

Watching the wild, tumultuous tumblings of a dogfight, one might envision violent manipulation of the controls to be part of the action. Nothing could be further from the truth. It is the person who brings his aircraft smoothly up to the edge of maximum performance *without exceeding it* who has the advantage. In a fight, anything less than maximum performance is an error, but that error (his or yours) need not be fatal if neither of you capitalize on it. Therefore, offensive thinking requires that you *assume* that the opponent is going to make mistakes, so that when he does, you will be prepared to reap full advantage of the situation.

In order to provide for mutual defense, a flight would typically proceed into hostile territory in combat spread, separated by 6,000 to 10,000 feet, each pilot continually clearing the other's tail. A bogie would most normally approach from the side, slightly aft of an abeam position, "perched" 5,000 to 6,000 feet high and a mile and a half abeam. He would likely begin his run by turning into the section and lowering his nose to pick up airspeed, planning to descend slightly below the near element and reverse at about a half mile out in order to cut the angle-off down to about 20 degrees. This would place him out of sight of the intended victim, and if no evasive action were taken, the intruder could hardly fail to knock his target down.

The counter to this begins with good lookout doctrine. As soon as the bogie is sighted, a turn *into* the raid is commenced, the severity of which is a function of the threat. If the bogie is spotted before he commences his attack, the turn can be *easy*—25 to 30 degrees angle of bank—forcing the bogie to do something (anything). Once the bogie has established in the attack and is approaching the reversal point, the defenders must go to a *hard turn* of 45 to 60 degrees angle of bank. If the bogie is not spotted until he is past the reversal, coming up on tracking, the flight is forced to perform a *break turn*, which is a maximum-performance, nosed-down, gut-wrenching panic maneuver meant to throw the attack off aim.

Regardless of the severity of the initial maneuver, the purpose is to get the bogie to *overshoot* the flight path of the section, and after he has been forced to the outside, the idea is to increase the angle-off and separation until it is the intruder who is the defender. The key to this is throwing him out of phase. Once you have gotten your energy up to his level, you can begin to nibble at him. When you see his nose come down, you pull yours up and vice versa, but you never *reverse* your turn unless you see that he is going to overshoot badly.

The base energy level of the engagement determines the extent to which maneuvering is accomplished in the vertical rather than the horizontal plane. Typically, the Phantom is maneuvered through a series of barrel rolls, performing what is commonly referred to as a vertical rolling scissors in order to cut down the angle-off and align the fuselage with the enemy's in order to get a shot. Often, the aircraft corkscrews through the dead vertical up as well as down, with the g-loading alternating between a half-g on the top to over 8 g's on the bottom. Despite the nibbling of prestall buffet well in advance of its critical angle of attack, the Phantom is an honest flyer and tracker all the way up to the moment of departure. Then

it can be a beast. Stall is announced by the "Phantom thing"—
an abrupt wing drop—and if the angle of attack is now lowered
immediately, a spin could well develop. One of the problems
with late-model high performance aircraft is that because they
are able to develop such tremendous kinetic forces, departure
from controlled flight can be spectacular and sometimes un-
recoverable. Features such as wing sweep, low sideplate area,
gyroscopic coupling, and low polar moment of inertia (to name
a few) can combine to make a pilot's life miserable if he chooses
to exceed the aircraft's critical angle of attack. In most cases,
the Phantom's spin—upright or inverted—is fairly docile,
masking the fact that the airplane is elevatoring down at a
horrendous rate. Even so, the spin may not be recoverable
despite the proper application of controls and deployment of
the drag chute. The handbook calls for ejection if the airplane
is not recovered at 10,000 feet above the ground, because
further delay might prove fatal.

Even while you are fighting for your life against one attacker, you never stop looking for his buddy. Surprisingly, the
Soviets and their allies have never placed much store in section
tactics—possibly because of their inferior equipment—but in
all too many cases they have won, because a second intruder
has jumped in to finish off a fight.

Because of its higher thrust-to-weight ratio and superior high
angle of attack performance against the MiG-21, the Phantom
should be able to go to the offense within two turns, going for
separation and bringing its weapons to bear in three. Because
of their own performance deficiencies, the Vietnamese pilots
wisely chose to come at the Phantom with a slashing attack,
making a single pass and hauling tail regardless of the outcome.
While we could look with pride at the relative lack of success
the North Vietnamese pilots had against our airplanes—even
the heavily laden Thuds and A-7s—we could not overlook the
effectiveness that their mere presence had in disrupting attacks.
The excited call of enemy aircraft airborne in a certain sector
was often sufficient to cause flights to jettison ordnance and
wheel in anticipation of an attack. It was something we had to
keep in mind ourselves as we proceeded to Vinh. Others depended on our ability to neutralize the antiaircraft site with our
bombs, and that was our job—not fighting MiGs.

Our flight slid into its base altitude of 21,500 feet at 325
knots indicated airspeed, which yielded a true airspeed of just

over 420 knots. Above and beneath us, the cloud cover was complete in all directions, though the upper deck showed some signs of breaking up. We were within five minutes of our scheduled refuelling time.

"Boilerplate One, contact Joyride on button six."

There was a method to our radio channelization: button one was our squadron's common frequency, used to transmit non-tactical information; two was for ground control; three for tower; four, departure; five, Panama, Da Nang's GCI site; and six for Joyride, which was the tactical air control center (TACC) located on the ground at Da Nang and responsible for or, more precisely, cognizant of all tactical flights within I Corps. (I Corps was the northernmost of four arbitrary zones of tactical responsibility in South Vietnam.)

"Joyride, Boilerplate One, two Fox-fours with twenty-four Delta-fives, four Delta-sevens, mission number foxtrot-charlie niner-five, two-two x-ray."

Why we had to tell Joyride all of that was beyond me. III MAF received its mission requirements from the Seventh Air Force in the evening and after sitting on them for a while, it divvied the missions out to the air groups by means of a missive known as the FRAG—fragmentary combat operations order. The FRAG was then transmitted to the squadrons late at night, detailing call signs, ordnance, target times and the rest. All the squadrons had to do was fill in the blanks with flight crews and aircraft, shooting a copy of their flight schedule back up the chain of command to III MAF—so whoever it was that was on the radio had all the information in front of him. As far as all this Delta-fives (500-pound low-drag bombs) and Delta-sevens (AIM-7 Sparrow missiles) hogwash went, the enemy monitored our frequencies and knew our ordnance codes as well as we did—probably better—so one was left to suspect that it served the purpose of making staff types feel like a "part of the team."

"Copy, Boilerplate One. Your Pigeons to Basketball One Nine, three-five-zero for thirty-seven. Remain this frequency until advised."

Basketball One Nine was a Marine Corps KC-130 Hercules set up for air refuelling. His orbit point was over the water about twenty miles south of the DMZ.

Configured with two 270-gallon external fuel tanks, the Phantom could have made it to the target and back to Da Nang without refuelling, but it would be so tight on gas that there would be little margin for error. Were we to have to take evasive maneuvers requiring afterburner, we'd be walking home.

It would have helped in the rendezvous with the tanker if our radar had been working, and at that time my repeater scope showed an attack presentation. For an instant, I took heart, but I quickly recognized in the movement of the aim dot that Jerry was going through his BIT checks again—in this case Test 2. The location of the closing velocity indicator was still wrong, which meant that we would have no Sparrow missile capability. If we got jumped, Mike would have to be the shooter and as a last-ditch maneuver I could always ram someone.

On the bottom of the Phantom's fuselage there are four recessed bays, sized and plumbed to house the Sparrow missile. The Sparrow is a "semiactive" air-to-air homing missile, differing from "active" missiles in the essential detail of who handles the guidance. In the case of the latter, the missile itself carries all of the equipment required to locate, track, and detonate against an enemy aircraft. With Sparrow, the aircraft's radar illuminates the target, tells the missile where to look and what to look for in terms of a Doppler frequency, and the missile uses its own radar antenna to home in on the target. As is the case with active missiles, Sparrow enjoys an all-aspect attack capability—meaning that it can be fired at the opponent from any relative position including (and optimally so) head-on, so long as range and angle-off parameters are met. The advantages of the Sparrow system relative to a fully active system are in cost and size. Its drawback is that the launcher aircraft must continually illuminate the target throughout the entire flight of the missile, meaning that the fighter can engage but one attacker at a time, and during that commitment he is unable to take any serious defensive action of his own. Moreover, if lock-on is broken after its launch, the missile will self-destruct.

Perhaps the best known and most useful missile system in existence is the infrared or heat-seeking family, of which the Sidewinder is the archetype and leader. Typically, these were carried two to a pylon on the inboard pair of weapons stations, though on this particular mission we had foregone Sidewinders in order to mount bomb racks instead. (A later modification to the pylon allowed missiles and bombs to be carried on the TERs, but that was still some time in the future.) The pilot tunes the missile to the ambient IR threshold and when the

seeker-head on the Sidewinder senses a heat source above that
level, it "locks-on" and tracks it until such time as a higher
source enters its field of view. It was named Sidewinder because, like its namesake, the sidewinder rattlesnake, it homes
on heat, but it is interesting to note that the analogy has been
taken a step further. The IR threshold is presented to the pilot
as a rasping tone, much as that made by a Geiger counter or
an agitated rattlesnake. The louder and more intense the growl,
the higher the IR source. Aircraft exhaust is extremely attractive
to the Sidewinder and though it is possible for the missile to
track aircraft inlet IR, it is essentially a rear-quadrant weapon,
meaning that the pilot must tuck in behind the enemy aircraft,
locate the IR signature with the seeker-head tone, and launch
while holding the tone.

Which is the better missile, Sparrow or Sidewinder? It depends on the mission. For point defense, where you must engage the intruder far enough out from the target to shoot him
down before he can deliver his weapons, the Sparrow is the
better choice *so long as you can separate the good guys from
the bad*. However, in a fighter-versus-fighter engagement, particularly one requiring the identification of the adversary prior
to shooting, the Sidewinder has a distinct advantage. In South
Vietnam for certain, and almost as much so in North Vietnam,
the chances were that *any* airborne target was one of ours, so
we couldn't go banging away blindly at anything coming down
the pike.

So confident were our politicians and planners in the superiority and utility of missiles that they steadfastly ignored
the pleas of the fighter pilot community for a gun. Just a bunch
of little boys longing for the good old days, they assumed, and
in one sense they were right. The desire to close with and blast
an adversary is part and parcel of the fighter pilot's make-up.
But until positive identification of all aircraft can be guaranteed,
the age of the push button is still a bunch of smoke. The
recognition of this truth is borne out by the fact that the Air
Force has configured its newer model Phantoms and more recent airplanes with internally mounted Gatling guns—so called
because, as their forebear, operation depends upon the rotation
of a number of barrels.

In slightly over three minutes we had gone nearly twenty-
five miles, and it was time to go over to the tanker's frequency.
As if reading my mind, our controller came up on the radio.

"Boilerplate One, contact Basketball One Nine on button eighteen." The tanker was in visual contact at about ten miles, heading in the opposite direction. Although his indicated airspeed was scarcely more than 200 knots, he was making good nearly four miles per minute. At roughly six and a half miles a minute on our part, the total closure was over 600 knots, so if he were to turn 180 degrees back outbound when we closed to eight miles, we would overtake him and be in position to plug in as he rolled out of his turn heading northwest.

"Basketball One Nine, Boilerplate One at your one o'clock position for eight miles, request port turn to outbound track."

"Roger, Boilerplate, commencing port turn to three-three-zero. I've got your smoke."

A notable feature of the J-79 is the trail of smoke that it leaves in basic engine. In friendly skies, this is beneficial in that it makes the Phantom highly visible from as far away as twenty miles, lowering the threat of a midair collision. The problem is that the smoke trail can be disastrous in a hostile environment where the trick is to see the other guy before he sees you. The wizards of General Electric were working on a fix to the problem (which would be incorporated late in the year), but in the meantime we were stuck with a workable (but decidedly unpalatable) solution. The smoke trail disappeared the minute you selected afterburner, so the idea was to go to minimum burner to kill the smoke and then use speed brakes to maintain the desired speed. The procedure almost doubled fuel consumption, so it was a technique that we reserved for the immediate target area or other high-threat situations.

As the tanker rolled into his turn, I signalled Mike to join us by making an exaggerated wing dip. As he moved in, I gauged my closure with the tanker. Through his first 90 degrees of turn (which took one minute), our relative closure had gone from ten miles per minute down to three, paring the distance to just slightly more than a mile. As he continued his turn, closure became more and more a matter of speed differential—initially 150 knots, but decreasing as we decelerated—to where it was eighty knots with 90 degrees of turn remaining. At a quarter mile out, and with 45 degrees of turn remaining, Mike was aboard and I signalled for speed brakes. Deceleration from putting the "boards" out is crisp at higher airspeeds, but as the speed bleeds off, their effect diminishes. The airframe entered into gentle prestall buffet at 240 knots indicated airspeed (IAS),

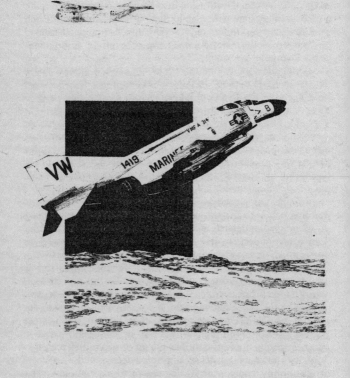

and it grew more insistent as we slowed to match tanker speed.

Flaps-up stall speed for the Phantom at that weight and external stores configuration was about 175 knots, rising to close to 180 knots because of the extra weight at the completion of refuelling. At a refuelling speed of 200 knots, we were not perilously close to stall, but there were other problems. In the first place, the plane was on the "backside of the power curve," which is to say that below a particular airspeed it actually took more power to fly slower because of increased drag. There are a whole bunch of interwoven physical principles involved, such as rapidly increasing induced drag, and spanwise flow and airflow separation, but for a quick visualization of things, consider that in order to maintain lift while flying slower, the aircraft must be cocked up to a higher and higher angle relative to its direction of flight. The effect is similar to opening a barn door into the teeth of a windstorm. Whereas we burned roughly 8,000 pounds of fuel per hour in cruise, on the tanker we averaged somewhere around 12,000 to 14,000 pounds per hour, or more than 200 pounds of fuel a minute. If we were allotted 5,000 pounds of fuel by the tanker, we would burn a thousand of it in the process of joining, tanking, and departing, but it was a cost that had been considered during the mission planning.

Of more immediate concern was the severe deterioration of the Phantom's handling qualities, a function of the reduced airspeed exacerbated by the bomb-laden configuration. Every aircraft design is a compromise between stability and control, but each aircraft must exhibit at least some of both, with the mission defining the relative weighting to be considered. In general, stability receives greater attention in transport design; controllability, in fighters. Among the several competing design criteria for the Phantom was that it perform well at supersonic speeds, fly slowly enough to land on aircraft carriers, and yet show agility as a dogfighter. These are very dissimilar requirements and their achievement stands as a monument to the creativity of the aerodynamicists at MAC.

At 200 knots with the flaps up, even a "clean" Phantom can be something of a handful for close-quarters maneuvering. This has to do with a bunch of esoteric factors such as center-of-pressure location, thrust-axis offset, roll-center displacement, and other such tedious details. The trick is to do as little as possible with the stick, which provides primary inputs for pitch and roll commands. Once displacements in pitch or roll occur, the sensation is akin to being on a three-dimensional teeter-totter. Adding external stores (particularly those with lots of bumps and protrusions such as bombs) disturbs the airflow to such an extent that the aircraft is further destabilized. Under extreme conditions, as in the case of what we called the "super-bomber" (a Phantom loaded wall to wall with twenty-four bombs), the stability index was lowered to such a point that the airplane could become virtually unmanageable at refuelling speeds.

During daylight and free from the clouds, the refuelling operation is fairly straightforward. The tanker aircraft deploys a drogue (in the case of the KC-130, there is a drogue from each wing) composed of a 125-foot hose with a female spring-loaded receptacle guarded by a two-foot-diameter basket having the dual function of stabilizing the drogue in flight and pro-viding a guide to the probe for plug-in. In the case of naval aircraft, the receiver inserts his probe into the locking collar and drives the hose forward several feet to activate fuel flow. The Air Force reverses the process by putting a specialist in the tanker aircraft to "fly" a boom into a female receptacle in the receiving aircraft. It is a change in sex roles based on the premise that the specialization of the boom operator makes the process more reliable. For my part, I believed that the need of the receiver is so much greater than the need of the donor, that his motivation is bound to be higher, but I'd have been willing to go to the Air Force system if it meant standardization. Here is another case where interservice rivalry has created a serious and entirely unnecessary problem. A Navy tanker cannot refuel an Air Force fighter, nor can an Air Force tanker give fuel to a Navy receiver except in the remote circumstance that the tanker happens to be configured with a rinky-dink afterthought drogue attachment that bounces around like the Good Ship Lollipop, and is nearly as impossible to plug into. That even one fighter should be lost because the proper tanker was un-available is stupid.

In any event, the Phantom's probe is housed in the starboard fuselage just below the cockpit section. When it is fully ex-tended, the tip of the probe is just slightly forward of the pilot's head and about three feet out, placing it out of the normal line of sight. I found that the trick to refuelling a bomb-laden Phan-tom was to ignore the handbook, which told the pilot to es-

tablish a position aft of the tanker and allow the RIO to talk
him into the drogue. With the airplane wallowing around, re-
acting to voice commands is not merely difficult, it is liable
to aggravate the situation even more.

For me, the answer was to stabilize the probe about ten feet
left, ten feet behind and slightly below the drogue. The approach was commenced by adding power to create a three-to-
four-foot-per-second closing rate and using right rudder to
maintain a constant sight picture between the point of the probe
and the outside lip of the drogue until the probe was lined up
directly behind the drogue. Here, I would feed in left rudder
to stop the starboard drift and allow the probe to engage the
drogue. It may not have been the handbook solution, but it
worked a lot better for me.

At night or in the clouds, things are tenser. Radar can be
used during the initial part of the rendezvous, but the system
was so designed that it would break lock-on at a half mile in
trail. From there on in, you had to grope, praying that you saw
the tanker before you either passed him by or rammed him.
Once you picked him up and transferred your scan from your
cockpit instruments to the drogue, you were in for what seemed
like a lifetime of mind-warping vertigo. I've spent the whole
time absolutely convinced that we were doing slow rolls down
the refuelling track, unable to arrest the sensation until I'd
backed away and gotten on the gauges again.

Our closing rate slowed to a walk, until just as the tanker
rolled wings-level on his outbound track, we stabilized up on
the left drogue. The port lookout relayed our position to the
tanker pilot.

"Boilerplate flight cleared to plug."

Mike's refuelling probe was already out, indicating his readiness to proceed. Patting the visor of my helmet and pointing
towards him, I signalled Mike to remain on the left drogue
while I drifted to the other side. The right drogue is a little
harder to plug into because, with the probe on the right side,
both the wingman and the tanker's fuselage are hidden from
view, making for an uncomfortable situation.

As occasionally happened, the response system on the starboard hose was not working, so as I drove the drogue forward,
the hose buckled instead of rewinding into the refuelling pod.
In this condition refuelling could not take place and there was
the danger that the buckled hose would strike my airplane and

perhaps even tear the probe off. I backed out gingerly.

"OK, Boilerplate One, we've reset the response. Give it another punch."

This time the hose went in smoothly and the green light at the rear of the pod came on, confirming fuel flow. My only concern from there on (other than maintaining a proper position on the tanker) was that the fuel went where it belonged. Any time valves are cycled, there is a chance for malfunction and even damage to the fuel cells. Were a valve to have stuck, permitting fuel (for instance) to transfer to the external tanks from the number one feed cell, we could have flamed out even while we were plugged into the tanker, but such problems were not critical if caught soon enough. There are emergency procedures to cope with most any fuel management problem imaginable. A glance at the fuel tape/counter display confirmed that all was well, so there was nothing for me to do for the next five minutes but hang on in the proper position and let the systems do their thing.

The green light on the tanker pod flickered and went out, indicating the transfer of the allotted 5,000 pounds of fuel. I disengaged from the basket by coming back on the power, drifting aft with about the same differential speed as during the plug-in, while concentrating on detaching from the drogue at its normal trail position to avoid being struck by its whip. Dropping aft of the tanker by another 100 feet, I retracted the probe and checked my fuel transfer. Mike was backing out.

"Basketball, Boilerplate One flight disengaged, departing your starboard side. ASP, button six."

The time was 0628, which was right on schedule. We would rendezvous with the Whale in fifteen minutes, en route to the target area, but well south of the SAM rings.

— 4 —
Asp on a Tear

Our scheduled target time was 0703, two minutes prior to the time that Tricky Six-Five and his flight of four F-105 Thunderchiefs (Thuds) out of Korat would be coming in at high altitude from the southwest to hit the marshalling yards at 0705. The idea was for our bombs to be exploding on the antiaircraft gun positions just as the Thuds hit the pushover point. With Willie pinning down the radar, and with us beating up the gun positions the 105s should be able to make their high angle attacks without getting shot up.

The Air Force tactic was to "stairstep" down to 15,000 feet and from there make a 60-degree dive delivery on the target, releasing at 8,000 feet and bottoming out at 5,000 feet. I felt that there were several problems with this approach. First, it meant that each airplane was exposed for an inordinately long time in the dive itself. If the run were established by 13,000 feet, each would be flying a straight track for nearly two miles, meaning that the wings were level for from twelve to fifteen seconds. That was way too long against fixed antiaircraft sites, even if they were not controlled by radar. But against radar, it was suicidal. Second, the slant range to the target at roll-in was 30,000 feet, or roughly six miles. Even at release, the planes would still be nearly three miles away, too far for the pilots to pick out most targets, much less hit anything.

Our attack profile was almost the dead opposite. We'd be down on the deck by about twenty-five miles southwest of the target, running pretty much due north until we hit the Ca River. There were good landmarks on the river, so we expected little trouble pinpointing our position for the final leg to the target. Crossing the river on a northeasterly heading, we'd drive straight in towards the antiaircraft site, which would by then be seven miles away over two low ranges of hills. Going to minimum afterburner, partly to eliminate the smoke and also to accelerate to the attack speed of 525 knots, I planned to split the section at four miles out, sending Mike left to a heading of north while I turned east, putting the target 45 degrees between us. After thirty seconds, with the range down to two miles, it would be time to pop the aircraft 45 degrees nose-high and, passing 2,000 feet, roll left 135 degrees to pull the aircraft around onto its back. At the apogee of the maneuver, I would be at 3,200 feet, inverted, looking down at the gun position. As the target reached the canopy bow above my head, I would pull the nose down until the target was in the center of the windscreen. Stopping the nose with forward stick and rolling the aircraft back to the upright position using crossed controls (left rudder and right stick to roll the aircraft around the sight axis rather than around its own longitudinal axis), I would then hold the pipper on line with the target. There should be no more than a half-second of track time before reaching the release point at 2,200 feet with 450 knots of airspeed and a dive angle of 30 degrees. Pausing just long enough for the bombs to clear the racks (1.2 seconds), I would commence the escape maneuver with a 5-g pull-up. As the nose came up through the horizon I would relax the pull while rolling into a 75-degree right bank to bring the bird around to the escape heading of southeast.

Mike would delay his pull-up for an additional fifteen seconds to clear my bomb fragments, and in doing so achieve a final run-in heading of around 120 degrees. Hopefully we would stitch a cross on the target area, ensuring good coverage. The element of surprise coupled with diverse run-in headings would aid our escape, and there should be enough noise, smoke, and confusion to allow the Thuds to make their runs in peace.

I rehearsed the procedure during the departure from the tanker, because I wouldn't get another chance before we hit the target. It helped to have been up to Vinh before, but mentally picturing the terrain and attack sequence was even more important. The real trick in prosecuting a successful attack lies in the ability of the pilot to visualize what is going to take place and then to follow the script. The more experienced you become, the more flying seems to be a matter of acknowledging the accomplishment of a preconceived set of milestones. It's what I referred to as my "automatic mode" where, as I entered the target area, I felt myself withdraw from the immediate tasks at hand and assume a monitor role. I became aware of the feel of the stick grip beneath my gloves. I heard myself breathe. At some point, the airplane became an extension of my body and for a magic few moments, I was at one with my surroundings.

We dropped below the tanker and moved off to his right, accelerating in a slight dive to our optimum climb speed, which for our present altitude, configuration, and weight was 350 knots. Signalling Mike to reestablish himself in combat spread, I took us over to Hillsborough, an Air Force EC-121 airborne early warning and command ship (AWACS) that controlled all U.S. air activity in North Vietnam. It was the one that looked like a submarine with wings, the radar antenna rising from its back like a conning tower.

"Hillsborough, Boilerplate One over the fence with twenty-four Delta-fives for your control. Mission number foxtrot-charlie five-niner-five, two-zero-x-ray."

Inside the dimly lit fuselage of the primordial monster I could visualize the rows of consoles manned around the clock by phlegmatic young men bathed in radar-scope green. Theirs was the unenviable (and probably impossible) task of keeping track of all the flights in the North, separating not merely the bad guys from the good, but distinguishing between the friendly flights as well. They did amazingly well, but they'd be the first to admit—insist as I found out from a controller one night over a beer—that the system was far from foolproof. In the first place, there were airplanes zipping all over the place, cycling in and out of North Vietnam on alpha strikes, coming from the ships, from Thailand, and from South Vietnam. There were photo-recon flights with escorts running along all of the supply routes. There were tactical strike-fighters beating up the area looking for targets of opportunity on the route packages. There were SAR (search and rescue) helicopters and their escorts

fishing downed crewmen from rice paddies and even from
downtown Hanoi. There were North Vietnamese transports that
were off-limits, and fighters that might or might not have been
off-limits depending on the circumstances. The chances were
that during an alpha strike, our controller would be responsible
for from six to ten flights, and it was his job to follow their
progress, often monitoring them on their discrete tactical frequencies.

"Roger, Boilerplate One, I hold you radar contact twenty-
three northwest of Quang Tri. Playboy One One [Willie] is at
your ten-thirty for fifteen. Come left to three-two-five, maintain
present altitude and airspeed. Amend time on target plus one-
zero minutes."

There was the temptation to ask Hillsborough if the Thud
flight had encountered heavy headwinds over Laos. If *we* were
ten minutes late for a target time, you can bet that the Air
Force would have torn us a new one. It was the problem of
being bottom dog.

The high overcast was beginning to dissipate, and ahead
there were large patches of blue sky. That was good, of course,
but the undercast was the problem, and there was no indication
that it had any intention of breaking up. Out at ten miles,
slightly above the horizon, Willie chugged along at something
around 360 knots true airspeed. We were indicating 320 knots
at 20,000 feet, so with an outside air temperature of minus 5
degrees centigrade, we were actually making good a true airspeed of slightly over 400 knots. Thus, we picked up two-
thirds of a mile every minute. With our angle-off, the rundown
distance was actually around seven miles, meaning that it would
take us about ten minutes to move into a one-mile trail position.

"Boilerplate One, contact Playboy One One on black. His
position is forty left for six miles." Black was one of several
tactical frequencies in normal use in the North and corresponded
to our button thirteen.

"Playboy One One, Boilerplate One at your three-thirty,
four and one half miles. Did you receive the revised time on
target?"

"That's affirmative, Boilerplate. I plan to proceed another
twenty-five miles on present course and set up a port racetrack
to kill the extra ten minutes this side of the SAM area." That
should hold us about ten miles from the southernmost SAM
ring and during that time, Playboy would be trying to get an

absolute fix on the radar position by triangulation during the orbit.

"Asp, set point six-two." Slowing from .66 to .62 mach would keep us from overrunning Willie, while putting us at our most efficient loiter speed for the present configuration, allowing us to reduce our fuel flow from 7,600 pounds per hour down to 7,000.

Even though we couldn't see the ground, it was mandatory that we knew where we were at all times. Orientation was maintained by various means. In South Vietnam, much as in the United States, there were numerous navigation facilities to present us with a positive fix over the ground. More than a decade before, the Navy had turned almost exclusively to TACAN (tactical air navigation) for its combat aircraft position referencing. The TACAN ground site sends out coded information that allows the aircraft equipment to determine the direction from which the aircraft lies relative to the station (radial), and by transponded pulse, to give it the distance. Since the position of the station is a known factor, the pilot can plot his own position using this information. The accuracy of the TACAN system is basically a function of range, but there are both inherent and local degradations that add an element of uncertainty. Be that as it may, TACAN was an invaluable aid as a double-check for the pilot as to his aircraft's position.

Things were different in the North, where we were quickly out of range of navigation stations, because signal reception is strictly a matter of line of sight. There, you had to revert to the primary mode—dead reckoning. The key to this lay in maintaining an ongoing record of where you were, and when, and what you'd done since. It's called a "howgozit," and it works something like this. If you know that you were over a specific spot on the ground two minutes ago and that you have been on a northerly heading making good 400 knots, you know that you have to be some thirteen to fourteen miles north of where you were. The more often you are able to update your position, the more accurate you're bound to be. If you had to go fifteen minutes between fixes (as we often did when the weather was bad in the North), you had to really concentrate—particularly since you were continually jinking to keep from being an easy mark for radar-controlled antiaircraft fire.

I tried to pinpoint my position at least every three minutes—more often if there were good landmarks—but by the same token, I didn't want to get bogged down into having to worry where I was every second of the way. In the same way that I had a thirty-second twitch when it came to jinking, I responded to a roughly three minute navigational jerk because it represented something in the vicinity of twenty miles of real estate. What I did was plant in my mind what I should be seeing in about twenty miles, and let that trigger my jerk. This is where that subliminal sense of time became important, particularly in adjusting for circuities in the route of flight. You learned to use every clue, so that even though I couldn't see the ground beneath me, I was not totally in the dark. The tops of the mountains to the west were clear, allowing me to estimate how far north I'd come. Though not quite as reliable, there were often patterns in the clouds that allowed you to discern features such as the coastline or boundaries between topographic regions. The main thing was to develop as many options as possible so that the loss of one set of clues didn't leave you in the lurch. When all else failed, you fell back on dead reckoning.

At last there were some good-sized breaks beginning to show in the undercast, but still not enough to get a good look at the ground. Without Willie, it would have been stupid to run along at 20,000 feet above a cloud deck that far north. As it was, Willie would keep radar from tracking us, but it would have been better still to see the ground. Though 57mm and 87mm antiaircraft fire could reach us at our cruising altitude, our random jinking was enough to render it relatively harmless. The main threat was a surface-to-air missile. The SA-2 was the kind of missile that brought down Gary Powers' U-2 over the Soviet Union. It was a large missile, designed to go to extremely high altitude, which is why it had a two-stage system with both a booster and a sustainer rocket. The booster carried it off the ground, burning for the first several seconds, during which time the missile could not be guided. Guidance commenced once the sustainer kicked in and the missile was guided through a *pursuit* curve (by ground-based track-while-scan radar), which differs from a *lead collision* profile in an important way. Whereas the lead collision approach calculates an aim point in front of the target, the pursuit curve vectors the missile to the rear of the target.

Because the SA-2 had to continually respond to target position updates from the ground-based radar site as it sought to follow its target, it could be treated in much the same fashion as an enemy aircraft. Turning into the SA-2 would throw it to a higher and higher angle-off, forcing it more and more to the outside of the turn. While it was capable of higher speeds than an aircraft, its turn radius was incapable of dealing with a fighter's maneuverability. As the missile was forced to an ever-increasing crossing angle, its closing rate decreased as it fell farther to the outside of the turn. The firing circuit in the missile warhead was designed to fire when the closing rate dropped off to a predetermined value. Regardless of the actual proximity of the missile to the target, when the Doppler value dropped below a certain level, the warhead exploded.

"Playboy coming port one-eight-zero." We'd closed to about a mile and a quarter, so by holding my present course until I cleared his radius of turn before commencing mine, I'd follow him into orbit. This would maintain my nose-to-tail separation on him, allowing me to keep him in sight. Mike, anticipating that our turn to the outbound course would be less than 180 degrees, fell slightly aft of his normal bearing, a maneuver calculated to move him forward again when we rolled out on the new heading.

"Asp, come port to one-eight-zero." In order to limit the amount of time that our mutual defense capabilities were degraded by the maneuver, we made part of the turn using the vertical. As I lowered my nose and started to turn into Mike, he pulled his nose up with his wings still level, bleeding off airspeed before commencing his turn. Once he started his turn, there was no way for him to keep from losing sight of me. He had to judge when it was time to lower his nose and tighten up his turn to cut back inside my radius of turn and reestablish his position abeam and to my left. As I watched him roll his bank up, allowing his nose to slice below the horizon, I brought my nose up to slow again to the base airspeed, playing my turn to help him out until he reacquired me.

For the first half of the turn, Mike had been between me and Willie, allowing me to keep them both in sight. During the last 90 degrees of turn, I had to spend more and more time looking out behind me to pick up Mike as he moved up to the abeam position, so that when there was a flash off to my right, it was at the limits of my peripheral vision. It was in the area where I knew Playboy One One was, but as I turned my attention to the spot, there was nothing there but a puff of smoke. He'd vanished. There was just the slightest temptation to dwell on what might have happened.

"Asp, port hard! Willie's gone." Almost instantly I was looking at Mike's planform as he reefed his bird quickly into a 90 degree angle of bank turn, dropping the nose far below the horizon and drawing streamers of condensation off the wings.

No sooner had I rolled to 135 degrees and pulled the nose down deeply below the horizon to move to the inside of Mike's turn than I saw something in motion coming out of the cloud deck well below us, heading from right to left.

"Keep your nose down and wrap it up!" I relaxed my pull a little and started my nose up in order to keep the SAM in sight. I caught another ripple. There was a second one airborne, displaced to the outside of the first! It was probably heading for me, because the first one seemed to be trying to get around behind Mike.

"OK, Asp, nose to the horizon and honk it on! SAMs in the air at four and seven." I was about to lose sight of the first one, so I barrel rolled back over the top, so that we were canopy to canopy as I moved to the outside of Mike's turn. There was by then no doubt that the first was heading for Mike, but just as certainly, the angle-off was already so high that it was actually more of a threat to me than to him. At the high crossing angle, and with its first stage gone, the missile seemed smaller than I remembered.

Then it was gone in a flash, leaving a multicolored smoke ring pierced by a corkscrewing white streak. My nose had now dropped far below the horizon as I worked to regain the inside of Mike's turn and force the second missile to follow the fate of its partner. Still inverted, I pulled hard into the buffet with the SAM looming larger above and behind the aft canopy bow.

Come on, airplane, bend . . . nose down lower . . . turn, you mother!

My airspeed was nearing 500 knots and still the Phantom was galloping in the buffet of the 6-g turn. The missile was growing at an astonishing rate.

Have I underestimated its performance? Keep pulling, dummy . . . ah, there it goes.

Sliding down the wingline, well outside the turn, the missile seemed to be acknowledging its failure. Then it too was gone,

the debris passing quickly from sight astern. Was there another?

"Bring your nose up and ease the turn, Dash Two. I'm passing inside at your eight. You're clear." I flashed in front of Mike on his right side, and pulled up high, inverted, looking down to make sure that there were no more missiles.

It had been less than three minutes since we started our turn to follow Playboy One One—probably no more than a minute since he had taken the hit—yet the numerous images registering in my mind's eye were remarkable, not merely for their clarity but in their vibrance, which put all that had happened before into a dimly remembered past.

"Bring it on into recce . . . speed brakes . . . NOW!" It was time to get down below the cloud deck and sort things out. Recce is a formation in which the wingman closes up to within 1,000 feet, stepping down and falling slightly aft of the abeam position, allowing for nose-to-tail separation. In hard maneuvering, Mike would end up locked onto my tail so that we could act essentially as a single aircraft. There is a loss of lookout doctrine from the standpoint of air-to-air engagements, but this is offset by an increase in section maneuverability and terrain lookout.

The SAMs had come up from east of where we made our turn. We were actually lucky that they hadn't gone for us first. Either the missile crew waited until Willie was into his turn with his jamming gear antenna blanked out by the angle of bank, or his gear wasn't working at all, otherwise he would have given us a warning. I had continued the turn around until we were heading south and this time I reversed to move out to the west, away from the SAM site. Down we plunged into the clouds, descending at 10,000 feet per minute, and popped out into the clear at 2,500 feet. The visibility was far better than had been briefed, and as if by plan, we were pointed straight at a column of trucks snaking through the low foothills still half a mile from the refuge of the treeline. We were ten minutes south of the initial point and another three to the target, so we were still six minutes early. I dropped the section on down to 750 feet.

"Asp, reverse hard to one-eight-zero." I wanted one more check to make certain that we were clear of the missiles while at the same time I wanted to displace ourselves another three miles to the west.

"Asp, button seven." We'd better inform Hillsborough about

Willie and the SAM site. "Jerry, can you get me some coordinates where Willie got hit?"

"Coming right at you. How about 18 degrees, 10 minutes north, one-zero-six degrees, 10 minutes east?"

"OK, if we figure that the missiles came from about 7 miles east of there, it should be at one-zero-six, seventeen or so. Sound about right? How about chutes, did you see any?"

One of the problems was that I hadn't seen the Whale get hit. I think that I saw something, but I'm not sure what. As far as Jerry was concerned, he had almost no forward visibility out of the rear cockpit, and when I called the hard turn, the area where Willie had been was lost from view almost immediately. One of the reasons that I doubted that anyone got out was that I didn't see any wreckage sheeting down. There was just the smudge of smoke, suggesting that it was a direct hit that blew the Whale into dust. If the crew got out, their chances of escape were almost nil. The area they were over was cleared farmland with signs of life all around. Worse than being caught by NVA troops was the spectre that the local farmers might well have strung you up. For certain you could expect no help from that quarter, or compassion either.

"Hillsborough, Boilerplate One. Be advised, at least three SAMs launched in the vicinity of eighteen-ten north, one-zero-six, seventeen east. Playboy One One destroyed. No chutes sighted. Is Tricky Six Five up this freq?"

"Roger, Boilerplate, this is Tricky Six Five."

"The bottoms of this trash are at about two-point-five, thirty-five miles southwest of the target. Without Playboy One One, I'd detour north if I were you until you can see the ground."

"Roger, Boilerplate, concur. We should still be able to hit our estimated target time."

"Hillsborough, Boilerplate returning button black. Asp starboard zero-one-zero."

The fifteen-mile detour to the west of the new SAM site had put us five miles west of my planned track, but it wasn't going to make much difference because it would be easy to pinpoint ourselves at the Ca River. Right there, the land was rolling and only occasionally rugged, but farther west was some of the most desolate and forbidding real estate on the planet. On our superzoomy maps, it was labelled "Karst," great limestone outcroppings with the added notation that much of the area was unexplored. Here on the coastal side, the hills vibrated with a profusion of greens with more subtle variations than any palette. The flatlands were basically a medium green typical of elephant grass, showing the stigmata of man in the intricate network of trails worn into the reddish soil. Farther east toward the coast, the land was a patchwork of fields and paddies with hues of blues and greens that were almost painful to the eyes in their richness.

My fuel counter showed that I had burned down to 9,600 pounds of fuel—all of the external fuel had been transferred into the internal tanks—about 700 less than planned. This was mostly because of the evasive maneuvering but also because we had dropped to low altitude earlier than expected, causing us to burn about 25 percent more fuel for the same distance than we would have at higher altitude. As it now stood, we would burn 2,000 pounds to go to the target, a thousand more performing the attack and withdrawal to the coast, and another 3,000 returning to Da Nang—a total of 6,000 pounds, or approximately a thousand gallons.

Fuel planning is important in any form of aviation, but never so critically as in the stovepipes. The variability in fuel consumption in the Phantom is enormous and any deviation from the planned mission could make a profound difference in the number of alternatives available to the pilot. Just as an example, were something to happen to close the runway at Da Nang, the nearest divert base would be Ubon, Thailand, 195 miles to the west.

In an emergency, the external stores could be jettisoned to lighten the aircraft and reduce drag. The aircraft would be climbed to its optimum cruise altitude of 39,000 feet, where it would remain until time to begin an idle descent to arrive overhead the field at pattern altitude. In this manner, the divert would take something in the neighborhood of 2,000 pounds of fuel, leaving roughly 1,500 pounds with which to play. At low altitude in the landing configuration, this is good for ten to twelve minutes of flight time. The point is that my options were predicated on the rest of the flight going pretty much without incident. Were I forced to spend as little as one minute in afterburner, I would suck up so much fuel that divert to Ubon would no longer be an option, and any time there were heavy strikes in North Vietnam, there was a possibility that Da Nang's only runway (a second was being built) might get closed by a disabled aircraft.

For the third time since departing the tanker, I went through the armament switches, making certain that nothing was out of place. Because of the diversity of weapons available and the variety of delivery options, the Phantom's weapons select panel—called the dog bone because of its distinctive shape—is fairly complex. As presently configured, my airplane had six bombs on the center station beneath the fuselage and three more on either inboard triple ejector rack (TER) station, for a total of twelve 500-pound bombs. Bombs are literally kicked off the racks in a set sequence and interval by ejector feet that are actuated by shotgun shells. This positive separation is important not merely for accuracy, but because of the uncertain airflow patterns about the bottom of the airplane, there is the danger that a bomb could get tossed into the aircraft. Thus, the ejector sequence and interval provide a predictable pattern on the ground while ensuring a safe separation between the bombs and the airplane, and between the bombs themselves.

The bombs are detonated by mechanical fuses with arming vanes that screw into both the nose and tail of each bomb. For this mission, our bombs were configured with "daisy-cutters"—twenty-four-inch-long fuse extenders—designed to detonate the bomb above the ground. Their purpose was to maximize the fragmentation pattern, and they were thus an anti-personnel feature. Were the target *hard*, daisy-cutters would be useless, but were our mission to be changed en route, we could still work effectively against hardened sites by electing to arm only the tail fuse, which is set up with a slight delay, that would allow the bombs to penetrate before detonation took place. A wire held to the bomb rack by a latch (which closes only when the arming circuit switch is placed in the on position) passes through the arming vane, preventing it from spinning until the bomb has been booted clear of the rack. Each fuse is armed by the rotation of the vane, which mechanically withdraws a safing lock from the firing pin. Upon impact with the ground, the firing pin detonates a charge in the fuse. Unless the fuse explodes, there is virtually no way that a bomb can be made to go off. Even in the case of heavy impact or fire, if the fuse fails to detonate there will very likely be no explosion.

With the center and inboard racks selected, 140 milliseconds delay in the ripple mode, and nose and tail arm switch on, all that remains is to select the master armament switch to the on position and depress the bomb pickle on the stick.

The bombsight setting is determined by a number of factors having to do with weapon selection, delivery mode, aircraft dive angle, airspeed, and release height, and to a lesser extent, aircraft gross weight and distance from the target at release (the last is a function of parallax, which results from the physical displacement of the sight axis from the bomb-rack axis).

Wind has an effect on where the bomb hits, but the wind of concern is that which influences the aircraft's vector at the instant of bomb release, not the winds through which the bomb will drop. The aircraft is an aerodynamic entity, flying in a sea of air. The bomb is a dart, cutting through the air, following dumbly the vector established for it by the aircraft as modified by the force of gravity. Where it hits is determined at the instant of release by its height above the ground and vector established for it by the aircraft. In turn, that vector is a function of the dive angle and airspeed of the aircraft and the induced target movement introduced to the aircraft by the wind as it dives to the attack.

Different pilots had different theories about how to deal with the wind. Some people buggered their sight settings on the basis of predicted winds at the target, but those predictions were often wrong. Most of the experienced bomber pilots cranked in a little fudge factor—mine was about one-half of what the correction should have been if the weather guessers got it right for a change—trusting in their own ability to analyze the aircraft's vector in the middle of the bomb run and make corrections as necessary.

Where antiaircraft defenses were not a real concern, the pilot could afford to increase the amount of tracking time in the bomb run. In most of South Vietnam, where the main threat was smallarms fire augmented with occasional 23mm cannon, the most accurate delivery method made use of a 30-degree dive, entering at 7,000 feet and releasing at 3,000 feet with a two-to-three-second wings-level track time. In this type of run, there was time to pick up the wind drift, analyze its vector, reposition the sight picture and stabilize prior to release. In a hostile environment, any more than one second at wings-level was dangerous. At that, there would be just enough time to pick up the drift and make one immediate correction to readjust the aircraft's instantaneous vector. If you had changed your sight setting to compensate for predicted winds and then found out during the run that the meteorologists had been wrong, there was little you could do to salvage the situation.

Because the flak site was an area rather than a point target, the corrections were not too critical, but it didn't pay to become complacent. There was just no sense going to all the trouble to arrive at the target only to make a bad hit.

The Ca River was coming up ahead with the Route 8 bridge about a mile to the east. It was extremely broad at this point—almost a mile across—with junks and rafts dotting the waterway and lining the banks. Our turn towards the target took us right over the top of several trucks heading for the bridge. If we had been out on a poop and snoop mission, they would have made excellent targets of opportunity, particularly once they got out onto the bridge. My excitement mounted, and for an instant there was this burning temptation to reallocate a couple of bombs. It was really rare that you actually got such an opportunity, and there was no doubt in my mind that this—like the convoy in the hills—was a far more lucrative target than what the Thuds were going for, but unfortunately, we had other work to do. At least I could content myself in imagining the thoughts of the truck drivers when we went roaring over the top of them. I'd have wet my pants if I were in their place. We were now four minutes from target and time to call Tricky.

"Tricky Six Five, Boilerplate four minutes out. Asp, starboard zero-four-five." Minimum afterburner stopped the smoke trail and we accelerated to 525 knots for the run-in to the target. Pressing down to 250 feet above the deck, we snaked back and forth to cut down on the chance of being tagged by an unplotted gun and to preserve the element of surprise at our destination if at all possible. (I was not at all convinced that the North Vietnamese didn't have all the details on our missions complete with TOTs and call signs long before we were airborne.) At this speed and altitude the Phantom was just a fraction of a second behind its sound, and the landscape beneath became a green and brown blur as we gobbled up nearly three football fields every second.

Popping over the top of a knob and following the contour down into the Ca Valley, we streamed towards the target, which was dead ahead now, less than three miles away over the next knoll.

"Asp Two, port to zero-one-zero. Out of turn, the target will be in your two-thirty for two and a half miles."

OK, let's go starboard to 090 . . . watch the hill . . . easy, don't overcorrect. Still twenty seconds till pop up . . . no ground fire . . . don't let it climb . . . ease it back down—

"Check master arm on." Jerry was going through the final weapons checks.

"Master arm is on."

Fuel 7,500 pounds . . . no warning lights . . . ten seconds . . .

"Check gunsight on and bright."

"Bright; 87 mils."

Five seconds . . . this takes forever . . . be smooth . . . NOW!

"Asp One at pull-up."

"Two, Roger. Fifteen seconds to go." Leaving the power levers alone, I thumbed the speed brakes closed and squeezed the stick until I felt 4 g's in the pit of my gut. Unleashed, the Phantom wheeled 60 degrees into the vertical, the altimeter needle a blur as it rushed through 3,000 feet.

Roll left to the inverted . . . keep the backstick in until the altimeter needle stops . . . easy . . . ee-easy . . . there we are . . . look for the dish.

In less than twelve seconds the Phantom had gone from its easterly low-level dash to its northerly 3,200-foot attack perch in a snarling arc. A dark cluster of guns slid into view just above the canopy rail, and beyond them to the left, the radar dish—my aim point. As the target drew towards the center of the windscreen, I continued the roll, coming to a wings-level inverted position just as the dish centered.

"Asp Two at pull-up."

Get some backstick in . . . pull the dish until it moves below the canopy rail . . . maybe just a little early . . . hold it up. OK, spike the mother, roll! . . . Forward and full right with the stick. Left rudder to the floorboard to hold the dish in place . . .

"Three thousand, 470."

That's it, Jerry . . . coming up on speed . . . a little shallow. Hello! Look at them running . . .

". . . twenty slow . . . 490."

Stop it there . . . run you turkeys . . . right on—

". . . stand by . . . MARK!"

Blap!

The airplane shimmied in the momentary asymmetry as the bombs were kicked from their perch on alternate racks. The rapid drum roll of the charges confirmed their tight departure and the airplane felt suddenly buoyant, liberated of 6,000 pounds—one-seventh of its present weight.

"Asp One off."

Mike would have been well into his pull-up by this time, but the transmission would help him pace himself. Even as I was talking, my bombs trained off, throwing dirt and debris a thousand feet in the air. It was behind and beneath me, blocked from my view by the airplane, but in my mind's eye, I saw perfectly where each bomb hit. Fragments would go out several thousand feet from the point of impact, though their threat to me or other aircraft diminished exponentially with distance. The main danger zone was along the extended flight path of my run, where the impetus of the bombs at impact propelled the bits and pieces in the same direction. Mike's run would bisect mine on an easterly heading, so my heavy trash would be out of his way even though a pall of dust and smoke remained over the target.

I flew straight ahead throughout my 4-g pullout, relaxing backpressure just long enough to warp into a 75-degree banked turn to the right to steady on a heading of 080 to watch for Mike coming off the target. The temperature and pressure gauges were all where they belonged, and the fuel tape and counter concurred in their readings of 6,500 pounds of fuel aboard.

"Tricky Six Five in."

"Asp Two off."

"Tricky, Boilerplate flight off target heading feet wet." More dirt and debris spurted up from the clearing, virtually ensuring that the guns would be out of action for a while. The timing had seemed good. All I could do was hope that losing Willie wouldn't make the Thuds meat on the table for some other SAM site in the area. Back at my three-thirty I made out a speck dashing towards the water. Dash Two was clear of the target area.

"Asp Two, I'm at your ten for two miles, say state."

"Asp Two, state five-six." Wow! Somehow he'd used nearly a thousand pounds more than I had. Three hundred, sure; five hundred . . . well, possibly; but a thousand? No way, Jose. Something was wrong somewhere.

"Asp Two, come starboard to one-one-zero. I'll join on you." I closed rapidly from abeam, and at a quarter of a mile I could see that there was a thin stream of vapor trailing from his airplane.

"Asp Two now state four-eight. How about looking me over." Closing swiftly from left to right, I slid underneath his airplane, taking in the devastation. The starboard external fuel tank was torn apart and there was evidence of damage in the wing, but it was the underside of the fuselage where the real damage was. The area just aft of the aux air doors was torn to shreds and there was vapor streaming from abeam the starboard forward Sparrow bay. At the rate that he was losing fuel, he'd never make it to Da Nang: in fact it was touch and go whether he could make it back below the DMZ. His only chance was to get to altitude in a hurry and find the tanker. If he could plug in, he could get a ride all the way home.

— 5 —
— Two Good Chutes —

"Asp Two, jettison all external stores and elevate angels two-four. You're blowing fuel from the starboard fuselage, and there're traces of hydraulic fluid on the belly." The tanks and racks peeled back from the bottom of Mike's plane and tumbled from sight behind. Cleaned and lightened, he drew slowly but inexorably above and away from me.

"Asp Two now state three-nine. Negative hydraulic fluctuations." Maybe what I saw was some fluid left over from a previous leak, but it looked as if it was pooling and blowing away in the slipstream.

"Take up a heading of one-five-zero, and shoot to pass close aboard the DMZ inboard of Tiger Island. Let's go button seven."

We punched our way through several layers of broken clouds before hitting a solid deck. Then, as before, we were in the clear between decks. Cut off from sea and sky, escorting a wounded bird, I was struck by a sense of loneliness, and I prayed that all would work out.

"Hillsborough, Boilerplate One flight off target at four-two, *winchester*, climbing angels two-four. Dash Two with a heavy fuel leak in the fuselage. We're heading direct to Basketball.

77

Request you inform Joyride of our intentions. We'll go to tanker frequency to effect rendezvous."

"Roger, Boilerplate, copy. We'll monitor your progress as long as possible. Say estimated flight time remaining for Dash Two."

"Stand by Hillsborough. Say state, Dash Two."

"Dash Two state two-nine." He was losing about 150 pounds of fuel per minute and burning another hundred in cruise, which gave him between twelve and fifteen minutes of flight time remaining, enough to go eighty to a hundred miles.

"Boilerplate One, Dash Two has twelve minutes fuel remaining."

"Copy, Boilerplate, cleared to switch frequency at this time."

"Basketball One Nine, Boilerplate One." It always seems to take forever for someone to answer when he isn't expecting you, but finally he rogered the call.

"Boilerplate One is sixty north of the DMZ inbound your position. Dash Two has approximately eleven minutes of fuel to flameout. Request you head northbound for rendezvous." The tankers didn't particularly like doing this since they had lost an aircraft going up to the BARCAP tanking station.

"Stand by, Boilerplate, let me clear this with Joyride. We are presently on our northbound leg twenty-five nautical miles southwest of Quang Tri." This was when I really wished that our radar was working. It looked as if we would get one chance at the tanker, and if we screwed it up, Mike and his scope were going to get a bath.

"Boilerplate, Basketball One Nine. OK, we're cleared to continue north, presently the zero-nine-zero for twenty, Quang Tri at angels two-zero. Say your position."

"Boilerplate flight is on the three-three-two for fifty, Quang Tri, angels two-four."

We were closing at almost thirteen miles a minute, meaning that we should be joining in just about five minutes—three minutes to spare. My plan was that when we got down to ten miles, we'd turn the tanker back to the south. With a little luck, we'd be joined on him by the end of the turn. The fuel was tight, but the main worry was that hydraulic leak . . . if it was one. The refuelling probe extension works off the utility hydraulic system, so if there was no pressure, the probe would not extend and lock in place, and if that were the case, he would be unable to tank. We'd just have to wait and see.

"Asp Two, let's drop on down to angels one-nine. Say state."

"Asp Two state one-three." It was getting down there. We were at thirty miles on the 345-degree radial.

"Basketball, say position."

"Basketball One Nine, the zero-one-zero for sixteen miles." That puts him off to our eleven o'clock for fifteen miles.

"Roger, Basketball, how about coming port to two-four-zero." It would take him one minute to turn, putting him on about the 355 for eighteen miles, heading perpendicular to us. We were by then in twenty-two miles on the 350-degree radial from Quang Tri. From there, we ought to be able to turn him southbound, completing the rendezvous halfway through his turn. We'd be all kneecaps and elbows getting slowed down, but it ought to work.

He was in sight at our eleven o'clock, still in his turn for about six miles, slightly high.

"Tallyho, Basketball, keep your turn going to a heading of south. I'm in your two o'clock for four miles. Asp Two, go to idle."

I figured that we might as well cut the fuel flow as we slowed to tanker speed. We were down to two miles with 170 knots of closure, but the overtake began to break as he continued his turn away from us.

We were inside of a half mile, still closing at more than 100 knots. It was time to deploy the probe. Cross your fingers.

"Asp Two, pop your probe and bring it up about 500 feet." As I started to cross to the starboard side to watch the probe come out, a large puff of vapor confirmed my fears.

"I've got a utility hydraulic light, and the probe is in a trail position." Mike's voice was steady despite the fact that he now knew that he was in for a bath.

"Basketball, Dash Two has had a utility hydraulic failure and will be unable to take on fuel. Would you alert the search and rescue folks and act as RESCAP?"

"Roger, Boilerplate. Jolly Green is heading out the zero-nine-zero from Quang Tri estimating feet wet at two-six."

It was hard to believe that it had been only fifteen minutes since Mike took a hit, and yet here we were embarking on a third course of action. Luckily, Basketball had been coordinating with Joyride for a rescue chopper just in case the air refuelling fell through. He should be on station by the time they hit the water.

"Thank you, Basketball, Dash Two will eject at the zero-seven-five for fifteen at one-zero-thousand. Estimated splashdown at three-five at the zero-nine-zero for fourteen. Dash Two, let's drop it on down to angels ten." If all worked right, their chutes would open almost immediately, and from that altitude it should take them close to six minutes to descend. The wind was from the northwest at fifteen to twenty knots, so they should move southeast one to two miles.

Ejection is never desirable, but in a modern high-performance swept-wing fighter there comes a time when there is really no alternative. When the engines quit, Mike's airplane would pick up a sink rate of 2,000 to 3,000 feet per minute. At altitude, the dead engines would windmill fast enough to provide hydraulics to the flight controls. There are no control cables to operate the various movable control surfaces in the Phantom; instead everything is done hydraulically or electrohydraulically. A displacement of the stick or rudders positions a control valve that allows a small amount of hydraulic fluid to flow to the actuator assembly of the particular surface to be moved. This fluid in turn positions another valve that allows a greater amount of fluid to go to the cylinder that actually repositions the surface. There are three separate hydraulic systems in the Phantom, each with its own pumps, reservoir, plumbing and actuators: two totally redundant systems (PC-1 and PC-2) for the flight controls, and one separate system (utility) to operate the peripheral devices such as the refuelling probe, landing gear, flaps, speed brakes, inlet ramps, auxiliary intake air doors, pneumatic pump, and radar antenna. It was this one that Mike had lost and for which there was no backup.

As a powerless aircraft descends to lower altitudes, the engine windmill speed diminishes, decreasing the output of the hydraulic pumps. At some combination of altitude and airspeed, there is insufficient flow to actuate the controls. Even if the pump output were able to meet the demand, unless the aircraft could be landed on a suitable landing site (and in the case of the Phantom, this meant a hard-surfaced runway or aircraft carrier deck) the crew would be little better off than if they were to plummet from the sky out of control. It didn't used to be this way in propeller-driven aircraft with their manual control systems.

Ditching and belly landing are now pretty much things of the past, not because pilots no longer have the stomach for such things, but because the aircraft are no longer constructed the same way that they were in World War II. In many ways, a modern jet is stronger than its predecessors, but in the matter of landing on unprepared surfaces, it is vastly inferior. A great deal of this is a function of engine location, which in the case of the Phantom happens to be right behind the main fuel cells, which in turn are behind the cockpit section. The aircraft itself is of monocoque construction with the fuselage forming a portion of the main structure. The strongest and heaviest elements in the aircraft are the engines and their attach trunnions. On the other hand, the cockpit, hanging out in front, is among the lightest and weakest sections. In an impact, the cockpit section decelerates quite quickly, crumpling in the process. The engines with their greater momentum tend to rip away from their mounts and continue forward through the fuel cells into the cockpit section, exploding the remaining fuel and gobbling up the occupants in the process.

Ejection seats appeared with the advent of jets, partly in recognition of the increased risks involved in ditching but also because their higher speed potential increased the hazards associated with bail-out. Another factor that may have been even more important in the long run was the change in attitude towards the relative value of men and equipment. During World War I, pilots were not equipped with chutes, on the presumption that having them might blunt their aggressive energies, leading them to prematurely abandon aircraft still fit for flight. For certain, it was easier to get eager young men to strap into a questionable assemblage of disparate parts than it was to come up with the parts themselves. By the beginning of World War II, parachutes were an accepted item of equipment everywhere except perhaps Japan, where many of the pilots refused to wear them, holding fast to samurai tradition of victory or death.

As the importance of the aircraft in battle grew, and the equipment became more complex, the demand for experienced aviators increased apace. It has become easier to build machines than to train the men to fly them. Clear as well is the fact that in terms of age, maturity, and education, the operator was fast

becoming a different breed of cat well before the end of World
War II.

One of the problems that began to crop up was that all too
many experienced aviators were getting killed in the stovepipes,
either because the airplanes didn't ditch well, or because the
pilot was cleaved by the tail section as he tried to go over the
side. Early ejection seats succeeded in blasting the pilot clear
of the aircraft, but often the injuries that resulted from ejection
and the subsequent chute opening were fatal or sufficient to
ground the pilot from future flying. In the mid-fifties, the United
States in conjunction with Great Britain began pouring massive
sums of money into ejection seat development.

The Phantom is equipped with a pair of Martin Baker rocket
ejection seats made in England, clearly the premier seat in the
world at the time. On the bottom end of the spectrum, it has
zero-zero capability, which is to say that the crew can eject
while the aircraft is sitting in the chocks. As a more practical
matter, this means that the likelihood of a safe ejection at low
altitude is greatly increased, and unless the aircraft is upside
down or coming down like a lead safe, there is a good chance
that the chute will open if ejection takes place before the plane
hits the ground. Unfortunately, arriving on the ground with the
chute deployed does not guarantee survival. All too often, in
a low-altitude ejection, the seat will work as advertised, only
to have the pilot flutter down into the aircraft's wreckage and
burn to death. At least he had a chance to live.

The other end of the spectrum, the high altitude/high-airspeed
ejection poses problems that, if anything, are even more complex. The fact is that without protection, the human body cannot
withstand the buffeting and tumbling that attend a supersonic
ejection, and if the chute were to open at too high a speed, the
pilot could likely be torn limb from limb in the awesome deceleration. For these reasons and because of the anticipated
disorientation attending ejection, the seat has a number of sensors and interlocks that prevent or enable the seat separation
and parachute-opening sequence.

What made the Martin Baker so much better than its com-
petitors was that its reliability was not merely a matter of events
occurring in their proper sequence but the manner in which the
seat functions were performed. Just as there is no telling in
what flight condition ejection will take place, it is impossible
to predict what the situation will be at the time of seat separation

and chute withdrawal. Martin Baker's system is totally positive, leaving nothing to chance. Ejection is initiated by pulling either of the two ejection handles installed in each seat. The primary handle is recessed into the top of the seat and is actuated by grasping its rings with both hands, pulling straight out and then down. This accomplishes several things besides firing the seat: it forces the body into an upright position, helping to protect the crewman's back against compression injury; it withdraws a face curtain for protecting the head and upper body from the airstream; and it initiates the sequence by blowing the canopy off. The alternate handle is located in the seat pan between the crew member's legs. In some cases it is the easier and faster method, though you sacrifice the body positioning and face-shielding features of the primary handle. Either way, in the Phantom, the RIO's seat must go first. Either he can initiate his own ejection, or the pilot can initiate it for him, but what is significant is that if the RIO's canopy or seat doesn't go, the pilot cannot eject either.

In the first few inches of seat travel, several small but important mechanical actions are performed automatically. The crew member leg restraints are drawn taut, holding his limbs securely against the seat bucket to prevent amputation by the dash panel on the way out and to restrain them from flailing in the wind. The seat belts are released so that separation can take place immediately. An iron rod is fired to draw the drogue chute positively from the parachute container, stabilizing the seat while putting an immediate load on the parachute withdrawal line. (This is the single most important feature that sets the Martin Baker system apart from others, and the one most appreciated by crew members despite the fact that they occasionally got pounded on the head by the iron rod in the process.)

The main interlocks that must be satisfied have to do with altitude and deceleration. The parachute withdrawal line is held in place and the pilot remains in the seat until deceleration decreases to less than 3.5 g's and the seat is below 10,000 feet above sea level (some interlocks are set at 15,000 or even 20,000 feet depending on the terrain). Until both interlocks are satisfied, the drogue chute remains fixed to the seat, acting as a stabilizer to stop the seat from tumbling. When the proper conditions have been achieved, the drogue line is released from the seat, permitting the drogue chute to withdraw the main parachute and snatch the crewman from the seat. At low altitude, this sequence takes less than three seconds, and in most cases, the chute is totally blossomed while the crew member is still in his upward trajectory. It is complex, but very effective.

Even under the most controlled conditions, the activities associated with the ejection, chute deployment, and landing sequences are violent, often leading to injury. Prior to the introduction of the rocket seat, ejection almost invariably meant damage to the spine. Even now, a compressed vertebra is not unusual, and almost everyone feels the effects of the strains associated with chute-opening shock for several weeks after the event. Sport parachutes are designed to ease the opening shock, provide a measure of controllability and make the landing about as shattering an experience as jumping off the roof of a car. Not so with the Phantom's chute. It is designed to snap open almost instantaneously and elevate down quickly. About the only time the crew member has any control over his descent is if the violence of the opening has ripped out a panel or two. This unintentionally duplicates the slot found in many sport parachutes, or so I am told.

Besides his parachute, the crew member separates from the seat with his seat pan, which contains breathing oxygen, life raft, emergency radio, flares, emergency supplies, rations, water still, and a Mongolian ghost trap—a do-it-yourself radar corner-reflector that is so intricate that by the time the crewman gets it erected, he has either been rescued or died of exposure. Once the crewman is settled into his chute, his next trick is to attach the lanyard from the seat pack to his torso harness and then let the pack fall free to dangle several feet below. The idea is that this will give fair warning to impact, a matter of some importance over water, where getting rid of the parachute as soon as possible can spell the difference between life and death. Despite a continuing effort, no one has yet succeeded in coming up with the perfect quick-release fitting.

This then is what Mike and his scope had to look forward to very shortly, and in a way I could imagine that the waiting was almost worse than having to eject in the midst of calamity. I felt my own gizzards churning, so it had to be a lot worse for them.

"Asp Two, leave it back at idle and drop it on down towards 10,000. If it starts to go on you, slow it up and pull the handle."

The optimum ejection speed is somewhere around 220 knots and the advantage of going on down to 10,000 feet is that with the interlocks satisfied, seat separation should occur almost immediately. If the automatic sequence were to fail they would have the maximum amount of time to go through the manual separation and chute deployment drill, a routine that Mike's RIO was probably reading out item by item at that very moment.

We were rapidly approaching the 090-degree radial from Quang Tri TACAN, still above 14,000 feet indicating 300 knots. The best bet now was to go ahead and slow it up, even if it meant ejecting a little high. That way, if the engine quit, Mike wouldn't have to worry whether or not he could keep control of the airplane.

"Asp Two, go ahead and slow it up to two-fifty, and start your turn outbound in one minute."

"Roger, One. I'm showing 200 pounds on the gauge, so it ought to go any time now. I'm going to slow it all the way down here and get it trimmed up just in case."

"You're looking good, Dash Two. You can get out anytime now if it quits. You should have no more than thirty seconds to seat separation once you're out."

I'd taken a position above and well behind Mike so that I wouldn't interfere with the ejection. He started his outbound turn on the 090-degree radial at twelve miles. The chopper ought to be coming up on frequency any moment, though there would be at least ten minutes before the pair of them splashed down.

"Boilerplate One, Jolly Green feet wet on the one-one-five for eight at one thousand five hundred. What's your status?"

"Roger, Jolly Green, Dash Two has just turned outbound on the zero-nine-two at thirteen. Estimate ejection in three-zero seconds. With the wind, they should splash down somewhere around the one-one-zero for twelve."

"Copy that, Boilerplate. The wind's kind of a bitch down here. Pushing six-to-eight-foot swells."

"Bye."

Just the one word, and in a ripple—canopy . . . seat . . . canopy . . . seat—they were out, falling rapidly behind the derelict airplane. It was all very eerie, and yet sad and lonely at the same time. It was such a waste. For a while, the Phantom continued straight ahead as if nothing had happened, but slowly at first, then dramatically, the stricken monster, which until just moments before had been the proud standard-bearer of

America's might, fell off on its left wing and entered its fatal plunge through the cloud deck to the sea below. For just an instant the event seemed larger than life, but quickly the thought faded.

Rolling up into a 90-degree bank I watched the figures streak towards the clouds, growing smaller by the second. *They ought to be separating now. Come on, seat, do your thing!* Then suddenly I was looking at two chutes mushrooming brightly against the clouds.

"Jolly Green, they've got good chutes. What do you estimate the bottoms?"

"They're kind of ragged out here, but anywhere between two thousand and thirty-five hundred. Some scud, quite a bit of spray. It wouldn't be all that bad except for the swells. We've got a swimmer who can help them if it comes to it. We'll just play it by ear."

Their main problem would be getting rid of the chutes after they were in the water. With this much wind, they'd be dragged along at a pretty good clip. The trick is to go into the water backwards, facing the wind so you'll be dragged face up where you can see to get at the release fittings. Breathing is not the problem because you would still have your oxygen mask on and several minutes of emergency oxygen left. The problem is getting tangled in the lines, and panicking. If you get a clean release with the fittings, the chute will carry out of the way, but if the fittings don't release, you get towed along until the chute finally decides to collapse and then you run the danger of fouling in the cords. I think that all of us had the fear of getting tangled up while being knocked around by the waves and dragged down by the chute.

"OK, Jolly Green, they just popped into the clouds, so you should have them in three or four minutes." I was tempted to drop down beneath the overcast myself, but it was better to stay high. The chopper was more apt to see them come out of the clouds than I, and I'd only be in his way. If Jolly Green failed to make contact within ten minutes, then I'd drop down; otherwise I'd stay at high cover and conserve my fuel, which was down to 3,800 pounds—enough for forty minutes of flight before flameout.

"I have a chute . . . I've got them both, Boilerplate. Right on the button. I'll watch to make sure they both get out of their chutes before going in for a pickup."

"OK, Boilerplate, they're in the water about a half mile from one another . . . the first one is out of his chute . . . he's inflating his raft, so he looks all right . . . the other guy's having a little trouble. I'll stand by with the swimmer . . . OK, he's free. I'm shooting the horse collar down now . . . no sweat, Boilerplate, he's on the way up."

"Basketball, will you ask Da Nang Approach for a one-five-minute extension on my block time?" It was almost 0040 Zulu and there was no need to get them all upset.

"Boilerplate, Jolly Green. Your playmates are aboard and in good shape."

"Bless you, sir. The drinks are on me."

The battle damage and subsequent ejection obviously were not in the script, but this by no means implies that it was unexpected—just as the possibility of a closed runway at Da Nang was not beyond consideration. From what Jolly Green had said, the weather was probably not much of a factor other than its adding to the aggravation by forcing me to perform an instrument letdown. A quick check of the transmissions on tower frequency was enough to confirm that the runway was open with no significant landing delays, which might have forced me to divert to Thailand.

"Joyride, Boilerplate One, mission number foxtrot charlie niner-five, two-two, x-ray complete. RTB."

"Roger, Boilerplate, you're cleared to Panama on button gold."

The penetration checklist is an opportunity to put into a final perspective the potential problems and options that remain for this last phase of the flight. Thus it is more than going through the cockpit heat full-hot and canopy-defog full drill, though failing to do so, particularly with so much moisture in the atmosphere, can be annoying and potentially dangerous. Descent into warmer moist air with the heat in the normal range will not only subject the crew to a barrage of ice pellets but opaque the windshield and canopy in fog as well. It's inconvenient if you're by yourself, but no way to fly smooth wing if you're not.

Even though I had made this particular instrument approach at least fifty times since arriving in Vietnam, I still refreshed myself on the procedures, and particularly the minima—the height and distance from the runway at which I had to commit to landing or execute a missed approach. I was now down to

3,000 pounds of fuel, which meant that the flight from here to landing would require about half that, putting us on the ground with 1,500 pounds: again, not enough to allow us to divert to Thailand. Had I any significant doubt about our being able to land at Da Nang, I would have rejoined with the tanker to take on a couple of thousand pounds more fuel for insurance. The option was still open and would remain so until I started my descent. After that, I'd be committed to landing at Da Nang. If something came up to close Da Nang's runway, I'd probably be screwed, and unless I were allowed to land on the taxiway, we'd probably have to eject, tossing away an expensive airplane because of what would come to be called my "poor headwork." Because it would be noted that I had had ample opportunity to take on extra fuel prior to approach, I would probably lose my wings—for sure I would never see a tactical squadron again— but that's "the breaks of Naval Air" as the saying goes. The situation could become a dilemma were it not for line one of the fighter pilot's creed, which goes "I can hack it myself." Heading to the tanker would be tantamount to admitting weakness. If I really needed the fuel, that would be one thing, but on such a remote possibility, no way.

It was amazing how flexible we were when it came to all-weather operations, but I never cease to marvel at the World War II pilots who flew around in weather as bad or worse than we did with rudimentary navigation and instrument-flight equipment compared to ours. It's all relative in a sense. We travelled a bit faster, and minor changes in attitude created rather impressive differences in climb or descent rates, but on the whole I'd rather have flown the Phantom in the soup than a Mustang. As surprising in another way was how far behind civilian equipment the Phantom was. I'd flown Bonanzas with more and better instrument equipment, and almost any light twin owner would have giggled at our humble assortment of all-weather stuff. About all you can say for it was that it was expensive for items that represent 1940's technology. From where I sat in 1966, it was liable to be years before the term *solid state* entered the military contractor lexicon.

"Da Nang Approach, Boilerplate One, two-zero thousand."

"Boilerplate One, Da Nang Approach, squawk zero-two zero-zero, say position." The IFF (identification friend or foe) code would give him a positive identification of my airplane on his radar scope. The 0200 squawk was the primary descent code indicating that there were probably no other aircraft returning at that particular moment.

IFF was developed during World War II to allow our air defense people to discriminate between hostile and friendly aircraft. In its basic mode, it senses a radar pulse and transmits a return pulse stronger than the normal return echo. While this increases the range and strength of the return, it doesn't really distinguish the blip from others that are on the screen as raw targets. The SIF (selective identification feature) permits the pilot to choose from among 4,096 discrete codes providing positive identification to the interrogating radar operator. Were other aircraft returning under radar control, the controller would assign discrete squawks to each plane to help him avoid confusion. Aviation is all too full of horror stories of controllers issuing instructions to the wrong airplane, with compliance ending in disaster. Assignment of squawks, frequencies, and sequencing is in the hands of the approach controller, who hands off aircraft to a final controller for the precision approach phase of the operation.

"Roger, Boilerplate One squawking zero-two-hundred, presently the zero-four-five for forty-eight, Da Nang TACAN, a single Fox-four at minimum fuel." The term *minimum fuel* informed Approach that while there was no immediate danger, an inordinate delay could put me into an emergency situation.

"Radar contact, Boilerplate, turn left to one-six-five, descend at pilot's discretion to 5,000 feet. This will be a radar vector to the GCA final approach course landing runway three-five. Da Nang weather is presently 800 feet broken, one and one half miles in rain. The winds are zero-three-zero at eighteen gusting twenty-five. Altimeter setting two-niner point eight-six. The morest gear is down."

The weather had deteriorated somewhat, but it was nothing serious. My main concern was still the left main tire. With the wind from the right, I'd have to worry about arcing downwind—particularly if I didn't get a good drag chute. The Phantom should touch down at about 130 knots in the present configuration and weight (30,000 pounds), which meant that it would be carrying a lot of kinetic energy. Brakes, particularly on a wet runway, are essentially useless, so you rely on the drag chute to haul off the first fifty knots. The trouble is that moisture, the very condition that demands the drag chute the most, is the same one that is most apt to give rise to a streamer—

a chute that either sticks in the well or flops out but doesn't blossom. Wet chutes are a bitch, and as a result, it was squadron policy to use the arresting gear when it was raining. Unfortunately, it was out of service at the moment.

The tailhook is such a real blessing that it amazes me that neither the Air Force nor commercial aviation has realized its potential. It was developed for shipboard use, but Navy and Marines rely on it ashore to snag overrun cables at the end of the runway. The Air Force believes in extremely long runways and pop-up barriers for overrun protection, and only grudgingly did they retain hooks on their Phantoms. In Da Nang, even the blue suiters became believers if for no other reason than the fact that the tailhook saved a lot of tires. Da Nang's morest unit was located at midfield—4,000 feet from touchdown— so we normally engaged it at less than 100 knots. At that speed and with the long cables (500 feet) the deceleration was gentle but firm. When there was a lot of water on the runway there was the possibility of encountering the phenomenon of hydroplaning, where the tire actually rides on a cushion of water.

The principle difference between the Navy and Air Force versions of the Phantom is in the landing gear. The Navy struts and attach fittings are beefier, as might be expected for carrier landings, but the wheels, brakes, and tires are smaller and lighter in order to keep the weight down. The Air Force tires have a larger footprint and are inflated to 150 psi. The wheels contain provisions for "no skid" brakes, giving them superior runway stopping performance. The Navy Phantom does have one advantage. Because it inflates its tires to 225 pounds, its tire hydroplaning speed is 135 knots, while at their lower tire pressures, the Air Force Phantoms run the risk of losing traction above 110 knots.

Normally, the drag chute helps in directional control, but in a crosswind there can be trouble; the chute wants to pull the tail of the aircraft downwind, slewing the nose around into the teeth of the gale. This is not a hopeless condition, but one that must be treated with care, particularly where the runway has a high crown to help the water drain.

In any event, I would have to pay particular attention on the landing and hope that I got a good chute. If the tire were to blow, I could probably keep the plane straight, but I might not be able to stop without catching the overrun gear at the end of the runway. Overrun gear is simplicity itself, consisting of a cross-runway cable stretched between heavy chains laid out along the direction of roll-out. The tailhook engages the wire, and as the aircraft continues along it picks up more and more of the chain, increasing the braking effect. It is a valuable safety tool, but one not without drawback. Aside from any embarrassment, an excursion like that would close the runway for up to twenty minutes while the airplane was towed out and the chains were restretched.

Crossing the 075-degree radial at twelve miles, I reduced the power to idle, lowering the nose to maintain airspeed. The feeling is like driving a car from the roadway off onto sand. You press forward firmly into the shoulder straps, conscious that without the might of the two J-79s, you are flying in something very much akin to a lead safe. I had delayed my descent until the last moment in order to save as much fuel as possible. In the States, there would be no sense doing this because regulations require all airplanes to slow to under 250 knots any time they are below 10,000 feet. In Vietnam we didn't have the same restraint, so the idea was to stay high for as long as possible, descending at the last minute to intercept the glide path for landing.

"Boilerplate One, continue descent to two thousand five hundred, turn right to two-six-zero. Lost communications procedures follow. In the event of no transmissions for one minute in the pattern or five seconds on final, proceed in accordance with TACAN One procedures, landing runway three-five. Copy?"

"Boilerplate One, Roger lost comm." The TACAN One approach procedure was a set of instructions involving the use of the Da Nang TACAN, an ultra-high-frequency (UHF) navigation aid that provided both azimuth and distance information to the aircraft's navigation equipment. Even though TACAN provides a reliable and generally accurate position, it is far less precise than GCA and is therefore subject to more stringent (higher) minima. In this particular case, whereas the minima for GCA at Da Nang were 200-feet ceiling (base of clouds) and one-half-mile visibility, TACAN minima were 400 feet and one mile.

At nine miles south of the field we arrived at the extended runway centerline, decending through 4,000 feet on our way to 2,500 feet. With my speed at 300 knots, I planned to be established inbound to the field and on altitude at about six miles and by then it would be time to lower the landing gear.

"Boilerplate One, turn right to three-five-zero, perform landing cockpit checks and reduce to approach speed. You are now seven and one half miles from touchdown approaching glide path."

At 220 knots, I slammed the gear handle down, watching all of the indicators flip and flop as they confirmed the transition. At 170 knots, I selected full flaps and advanced the power, first to 88 percent, and then to 92 percent as the speed decayed to 145 knots.

"Boilerplate One, gear down and locked, flaps down.

"Roger, Boilerplate One. No need to acknowledge further transmissions. You are five miles from touchdown, slightly left of course approaching glide slope. Come right to three-five-five."

The level of turbulence had actually diminished during our descent, which was a little surprising considering the reported surface winds, but we still locked in solid overcast.

"Still left of course heading three-five-five . . . up to and on glide slope . . . You're correcting nicely to course four miles to touchdown, come left to three-five-three. . . . Now going slightly above glide slope. Adjust your rate of descent."

The controller was feeding me information, but it was my responsibility to initiate corrections, not wait around to react. Thus, I anticipated my return to the glide slope. Initially, I had pulled the engines back to 89 percent and allowed the rate of climb to stabilize at 700 feet per minute descent—a nominal value for maintaining the glide slope. In his "slightly above" call, the controller was telling me that 700 feet per minute was not enough descent, and the amount of time that it had taken for me to go above the glide path told me that the divergence was not great. I took off another 2 percent to increase the descent rate to 800 feet per minute, planning to shoot for 750 when he called us back "on glide slope."

"You're now on course line, at three and one-half miles; come left to three-five-one. You're very slightly above glide slope."

The controller kept up a steady stream of information, rarely pausing for more than two or three seconds. Not only would this allow me to anticipate things, but it established the fact that we had not lost communications. Were we to lose contact,

in keeping with my instructions, I would immediately revert
to the TACAN One approach procedures.

"Two miles, on course. Coming down to and on glide slope."

I adjusted the power to 88 percent, holding 750 feet per
minute down, on-speed, with a one degree crank on the runway,
which, because it was less than I expected for the kind of
crosswind they were reporting on the runway, caused me to
suspect that we'd hit a windshear pretty soon. *There!* The
Phantom staggered in a gust, and without thinking, I added a
touch of power to go kill off 50-feet-per-minute of rate of
descent, while allowing the nose to drift right 2 degrees to 353.

"You're at one mile, on course, on glide slope. Tower has
you in sight. You're cleared to land."

At first I saw nothing, but gradually the threshold lights
emerged from the gloom . . . then the perimeter fence line . . .
Dogpatch . . . the mirror datum lights . . . and the runway with
its black scrub marks where thousands of tires had screeched,
each adding its contribution to the growing smudge. The runway was dead ahead at three-quarters of a mile and I was
holding a slightly high meatball on the mirror. The mirror is
to carrier aviation what the signal light is to traffic flow—you
can get by without it, but it sure makes life a lot easier. The
concept is simple: by reflecting a source light at a preset angle,
the mirror presents you with a visual cue of your relationship
to a desired glide path to the place of intended landing. If you
are on glide path, the meatball (the reflected source light) will
appear in the center of the mirror. If the aircraft goes high, the
meatball will be high. It allows the pilot to make a stabilized
approach to a spot landing aboard ship, and while such extreme
precision is less important on a long runway, the mirror still
provides helpful information.

Normally Marine and Navy pilots fly a constant airspeed
approach using angle of attack even ashore in order to maintain
their sharpness for carrier work, but at Da Nang we generally
held it a little fast in order to flare the airplane and smooth out
the touchdown. This helped save the tires from the violence of
a carrier arrival—an event that is little more than a controlled
crash—while cushioning the load on the bomb racks, which
had developed a cracking problem from all of the abuse.

Cocked up in the landing configuration, the Phantom's descent rate is a function of thrust. If you find yourself riding a
low glide slope, it takes an addition of power to climb back to

where you belong, then a reduction of power to below that
which you needed to hold the flatter approach. Landing dif-
ficulties seem to follow a predictable pattern of events, particularly aboard ship where precision is critical. When things start
to go wrong in an approach, you tend to get behind the airplane,
responding to one stimulus after another in fits and snatches.
Often, when you're playing "catch-up" with the glide slope
and airspeed, you neglect line-up, and that can be a problem.

"Tower, Boilerplate One is a quarter-mile on final. Is the
midfield gear still down?"

"That's affirmative, Boilerplate, the gear is still down. You're
cleared to land."

Even when you squeak the Phantom on, you know that
you've arrived on the ground with all the rumbling and shaking.
Just before touchdown, I raised the drag chute handle on the
left side of the seat bucket, setting it securely into its detent.
After that, all I could do was wait and pray that the chute
worked.

It didn't . . . I mean, why should it?

"You've got a streamer, Boilerplate. The north end overrun
is rigged and ready."

I was still at 110 as I passed the midfield gear, too hot to
touch the brakes yet. At the 3,000-foot marker, I was down to
ninety and able to gingerly touch the toe brakes. Not a very
dramatic sensation of deceleration. With 2,000 feet to go, we
were still hot-footing it at sixty knots, but the brakes felt better.
At the 1,000-foot marker, we had slowed to thirty and for the
first time I knew that we had it made. We slowed to turn-off
speed with 100 feet to spare.

"Da Nang Ground, Boilerplate clear of the active, taxi to
dearming."

The dearming area was adjacent to the runway, and oriented
so that the aircraft was pointed towards the harbor. This way,
if a missile went off, it would miss any populated areas. A
recent directive mandated that missiles were not to be plugged
in or unplugged except at either end of the runway in the
designated arming/dearming areas, but it hadn't always been
so. Several weeks before, we had been joined by an F-8E
Crusader squadron arriving by TRANSPAC (an air-refuelled
nonstop flight across the Pacific Ocean) from Hawaii directly
to Da Nang—quite a feat, even for what was surely one of
the proudest and most experienced squadrons then in existence.

The shark-snooter's engines had hardly clanked to a stop when their maintenance crews were hard at work getting each airplane ready for its first combat flight. No sooner would an airplane reach the tiedown area than ordnancemen were swarming all over, hanging missiles and loading the guns. At the height of the activity, with a flame-belching roar, a pair of Sidewinder missiles sizzled off, overflying our tiedown area before striking the headquarters building in the Vietnamese compound over a mile away. Two "suspected Vietcong" died in the incident. It was a matter of missed communications; an electrician happened to make a missile-firing-circuit continuity check at exactly the same time that an ordnanceman tested out the missile plug-in adapters. As the saying goes, "Ordnance rules are written in blood."

An ordnanceman scurried under my airplane with a raft of red-flagged safing pins to dearm the Sparrow missiles, emerging again with a thumbs-up to indicate that it was OK to proceed back to the flight line. As I continued my taxi, I unstrapped and packed my charts. Even before the aircraft had come to a complete stop in the chocks, a plane captain had clambered onto the wing to check the status of the canopy-actuating rods in both cockpits. A recent directive prevented crews from opening their canopies on the ground until a plane captain had made a visual inspection to ensure that the canopy-actuating mechanism had not disengaged and fallen into the top of the seat. This had been prompted by a chilling mishap in Thailand, where an Air Force F-4 pilot pulled the canopy release lever while taxiing back in from a flight. He'd wanted to let a little fresh air in to lower the stifling temperature that builds up in the Phantom's cockpit on the ground with the goldfish-bowl-like canopies closed. He didn't know it, but the actuating rod had torn loose, allowing it to drop down and lodge in the ejection seat firing sear. The canopy actuating-rod fired the seat, pinning the pilot in the eighteen inches that remained between the seat bucket and the canopy. Apparently it was not a very pretty sight, but the canopy was barely scratched for all the devastation. Now that the inspection had been performed, we were at long last able to crack the hatch and get some air into the cockpit.

There was one last functional check of the stabilator to be performed in concert with the plane captain, and after it was completed I snapped both power levers to the idle cut-off po-

sition. The purposeful whine dropped away, leaving in its wake
a lonesome sigh and then stillness. Already, ordnancemen were
beneath the plane stripping the racks in preparation for the next
launch.

Corporal Martin took my helmet and flight bag and stood
by to guide my feet into the footholds. There was more than
courtesy in the gesture. After a long or hard flight, you were
apt to be a little shaky on your pins. Falling off the canopy
rail would be a hell of a way to end a flight.

"We heard that number Five is in the drink, but that Captain
James and Lieutenant Slacom got out OK," he said with a hint
of challenge in his voice.

"They weren't in the water long enough to get their clothes
wet. They'll probably be back in time to make the night schedule."

Martin shook his head as if to say "what a waste," and
headed off to the tail section to check out the malfunctioning
drag chute.

Jerry was looking the plane over, and I could just imagine
what was going through his mind when he saw the tire this
time. It was showing nearly twice as much cord as before. A
gust of wind slammed through the flight line, overturning a
toolstand and scattering empty hydraulic fluid cans beneath the
tethered airplanes. The rain started down in sheets, obscuring
the hangar less than a football field away and soaking us instantly to the skin. There was nothing to do but make a dash
for the line shack to complete the yellow sheet.

"Hello, gunny. Eight is up and the radar is down. Do we
have any more tires?"

"Uh-uh, cap'n. Damned if we didn't put a new one on Five
this morning, too. It's not worth the trouble preflighting the
birds if you all are going to keep parking 'em in the boondocks."

Normally, we wrote up aircraft discrepancies in great detail
on the maintenance forms, but with Eight there was nothing
new to add, so I scribbled "see previous gripes" and signed it
off. Jerry would write up the radar, so I asked Sergeant Hodges
to call over to the hangar and have them send a radar technician
out so that Jerry could debrief him in detail. Just sometimes
the glitch was in the aircraft rather than in the equipment, so
it was possible that a face-to-face description by the RIO could
provide a clue to getting the thing fixed.

Corporal Gray, the duty driver, stuck his head in the door,

and catching my eye, pointed to his watch. "I'll come back for Lieutenant Wright, captain. You're already five minutes late for your next brief."

That was it. A hundred man-hours of labor for fifteen seconds over the target. We had expended 30,000 pounds of fuel and $2.5 million worth of airplane to put six tons of explosives onto ten acres of real estate, and that's probably as much as we'll ever know as to the value received for the price paid.

— 6 —

— Search and Destroy —

Two months later, in the early summer of 1966, the second runway opened, but there was hardly time to savor the luxury before the excess capacity was soaked up by the arrival of new squadrons. Da Nang, which during Alpha strikes was already the "busiest airport in the world," became even more so. The build-up in I Corps accelerated, and it seemed that every day, our mess hall was filled with troops fresh from the States. It was impossible to mistake them, not merely from their pressed utilities and spit-shined boots, but because they looked like corn-fed baby beef with clear skin and milk-white irises. Three weeks of heat would trim them down to where they looked like survivors of a concentration camp, and the antimalaria tablets would take care of the lily-whites.

Smartly dressed air police in their berets and bloused boots appeared, armed to the teeth with the new M-16 rifle, acting for all the world like the SS reincarnate. Checkpoints and sandbags and bunkers profilerated, and the III MAF and Wing headquarters areas developed an advanced case of urban sprawl. The first SEA (Southeast Asia) huts began sprouting up, replacing strong-back tents for some of the staff buildings, and our Lister bag was replaced by a real shower with four spigots and more than enough water to permit everyone in the squadron a shower every day. Up and down I Corps, things were heating up, and while the war remained episodic, the skirmishes became more fiercely contested. Khe Sanh was in the news and the stacks of body bags baking in the sun grew to match the burgeoning airlift support.

PanAm, with stewardesses and catered meals, flew into the base twice a week, then daily. Soon other contract carriers arrived, and one night one of them mistook the lights at Da Nang East (a helicopter facility with less than 3,000 feet of runway) for the main base and landed. He was saved by more than a heavy braking foot that night. High winds right down the runway shortened his runout to the extent that all he did was dribble slowly off the end onto the overrun. There was virtually no damage, which is not to say that it didn't create a tremendous problem, because there was no place to park the DC-8 without disturbing the operational capability of the base. It had to go. The plane was stripped right down to its gizzards. Every part not absolutely essential to flight was removed and the tanks were defuelled right down to the minimum amount needed to get the bird airborne and over to the main strip three miles away. Aluminum matting was laid to lengthen the runway as much as possible, and in the coolness of morning, with a stiff breeze on the snoot, the DC-8 was coaxed safely into the air. After that, the contract pilots paid more attention to what they were doing.

The level of escalation continued to increase without letup. Troops came in rivers, and by midsummer, groups of skinny earlybirds draped in oversized utilities began queuing up to return to "the world." Most were still cocky, though here and there you would see a grim face with a "hundred-mile stare." Some of our maintenance troops began to talk about "seventy-five days and a wakeup," but most were still into getting on with the job.

Bob Hope came and went, and here and there a headliner showed, but it didn't take Hollywood long to learn that Vietnam was a pariah. *Stars and Stripes* began to show up in the latrine, and Armed Forces Radio pumped out a variety of vapid shows four, then six, and eventually sixteen hours a day. The air group got a Protestant chaplain to go along with the Catholic priest, and just after the former got his duck pond, the headquarters area got a facelift.

It was so insidious that you couldn't see it happening until you stepped back. We were "going into garrison," which was a tacit admission that we had lost the initiative. The official designation for retrenchment was "enclave," the purpose of which was to limit American casualties. Since the flare-up between Ky and the Buddhists, critics began to demand that the bulk of the fighting be turned over to the South Vietnamese Army. At the very time that our guidance and help was needed the most, we began to disengage from our advisor role, holding more and more to ourselves. The more we pulled away, the less effective the South Vietnamese units became, until at last, our union was more one of rhetoric than practice.

We had stand-down days in which we flew no missions in either the North or South. Rumor had it that if the enemy didn't start things, we wouldn't either, and there were those who worried that the war might just end for lack of interest. The NVA, though, didn't leave a second's doubt where things stood. The final stroke of midnight signalling the end of an armistice period would barely have sounded when the NVA would cut loose with a vengeance, and the war would begin again with an even greater ferocity than before. In response, we stepped up our bombing of the North.

There was a lot said about the rules of engagement, but curiously what was more significant was what was implied. For instance, the letter of the law said that you couldn't attack a "nonhostile" aircraft in North Vietnam, which would seem to mean that you couldn't go around knocking down defenseless transports. In fact, not only could you not blast helpless trash-haulers, you needed permission to fire at fighter planes if they were not acting in a "hostile manner" at the time. Just what peaceful mission one could envision for a MiG-21 escaped me, but apparently Saigon knew something we didn't. Gradually this (like everything else) began to change, but there didn't seem to be any plan behind it. It appeared to us that each lessening of our restrictions was the impulsive act of our leaders, who were responding in anger to the fact that their policies were bearing bitter fruit.

At first, Haiphong's barge/crane was off-limits even though, aside from the ships engaged in hauling arms and supplies to North Vietnam, it was the only lucrative target in the area. The only targets we were allowed to hit were the transportation routes and facilities away from the area, storage areas and their antiair defenses. Then, one day we were turned loose on Haiphong's major power-generating station. Step by step, targets were added to the list and the size of the raids over the North grew apace. Then, for no apparent reason, we would cease our strikes for weeks at a time. The official word was that it was to show our desire to achieve a negotiated settlement rather than a military victory, but it seemed to us that these moratoriums came at a time that the defenses in the North showed signs of crumbling. As we would increase our level of activity, our losses would mount for a short period of time, level out and then dropoff. Just about the time that we seemed to be able to strike targets with virtual impunity, our raids would be curtailed for several weeks. When the strikes resumed, the enemy's air defenses were back in business, showing ready improvement as the conflict wore on.

For all of the activity up near the DMZ and west of Hue, life in Da Nang went on pretty much business as usual despite the continuing political unrest on the part of the Buddhists. To some extent, the city itself was of as much value to the NVA as it was to us, encouraging them to leave it alone. But mostly this had to do with the terrain, which to the north and west was forbidding. The approach from the south was wide open, but because it was under cultivation, it offered little in the way of cover for maneuvers by units larger than batallion size. Even so, towns like Tam Ky and Hoi An would come under bitter attack, and by the time we could respond, the attackers would disperse, making pursuit difficult and nonlucrative. It was a period of mounting frustration, as the gulf between enemy tactics and our capabilities widened.

What was curious was our resolute resistance to adapting our tactics to address the enemy's weaknesses. Instead of moving ground troops to interdict his supply lines along the Ho Chi Minh Trail at the exit points of Ban Karai and Mu Gia Pass, we serially widened the air war on a search and (if you found) destroy basis. Somewhere along the line, we confused road cratering and toothpick manufacturing with route denial and were surprised that the infiltration of men and materiel increased every year until the end of the war. Blinded by the daily battlefield reports with their glowing BDAs (bomb damage assessments) our leaders seemed to have been lulled into complacency, believing short-term tactical considerations to be a measurement of long-range success. In retrospect it is easy

enough to acknowledge that because North Vietnam's casualties were well within its capacity to persevere, all it had to do
to win was keep the pressure on. In its order of battle, the Trail
was the critical element, and dispersion the key to success.
Still, despite the fact that we could see how ineffectual our
efforts at closing down the Trail were, it never occurred to us
(at least me) that we weren't going to win.

Starting in late August, patrols began taking fire just beyond
the perimeter, and I flew one mission that took less than seven
minutes from takeoff to landing. A recon unit heading southbound from the base was jumped by an NVA unit of superior
firepower before they had even had a chance to settle their
packs. I was sitting outside the Hot Pad van enjoying an uncommon afternoon breeze tinged with the smell of salt, and
noting an unusual amount of dirt and smoke just beyond the
south perimeter, when the horn went off and we found ourselves
banged off the pad to make bombing runs inside the normal
landing pattern. It was wild. Gear up, flaps up, fuel dump
switch to dump. In our race to get the planes down to fighting
weight (there are severe g-load restrictions at takeoff weight
with full fuel aboard) we began dumping fuel right over the
base. After popping out full speed brakes with the throttles still
in the maximum afterburning positions, we went through three
controlling agencies on the downwind, setting up switches on
the fly, watching a second pair of Phantoms taxi onto the runway to follow us.

There was no need to call for smoke from the embattled
friendlies; eruptions of sand and dirt marked their positions
with all too much clarity. They were pinned down by mortars
and small-arms fire, and because they were themselves without
mortars, their situation was perilous in the extreme. While the
main body of the enemy assault force was located in a treeline
half a kilometer to the southwest, there was no telling where
the mortars were coming from. A resupply helicopter with a
shot-out tail rotor sat in no-man's land between the opposing
forces, and even as we watched, it broke into flames, flaring
brightly for less than a minute before dying away to a spent
pyre marked by a pall of black smoke. The crewmen lay hidden
in the elephant grass, safe for the moment from ground fire,
but the copilot was gravely wounded and badly in need of
evacuation.

We had seven napalm tanks apiece—the right selection for

once, considering that the enemy's disposition was along a broad front—so we set up to make our runs to the southwest, on the long axis of the treeline, parallel to the friendly position. Delivering nape is a piece of cake, except that the tanks don't always go where you want them to, making them tricky to use around the friendlies, particularly when there is no way to avoid dropping over or into them. Sometimes they "fly," and it's not unusual to watch tanks that have been launched in tandem land several hundred feet from one another—which gives you some idea of how careful you've got to be with napalm. The run is made in a 10-degree glide, which seems flat until you get right down close to the ground going like gangbusters. At 450 knots, you're covering a mile every eight seconds, or more to the point, the football-field-length straightaway to the target is gobbled up in less than half a second. Whap! The wings are level. Bing! The tanks're away. Whuump! The stick is back in your lap and your exhaust is blowing dust. If you're really pressing it on in close to the ground, the recovery is a last-ditch panic maneuver.

"Asp, set up pairs. We'll make three runs apiece starting at the western edge and working back to the east."

"Hold on, Asp, this is Grapestake Two Two. We've got to get in and pick up those chopper guys before the one bleeds to death. How about dropping all your tanks on your first run, and we'll go in and grab 'em?"

"OK, Grapestake, but this isn't going to keep their heads down for long. What's your ETA?"

"We're one minute to the north. When'll you be ready to drop?"

"I've got a tallyho, Grapestake, just keep it coming. I'll be in my run in one-zero seconds."

It was going to be quick and dirty. I homed the racks a second time to make sure that all the tanks came off, and brought the plane down to 1,600 feet heading perpendicular to the in-run. I would try to lay my napalm down so that the last tank would land at the western (far) end of the treeline. It would be up to my wingman to take care of the near end. If I were to drop short, most of the target area would be obscured from Two's view.

"Asp One's in hot."

OK, roll her on up . . . 90 degrees . . . you're a little too tight, so ease it out a little . . . that's good.

Until there were 30 degrees of turn left to the run-in heading, I held the nose up with top rudder, throttles to the afterburner detents to hold the speed to 420 knots. Then as I drew close to the heading, I overbanked, rolling up to 135 degrees while pulling the nose below the horizon to a 10-degree dive.

"440 knots at one thou."

Hold it in a little longer . . . OK, roll it back . . . the ground's coming up.

"On-speed . . . stand by . . . Mark."

Ease the nose a tad . . . now . . . get the nose up . . . boy, that's in the weeds.

Bending the bird back around, I saw that the main cluster of the tanks hit where I had aimed, but one had flown beyond the trees and into a rice paddy beyond. Dash Two was well into his run as the chopper touched down, and even before the weight was fully on the skids, figures leaped to the ground and raced to pick up the wounded man. A geyser shot up a hundred feet behind the chopper, and then another, ten yards closer. Three figures sprinted back to the helicopter, two carrying a litter between them.

"Run, you mothers," one of the chopper drivers yelled over the radio as if that could speed their progress. "RUN!" Another mortar round burst less than twenty yards away, then another, and another. Then the men were aboard and the chopper wheeled away to the south—legs still dangling from the open waist-hatch—with dust from the rotor-wash obscuring the site for an instant just before four more rounds creamed the spot where the bird had been.

Our maintenance people loved it (some had climbed to the roof of the hangar for a better view) because for once they could see the airplanes doing something. Most of the time they had to content themselves with sick airplanes and secondhand stories, but in this case it was all there for them to see. The second flight was on target less than a minute later, with a third on its way as I slugged the gear and flaps down and made a straight-in approach directly over the top of the friendlies' position. The tower personnel were having a ball telling flights to stay out of the area because the field was under attack. The fact that it wasn't didn't dampen their enthusiasm a bit, so when I called for landing clearance, the controller shot back, "Sierra Hotel, Boilerplate Seven flight. Cleared to land." But it wasn't Sierra Hotel . . . if anything, it was just the opposite.

The twenty-man patrol took twelve casualties, of which seven were KIAs, in addition to which two choppers were destroyed and two more damaged, adding five more WIAs to the score. Forty-four of the enemy were killed, but the mortar position was definitely located.

Two weeks before I was due to go home, we were hit with a particularly heavy rocket and mortar attack. It was September and the weather was great for flying. Doc Withers, my tentmate and the squadron flight surgeon, was accompanying himself on the guitar—his was a rare talent, combining an arcane sense of rhythm with an atrocious voice—when a sharp explosion lit up the area between our tent camp and the flight line, rending the night air with a menacing "WHOOMP."

"Oh, hell!" I thought aloud, "Someone's corked off another winder on the flight line."

Then they started coming in, one right after another. This was no hit-and-run attack, it was a serious "fire for effect" operation of a size and ferocity beyond any we had yet received. Dropping to the floor of the tent, I was taken by the sight of Doc's guitar still in midair, with him nowhere to be found. There was something surreal about it. The guitar and I hit the ground at the same instant and amidst the SWOOSHINGs and CRUMPINGs, I lay there laughing.

"You hurt or something?" The explosions stopped as suddenly as they had begun.

"No, I'm all right. How's your gee-tar?" I still had the giggles. "Man, I don't know what kind of mass attraction you're into, but it's a lot better than mine. That box of yours and I fell at the same speed, but you were on the ground in half the time. From now on out, you're 'Two-g' Withers, and you don't leave the hootch 'til you teach me the trick."

As it turned out, there were no casualties in our area and the only damage at the airfield proper occurred in a vacant meadow between our tent area and the airstrip, where several head of cattle stampeded into the concertina, tangling themselves so badly that they had to be shot. Charlie Med, the large medical evacuation center on the hill overlooking the base, took several direct hits with terrible results, setting a precedent that continued to the end. Hospitals were magnets for rockets and mortars, and whether or not this was by luck or design, I resolved never to go near one of those places while I still had the strength to resist.

The air wing came down with a policy that since statistics showed that the most dangerous periods in a pilot's tour were his first and last weeks in combat, the answer was to ground us for our last seven days before going home. It was stupid, of course, but logic never seemed to be held in high esteem. I got back on the deck from what was easily my most effective mission of the war, raring to get turned around to finish the job, when the operations officer met me at the bottom of the ladder with the tender message that I was through flying for the tour.

"Whatta you mean I'm through? We've got a convoy of twenty to thirty trucks caught in the hills west of An Hua and all we've got to do is go up and finish 'em."

We had been on a route package (RP-1) in southern North Vietnam looking for targets of opportunity when we stumbled onto a convoy snaking through the mountains nose to tail. It was a lucky sighting, coming when the setting sun flashed off a windshield. Unsure of what was there, I made a high-speed pass over the area and was greeted by the largest prize of the tour. There had to be at least two dozen trucks (it turned out later to be twenty-six), so the key lay in bottling them up at both ends before working the whole bunch over. Selecting pairs, I made my first run on the lead truck, plastering him and the truck behind. That end was blocked.

"Make a look-see pass, Asp Two." I wanted to make sure we had them penned in. "The tail end is about a click back down the road from the fire, in the middle of the bend where the road heads back north." I watched as he let down to treetop level before pulling steeply up just beyond the burning hulks.

"Got 'em in sight, Asp. There's one about a quarter of a mile farther back. Do you want to go after him?"

"Negative, Two. Let's get us a sure thing." He pulled back around the pattern and plunged down to nail tail-end Charlie, but nothing happened. "The bombs won't come off, Asp." His disgust registered over the air. "I'll reset and try again," but it was still "no joy."

I had ten 500 pounders left, and it was up to me. My next two bombs missed the last truck in line, but those that followed were on the mark. The remaining six bombs damaged or destroyed perhaps as many as a dozen more of the trucks, and those that remained were going nowhere for quite a while. It was frustrating to leave the job undone, particularly since "win-gie" was one of our better bombers, but at least the position was well marked for the flights, who were sure to follow. Passing the target location to Hillsborough, we hightailed it back across the fence to get turned around for another strike before it got too dark to see the target.

And that's when I got the word. "Your orders for home just came in. You leave on Saturday. You should have been grounded three days ago."

"You don't believe in that hogwash, do you?" I snapped back at him.

"Look, turkey, I don't make the rules, I just follow orders, and those are that you're off the schedule. Lawson can lead the flight back up there." He did, but it was almost dark, preventing them from assessing the full extent of the damage. Luckily, the trucks were still stalled there the next day, allowing flight after flight an opportunity to finish the job.

That was it for me. I had nothing to do but roam around the squadron area and stew. No more "zero-dark-thirty" briefs; no "late late shows" at the crossroads; no hours of acey-deucy on the Hot Pad or playing duty officer for the night; no more working out the flight schedule at two in the morning. I was through for the duration, and it was almost as if I had ceased to exist. It was awful. All the next day I stomped around the compound waiting for the day to end, but every time I looked at my watch, it seemed as if it was earlier than the last time I checked. What bothered me most was the inconclusiveness of my efforts. It was not only that I had more time on my hands than when I was flying missions, but that there was no longer any way I could improve on things. In retrospect, the surprising thing was that while I was quickly uncoupling from the local scene, never once did I think about what awaited me back in the States. It was out there, of course, and I knew for a fact that I had orders to the Naval Air Advanced Training Command as an instructor, but it simply didn't compute. There was so much to do, and just when the targets were getting better, I was finished.

I was saved from an acute case of boredom by an old friend from Skyhawk days who was flying Bugsmashers for Air America (as were half a dozen other ex-Marine aviator friends whose main fault lay in the fact that they never curried enough favor among the staff types to get promoted and were forced out). Air America was the CIA's none-too-clandestine Air Force in the jungle. My friend had agreed to take me with him once my flying days came to an end, so early the next morning (my last full day before I was scheduled to leave for Okinawa) he picked me up on the flight line and off we went into the boon-docks.

We went up and down like a yo-yo, touching down on grass clearings that were little larger than a couple of football fields placed end to end. People would get on and off, but the plane seemed always to be filled.

"Cong," he told me as two pajama-clad men of indeter-minate age climbed nimbly aboard, bowing to us. "Actually, they're commissars from the NVA down here working with the Cong, seeing that party discipline is preserved." And to them, "How're you doin', Tojo?" Both men grinned, and the leader pantomimed that he had it under control.

"What do we do now?" I asked, my apprehension mounting.

"Nothing. Everything's cool. They need to get to Ban Me Thout, and this beats the hell out of walking for five days."

"What if they try to take the airplane over?" In response to which I received an "are-you-stupid?" look.

"They won't. In the first place, what would they do with it if they did? They can't fly. In the second place, they've been riding with us for over a year, so we get on just fine. Their other buddy and I had a beer in Saigon last month when we ran into each other on the street. He speaks better English than you do and he told me a lot of things I never knew. Interesting guy.

"You'd think that they hated our guts—the North Vietnam-ese—but they don't. Without us they'd have a lot harder time taking over South Vietnam, because they'd have to do it through infiltration and subversion, which would allow the South Vi-etnamese to fight them on the same terms. Open warfare's a lot easier for them to cope with, particularly the way we fight it. The only fear they have is that we'll get tired of chasing ghosts through the forests along the Laotian border and march into Hanoi instead. But they know we won't do that and sooner or later we'll leave. When we do, not only will South Vietnam fall, but he thinks that North Vietnam will possess the strongest army in this part of the world."

Throughout the day, I learned more about the war than I wanted to hear or believe, and after a point, my receptor circuits plainly hit the overload point. On what was perhaps the tenth leg of the trip, just after we had been refuelled by a group of natives dipping bucketsful of av gas from a tub because the hand pump was broken, a tightly bound prisoner was brought aboard and thrust face down in the center aisle with a rifle barrel pressed menacingly into the nape of his neck. He was large for a Vietnamese and savage looking.

"Cong?" I asked, this time a little more sure of my ground.

"No, he's an ARVN deserter. Actually, he deserted when he heard that the NVA had killed his father. He was trying to get back home to avenge him when he was caught. They're taking him to Hue to shoot him after his trial for desertion." I wanted quit of the whole affair. Just get me the hell out of this rathole, my bludgeoned senses cried, but there was a final insult yet to come.

Hue Phu Bai airfield lay in deep shadows as we paddled abeam the lovely Citadel whose fame still lay sixteen months in the future. It was after dark when we rounded the point adjacent to Hai Van Pass, catching sight of Da Nang Bay and the city along its southern shore. Lapping waters reflected the soft lights in a shimmering wake of tiny sparklers, while neon lights winked with a more primal insistence in Da Nang's garish nightlife zone. To the west of the base, artillery flares lit up the hills, causing them to undulate in the flickering arc light, while the runway lights—white double rails trimmed with green and red and blue dots—beckoned with a cheery warmth. We landed long, exiting at the north high-speed taxiway onto the broad concrete passenger terminal area, mobbed even at this late hour by Vietnamese coming or going with a frequency that bordered on the absurd. While my friend secured the levers and switches for the night, I sat in silence, totally at a loss with all that I had seen and experienced. Though there were numerous Vietnamese working on our base—indeed, some of them scrubbed the pots and pans in our mess hall—it was the first time that I had ever been truly close enough to be aware of them without even having to look. Sitting within five feet of two of "the enemy," I'd been unnerved throughout the flight that either could easily slit my throat—and amazed that they didn't do it (after all, wasn't I one of those devils who rained down metal and fire before retreating to the safety of the upper air?). I watched and listened as these people spoke, surprised that their conversation didn't mirror the refinement of their physical selves, but after the initial jolt, I found their animation to be intriguing. Mostly I was overwhelmed with the awareness that after a day of observing their movements (even watching them squatting by the runway in seeming indifference as the aircraft's wingtip sliced closely past), I had gained far more insight into the nature of our hosts, as well as that of the enemy, than I had received from all the briefings and pamphlets provided by our intelligence experts. Finally, I was stunned by the realization that in the more than 100 night landings I had made at Da Nang, I had never once noticed the lights of the city. How more provincial could you get? Later as I lay awake far into the night, churning through the multitudes of sights and impressions gathered in that short day, I came upon the sobering realization that a part of me was forever left in that ridiculous little airplane.

On the day that I left, I looked around at our humble tent camp, seeing it as if for the first time. This never-never land enclave, which we had thrown together out of wood and canvas and concertina in the sands of the Vietnamese coastal plain and which I had called home for what seemed almost an entire lifetime, was already a part of a retreating past. Could it all have been a fantasy? Could I have hallucinated the whole thing? It just wasn't the same ... or was it? And there and then, for the first time, I began to suspect that I was no longer that right person in the right place at the right time with the right tools, and that perhaps I never had been. So powerful was this sensation that I could hardly bring myself to say good-bye to old friends and tentmates. It made little difference, because to them I was already a part of that other world—the world that little knew and cared less what went on in this squalid little piece of turf half a world and a thousand light years away.

— 7 —

Wings of Gold

Everyone I've spoken with has some sort of horror story about his return from Vietnam. Spitting was the rage—almost the official form of welcome—but when it happened to me, not only wasn't I prepared for it, I took it quite personally. Veterans came home expecting to be loved and admired for the privations and danger they had accepted and endured in Vietnam. Instead they found a lack of concern for what the troops were going through; ignorance of what was happening beyond the "2-D" representation of the war on the tube; resentment that the war was not over ("we won our war back in the forties against *real* enemies, so whatsamatter with you punks?"); resentment that because the war was still going on and deferments wouldn't last forever, others would have to go too.

It made a lot of difference where you went when you got back from Vietnam. After surviving the "moist" reception at the airport, I found myself involved in quite a different situation. I was posted to the Advanced Training Command in Kingsville, Texas, as a jet flight instructor, settling down in nearby Bishop, Texas—a town of some 300 people who epitomized what were coming to be looked down as mid-American values. Not only was I warmly and immediately received, but because I was among the first returning war veterans in the area, I found myself accepted warmly into a community made up primarily of fourth- or fifth-generation citizens. Actually, my neighbors in Bishop had no clearer picture of what was going on in Vietnam than the legions of activists who glared defiantly from the tube, but what they did know was that good American boys were going "over there" and doing a good American job. If things weren't going right, the fault was bound to be with those idiots back in Washington. I was pointed to with pride by my neighbors as one who "saw his duty and did it."

The training command was gearing to the task of cranking out students at nearly twice the rate as it had when I was a flight student. We worked ten to twelve hours a day, eight days at a crack to meet the schedule—and loved it. The flying was a good way to mellow back out of the grinding pace of combat operations, but perhaps more important was the fact that it kept me busy to the point where I could avoid thinking about Vietnam and what it meant. While my own beliefs were in the process of undergoing a fundamental change, my exasperation with the tactics of the antiwar activists and what I felt then (and now) to be slanted coverage of the war prevented me from acknowledging a central truth in their allegations: that the war was immoral. It wasn't the war itself but the manner in which we waged it that constituted the sin, but that recognition was still several years in the future. Nonetheless, I was willing to accept as an alternative to the belief that Ho Chi Minh represented a danger to America that Vietnam was important to the experience level of a new generation of pilots, ensuring that there would be plenty of blooded pilots for the next war. This was a sneaky kind of callousness, because I didn't have to acknowledge that at best we were using other people and other turf for our live-ordnance exercises.

Creation of an aviator is no trivial task. It is a step-by-step series of challenges designed to reorient the candidate's entire thinking and response patterns. The program starts at Pensacola, Florida, the home of the Naval Air Training Command, whose syllabus will in roughly eighteen months time take the fledgling through four separate stages, at as many bases, flying three different airplanes. When he completes the syllabus and graduates with his wings, he is a Naval Aviator, but he requires still further training in operational aircraft before he is ready for a fleet squadron and combat.

Preflight, conducted at NAS Pensacola, is half study, half physical torture designed to weed out what are uncharitably referred to as "weak sucks." The cost of training an aviator is so enormous, and the risks in military aviation so severe, that the earlier a potential dropout or incipient statistic can be removed, the better. The proof of the thoroughness of the screening and weeding process is the fact that once a student begins to fly, his chances of completing the program are excellent. Aside from the "need-to-know" courses on meteorology, aerodynamics, and Morse code, there are some weirdos thrown in to make things interesting. The one I remember best was "How to Go to Sleep," in which grown men spent forty-five minutes breathing deeply and relaxing their every part. And there were others like "Speed Reading" and "World Affairs" and "Etiquette," but they paled in comparison to the physical activities organized on behalf of the students. First, there is the Dilbert Dunker (Dilbert is naval aviation's equivalent to Freddie Allthumbs), which is a makeshift cockpit section attached to rails that run from a high platform steeply down into a training pool. The student is strapped into the contraption, which is then pushed over the brink to accelerate down the track, smack noisily into the water, and turn turtle. The object is for the stunned student to unstrap, open the canopy, and claw down through the murk to clear the cockpit—all without drowning. As spectacular as it looks, it's really kind of a prize bore. Ah, but then there's the Step Test, a simple little routine requiring the student merely to step rhythmically up and down from the floor to a two-foot-high platform to the accompaniment of a tone generator. Beep . . . BEEP . . . Beep . . . Beep—120 beeps to the minute for only five minutes. If the procedure isn't hard to grasp, neither is the rationale: complete it and you go on to Primary; fail and you wash out. Simple.

People who wash out of Preflight most often are assigned to line units, but those who do drop out after they have started to fly are encouraged to remain in aviation (often as RIOs or B/Ns) in order to recapture some of the investment. Happily for all concerned, the desire to fly is not easily extinguished. Once a pilot trainee gets past Preflight with its rigorous academic demands, seldom is he washed out by his instructors, who tend to bend over backwards to give him every opportunity to succeed, even to the point of allowing him to kill himself.

More often than not, washing out is not the result of rational appraisal, but a momentary loss of confidence, where, in a moment of doubt, the DOR (drop on own request) throws in the towel, justifying his actions by whatever seems appropriate at the time. In more cases than not the DOR feels remorse— after all, he didn't get into the program in the first place because he was a shrinking violet—and when he realizes that the most he's going to get from people who were once his closest friends is an insincere "gee, Dilbert, that's too bad," he is forced to view the tatters of his dreams from an unacceptable perspective. He had his chance and he blew it. By providing a second chance, the Naval Flight Officer Program is a blessing to all concerned.

Ten miles down the road from "Mainside" Pensacola is Saufley Field, home of the Primary Training Command where the student learns to fly. Perhaps as many as 30 percent of the trainees have some flight experience—10 percent are already rated pilots—but the previous experience is if anything a problem, because Navy training has a particular product in mind. Here the ground school training gets down to the specifics of the airplane and the syllabus at hand. The student is introduced to a new thing called Procedures, which have to do not only with the sequence of actions but, for some strange reason, the manner in which the actions are accomplished. This is the initial transition in the world of aviation, serving to redirect the students' habit patterns towards applying a set of planned responses to a stimulus. There is a catechism for everything— pithy jingles designed to keep the kiddies out of the weeds —such as "one-ten, chop-drop-prop," which reminds the pilot of a T-34 that at 110 knots, he is to reduce power, lower the landing gear and flaps, and advance the propeller control to its low-pitch (high-speed) position. Walking into the procedures training room at Saufley can be as startling as coming upon some kind of religious happening—Ohh-unnn . . . Te-enn . . . Chop . . . Drop . . . Prop—only incense is lacking to complete the image.

Saufley is a madhouse of runways, and a veritable cornucopia of little red and white airplanes that snarl their way through a set of procedures known as Course Rules into the wilds of the training area, which encompasses most of the Florida panhandle west of Pensacola. Flight training begins with A Stage, where the student gets his feet (and occasionally other things) wet, learning such basic skills as straight and level, climb, descent, turn, accelerate, slow down, and land. After these, he's ready for stall, spin, loop, barrel roll, wingover, slow roll, Immelmann, and Cuban eight, and when he has gained a broad grasp on these skills, he's booted out of the nest on his first solo.

This milestone comes somewhere around the twelfth night when the instructor climbs out of the airplane at one of the outlying practice fields, having satisfied himself that the student has it under control. He tells the student to take off and fly around for fifteen or twenty minutes and then come back and make several landings, the last of which is to be a full stop to retrieve the instructor. There is a legend floating around from the days of the mighty North American SNJ trainer about the instructor who loved to detach his control stick in the rear cockpit (a normal procedure for solo cross-country flights to ensure against its becoming hung up during flight), and after rapping the student on the helmet with it for added emphasis, would toss the stick overboard to signify that it was up to the student to take them home and land. One day, a student sneaked a spare control pole aboard so that when the instructor did his thing, the student mimed puzzlement before nodding his head in understanding. After several more moments of apparent indecision he pretended to fumble around for a bit, before brandishing the spare stick aloft and sending it to join its cousin. There are stories like this for virtually every stage of training—most of which are apocryphal—but they are part of the lore of naval aviation, and I would expect that the story will be told long after people have ceased to remember what an SNJ looked like.

Chaos is the rule on any normal day in flight training, but when a thunderstorm blunders into the pattern, the base issues a general recall, turning mere madness into a Chinese fire drill. Planes stream back in from all over the area, bent on beating the weather to the field. Adherence to the course rules becomes inversely proportional to the storm's distance from the field, divided by the intensity of the "crash-static" from lightning discharges erupting in student headsets. When I was a student myself, one of my classmates became the first solo fatality in the T-34 when he arrived at the field in a dead heat with the leading edge of a squall line. One moment, he was crossing overhead at a thousand feet, and the next, he was diving steeply, nose-down, into the center of the field. Whatever noise the crash made was lost in the pummeling of the storm, and instead of billowing flames, there was a tiny puff of smoke to mark the impact. The smoke was quickly gone, vanishing into the turbulent air like a fast departing soul. The debris was removed to a hangar for inspection, but the field showed no sign of the event, so that after a day or two of ritual whispers, his name and memory faded as well.

Aviators are funny about death, considering it the avenging angel for the inevitable cause of all accidents: pilot error. You'd think that they would bend over backwards to pin the rap on the weather, or material failure, or lousy design, but that misses the point. To admit that those factors are capable of separating an aviator from his life is to suggest that he is not the master of his fate. This response to death is irreverence, pure and simple, like drinking blood from the brainpan of a vanquished enemy. "Dilbert bought it because he was panicked by the storm"; or, "he should have caught the missing lock-nut on preflight." Or when nothing else fits, "he just couldn't hack it," and that's the end to that. Aviators should never be asked to visit the close relatives of a dead colleague, no matter what the relationship has been in the past. Whatever empathy he might have for the sadness of the friend or relative is tinged with the sure knowledge that the cadaver is mute testimony to the fact that good old Dilbert "screwed up." Even in Primary, the watchword is "I can hack it."

Whereas A Stage is concerned mostly with getting the student to the point where there is a high probability that he can take off, fly around, return, and land without mishap, B Stage concentrates more on the student's qualitative skills. While grades are assigned to the performance of maneuvers and procedures throughout the program, from B Stage on, students are increasingly rated in terms of their attitude and headwork, neither of which has any exact definition to my knowledge. These are subjective evaluations, and often the instructor is lost for a rational explanation for a poor (or superior) grade. It all has to do with how one lives up to some mythical standard of response that is in keeping with "the Navy way."

Flight training has what are known as pipelines—syllabi directed towards a specific fleet mission. "All Naval Aviators are equal" may be true before a promotion board, but the difference between helicopter training and jet training is enormous. While "needs of the service" exercise the greatest influence over which pipeline a student enters, his grades do make a difference where the element of choice exists. The first cut occurs at the end of Primary, where those bound for jets go to Meridian, Mississippi, where they will fly the T-2B Buckeye, while prop students (bound for helicopters or ASW or transport assignments) travel sixty miles east to Whiting Field to fly the North American T-28B.

Aside from transitioning the student into a new and vastly more complicated aircraft, basic training introduces him to the disciplines that are unique to the military aviator. After the obligatory transition, precision, and basic instrument stages, the student embarks on his great adventure, starting with formation, low level navigation, gunnery, and carrier qualifications. It is an exciting time for the student, full of hard work, thrills, and occasional terror, but the rewards are terrific as his hamfisted ineptitude gives way to rough-cut competence.

Formation flying is the first skill that begins to set the military flight student apart from his civilian counterpart. Most people who are familiar with formation work owe their awareness to the precise and occasionally spectacular exploits of flight demonstration teams such as the Navy's Blue Angels or the Thunderbirds of the Air Force. What they are seeing is the extreme edge of what all military pilots are trained to do. An obvious utility of formation flying is that it allows two or more aircraft to travel from one place to another at the same time and in roughly the same airspace, but if that were all there were to it, it probably wouldn't be worth all the bother. Formation flying is the classroom for the study of relative aspect and relative motion and is, as such, the laboratory for teaching the pilot how to place his aircraft in a position to launch his weapons against the enemy, be he on the ground or in the air.

The first thing to understand is that formation work requires total, undivided concentration on the part of the wingman. He has only one focal point and that is a spot on his leader's airplane. There are all too many disasters that point up the narrowness of the wingman's perspective, in which entire flights have hit the ground in perfect formation. This is not tragedy; it is adherence to flight discipline and is thus to be lauded, not pilloried. The two laws of formation flight for the wingman are: keep the leader in sight at all times and never ever hit the leader with your airplane. It's simple enough to understand— doing it is the trick.

Even though formation flying is highly reflexive, the responses are not haphazard. Any change away from a steady state involves a series of responses varying in magnitude with the amount of change and the timeliness of response. To the wingman, all changes are changes in relative aspect or relative motion of his aircraft with respect to the leader's. A small, smooth change by the leader can be met with only slightly greater response by the wingman, providing he picks up the change in aspect before too much relative motion has developed. The longer the wingman delays his response, the greater the relative motion will be, increasing the severity of the required response. The leader can do much to help the wingman by making his maneuvers as smooth as possible and by communicating his intentions by use of hand signals or head nods, but neither is required—merely "good form." The more familiar the wingman is with formation flying in general and a specified leader in particular, the more able he is to anticipate maneuvers, but anticipation has its limits. Leaders lead and wingmen follow—and that's the way it is, folks.

Formation is such a good training ground that it is used to impart a wide variety of insights. One of the first things a flight instructor does with a formation student is to place his aircraft between the student and the sun—and keep it there for a while. This is not sadism, though the student (or any wingman placed in such a situation) may tend to disagree. The purpose is to point out that "the sun is there every day" and you have to learn to live with it.

After he has mastered the techniques of joining up, holding position, and performing break-ups and rendezvous, the student is ready to try is luck at air-to-air gunnery. It's a thrill a minute for everyone concerned, as pass after pass is made against the jaunty banner with a "meatball" adorning its middle, and when the student has slung his ration of ammunition into the Gulf of Mexico, he's ready for the boat.

Basic training ends with carrier qualifications (CARQUAL), where the student gets to throw his fragile aircraft against a bobbing monstrosity of aluminum and steel. The intense training leading up to this act of insanity is among the most demanding and difficult the student will face, but the confidence it instills in the fledgling is enormous. So while he arrives at advanced training with more than a third of his training to go before he receives his wings, the distinction is one of degree rather than kind. What stands in his way, after transition to the Grumman TF-9J Cougar—a two-seated, swept-wing variant of the Korean War-vintage Panther—is the dreaded Advanced Radio Instruments syllabus known as C Stage.

There are eleven stages in advanced training, including among the variety of wonderful activities bombing, air-to-air gunnery, air combat maneuvering, and as before formation, low-level navigation, and carqual, but before the student gets to wallow in the ecstasies of his chosen profession, there is this one last, most painful, experience of his training command life: when he qualifies for his instrument card.

Aside from the obvious utility of being able to drill around in the soup, there is another value that instrument training imparts. The secret to any kind of flying is anticipation, but in a jet, anticipation is a long-range affair and often the cues are insidious. At high altitudes and airspeeds, even in CAVU (clear and visibility unlimited) conditions, you just have to know what will happen in a given situation and react to the knowledge long before you have any confirmation that a change is taking place. In some cases, the only proof you have that your reactions are correct is that nothing appears to happen. Getting set up and stabilized is the key to precise airwork—that and holding down the number of variables with which you have to deal at a given time. The worst thing that can happen is to find yourself transitioning through large changes in airspeed, altitude, configuration and heading all at the same time.

"Keep your scan going, Dilbert." There is this two-month period in the life of a fledgling when scan overtakes procedure as the number one source of pain and frustration. In truth, scan is procedure. It is learned by rote and perfected through seemingly endless periods of repetition in the Link trainer and then in the aircraft itself. The scan pattern is determined by the circumstance of the moment and reflects the fact that all instrument flight is a correction back to a desired situation.

At jet altitudes and airspeeds, the pilot/static instruments (airspeed, altimeter and rate of climb) lag behind aircraft performance, and the gyro indications provide little more than a broad hint as to what is to follow. As a consequence, it is possible to have excursions of a hundred feet in altitude and still be flying "good" instruments. For a student, maintaining the aircraft within 250 feet of the target altitude is often quite remarkable.

While the F-9's attitude gyro is too imprecise for fine control of pitch or heading, it is still the primary instrument for determining the general flight situation, which is why the airplane was equipped with a switch for failing the instrument in the student's cockpit. This condition, known with terror as partial panel, is routinely selected at the most inopportune time by the instructor. In fact, students find themselves on partial panel so much of the time that it is tempting to drop the attitude gyro from the scan pattern altogether, so as not to get fouled up when the duty "failure" occurs. This drill was so burned into my memory from student days that I rarely subjected anyone to it, relying on the fact that other instructors would take care of that detail of their training.

Every instructor has been treated to all sorts of broken scan whifferdills, but the one that I remember best (possibly because it approximated my performance as a student) came towards the latter part of an instrument check flight when I failed the gyro on a particularly good student just to make sure that he could respond to its loss. Unfortunately for him, he believed the student "book" on instructors, which had it that I never failed the gyro. In his complacency, he never saw the "off" flag come out. We were at 25,000 feet when he lost control, entering a descending spiral to the left. At first, the rate of climb indicator buried itself at 6,000 feet per minute down with the altimeter unwinding at a horrendous rate, yet the attitude gyro showed nothing more exciting than a gentle left bank. Rationally, he knew what had happened and recognized the need to get off the gyro and recover from the "unusual attitude" on the basic instruments (turn needle, airspeed, altimeter and rate of climb), but for at least half a minute, he stayed glued to the gyro, pulling completely through a maneuver known as a split S (the bottom side of a loop in which we went supersonic) before pressing up into a steep nose-high climb. Only then, with the airspeed needle plunging to the "zero" peg did he effect the transfer of scan and begin recovery. He brought it under control once, and then lost it, plunging us through a second set of octaflugerons to 8,000 feet, where again he seemed to regain control. After several seconds of straight and level, the left wing started down again until we were once again on our back with the nose steeply down. For the third time we pulled through a split S, this time bottoming at 1,500 feet, and by the time that he had it completely under control, we were at less then 300 feet. "Pop your hood," I told him, just to let him see what a close thing it had been. Not everything was that hairy, fortunately.

After instrument stage is completed, formation work begins, with discernible improvement on every flight. The difference between Basic and Advanced formation work is that whereas the former stresses the ability to maneuver confidently and safely in close proximity to other aircraft, the latter is more concerned with tactical considerations. Beginning with two-plane flights and graduating to four, the students adapt to the insidiousness of the high rates of closure developed by a swept-wing jet fighter. About the same time they develop proficiency in the daylight, they go out and terrorize themselves (and their instructors) at night. It's a real thrill to watch some solo student come pounding aboard in a turning rendezvous, hot, fast, and at a high angle-off. By the time he sees the tremendous closure rate, it's too late, and you watch helplessly as the student tries to salvage things by honking off all the power and racking the airplane up into a 90-degree angle of bank to try to bend around to your heading. Happily, most students realize the hopelessness before hitting someone, responding to the shame by rolling wings-level and shooting to the outside of the turn. If they've really messed it up, they'll forget that they have pulled the power, and by the time that they get things sorted out, they have overshot by half a mile and bled the airspeed off to a stall buffet. At 25,000 feet, it might take as much as ten minutes to come back aboard. When you see it happening, you have to trust to divine intervention and maintain a good sense of humor. Otherwise, you're liable to end up a basket case.

There is an "old-timer" tale in the training command about a Navy lieutenant junior grade with a penchant for becoming highly agitated in the air, often venting his frustrations over the radio. Students were terrified to fly with him, and his fellow instructors were getting so tired of the streams of vituperation that poured forth over the headsets day after day that finally a group decided to take matters into their own hands. When it came time to embark on a four-plane formation flight, instructors rather than students manned the cockpits.

As the airplanes taxied away from the flight line, instructors, students, and all the off-duty squadron personnel in the area crowded around the ready-room base radio to listen in on the fun. They hadn't long to wait. Immediately after takeoff, the flight switched onto its assigned tactical frequency in preparation for the initial flight rendezvous, but instead of making orderly, stabilized approaches towards the instructor's plane, they took turns making kamikaze runs from all directions and in all attitudes. The airwaves were alive with graphic epithets:

"What are you doing? . . . You're too hot! Wave it off! Wave it off! Watch your angle-off, Dash Three. Don't let it . . . don't . . . oh God, he's inverted! Dash Three's making an inverted rendezvous! You can't do that!"

And finally after ten minutes of screaming came pleading and swearing: "Go home, you miserable bastards, go home! You've all got downs! I'll get you all washed out of the program unless . . . ohhhhh sheeeit, HERE THEY COME AGAIN!"

The instructor came roaring into the ready room, eyes ablaze, set to skin a bunch of students alive, only to be greeted with the loud guffaws that accompanied the first of hundreds of replays of the tape. Realizing that he'd been had, our erstwhile hero fled from the ready room in full retreat.

Next in line is low-level navigation, where students practice blowing dust and sagebrush all over the King Ranch and making runs on highway patrol cars cruising the south Texas roads between Robstown and Falfurrias. It's not unlike a sports car rally, except for the fact that you're making it across the boondocks at 400 knots without benefit of road signs. Students are likely to head off most anywhere on their first couple of attempts, but after a while they get quite good at it. While the concepts and techniques involved are applicable to all forms of flight, they are most appropriate to the nuclear weapon delivery.

Next is air-to-air combat maneuvering and gunnery. It is here that the transformation from student to aviator manifests itself. Somewhere on the way to the target banner, the student self-image gets lost, and with the suddenness of the "bounce" crossing behind the banner, there's a new being behind the controls. It's magic, and though the fledgling still has a long way to go before he can issue a laconic "check your six" to a fleet-rated hotdog, there is no greater reward for the flight instructor than to watch this creation—this tiger—emerge from the cockpit to take its first steps on earth.

Below on the hangar deck, the armorers smirkingly insert the ammo pans for the "hot" flights, possessed of the knowledge that it is about one student in seven who succeeds in piercing the banner with so much as a single round. How well I remember the feeling from my student days when I would have sworn that there was absolutely no way that the target could have escaped the daring and savagery of my attack—indeed on one of my final runs, I almost speared it with the refuelling probe—but like many a duck that has come my way, it "flew on with its heart shot out," arriving back at the base pristine and ready to humble the next batch of students.

The final test before the student gets his wings is CARQUAL in a bent-wing jet. There are hours of boring bounce drill, the nerve wracking and frustrating field carrier landing practice (FCLP) sessions, during which students are humiliated by their inability to make good landings. The precision required to plunk a six-ton, bent-wing conglomeration of metal, fuel, and viscera into a 40-foot-by-200-foot box at 130 knots—particularly one that occasionally decides to buck and roll—is exacting. Because all of the factors involved in maneuvering flight are interrelated, and because the margin for error is so small, even little mistakes are magnified. But gradually, all of the skills come together, and one fine day it's time to head out over the Gulf of Mexico for a date with the ship.

The modern aircraft carrier is a miracle of engineering and efficiency, packing more firepower than the massed weaponry of two-thirds of the world's nations combined. Bringing the firepower to bear is no trivial matter, because if you can't get the aircraft up in the air and back again, you might as well stay home. The critical path is through "cycle time," the time that it takes to launch and recover flights of aircraft. The longer the sequence takes, the less effective the weaponry becomes, not merely because fewer aircraft can be cycled in a given time but because the carrier itself is trapped into steaming longer into the wind.

Efficient operations require teamwork and skill that are a product of practice and adherence to procedure, and these in turn demand strict attention to safety. You can't go around banging up equipment and tossing away lives if you want to stay in the carrier business.

With all of the landing aids and safety measures that came into the fleet in the sixties, carrier qualification in the F-9 is pretty much a piece of cake. The approach is flown at 120 to 125 knots, and with the ship putting 30 knots of wind over the deck, the closing speed is something less than a hundred knots.

Although it takes a considerable amount of sawing the throttle back and forth, glide slope control is actually easier over the water than on land, right up until that magic moment before reaching the fantail when the airplane flies through the burble from the island (the above-deck structure of the carrier containing the bridge, masts, radar antennae, and exhaust stack). There, the pilot experiences a slight sink lasting for perhaps half a second—just long enough to light off the adrenaline factory. The hardest part is remembering that because you are landing on a deck whose angle is 12 degrees offset from the direction that the ship is heading, you need to continually correct to the right to maintain line-up with the extended centerline. Unless the ship is driving into a left quartering crosswind, the pilot experiences the sensation that the boat is running away from him to the right—which of course it is.

The student's first two landings are touch and goes, with the hook up to acquaint the neophyte with the feel of the ship and the experience of what it's like to bolter. It's funny how small the ship looks the first time you roll out on final to work the meatball down to touchdown, a sensation that remains every time you return to the boat after a prolonged absence. Everything looks normal-sized when you're travelling upwind during the look-see pass along the starboard side, and even on the downwind abeam position, it appears almost larger than life. Only when you roll into the groove a quarter mile behind the ship are you struck by the realization that large as it is, it's no "steady as she goes" 10,000-foot hunk of concrete with lots of margin for error. In its foreshorted aspect, it can be seen for what it is—a bobbing and weaving postage stamp with a thousand and one ways of snuffing your promising career. After the touch and go passes, you're ready for the first of six arrestments. As you approach the abeam this time, you deploy the tailhook along with gear and flaps. (Failure to do so is an automatic bottle of hootch for the LSO.)

"Three Foxtrot Two Four Six abeam. Hook down. State two point nine." The last allows Pri-Fly to keep track of your fuel weight to determine whether to strike you below deck for fuel rather than chance having to bingo you back to the beach without completing the qualification session. Your altitude from here until you acquire the ball midway between the ninety and final is a constant 500 feet with stabilized airspeed. Speed control is maintained with reference to the angle of attack indexer, a three-position light indicator mounted on the wind-shield bow in the forward field of vision. The center circle indicates "on-speed," lower chevron, "fast," and upper, "slow." There is about a five-knot differential from one to the next at wings-level. Because the approach turn to the groove is nom-inally 22 to 25 degrees angle of bank, on-speed is roughly five knots faster than for wings-level. With this means is that the minute you roll out a quarter mile astern, you're going to be fast unless you've anticipated and already begun to decelerate.

"Two Four Six, ball."

"Roger ball. Watch your line-up, Two Four Six." This is pretty much of a routine reminder during a student session, because it is easy to concentrate so hard on the glide slope that line-up drops out of the scan. Moreover, pilots develop char-acteristic passes with which the LSOs become familiar. Mine, for instance, is typically slightly slow out of turn ("SLOOT" in LSOese), coming on-speed about halfway down the glide slope and ending with an OK at the ramp and a number three wire trap. There is a point just inside the burble when you have this sensation of stretching for the ground—the feeling that you're too high—and then BAM! The plane thumps on, just the way it's supposed to. You are trained to ram the throttle to the fire wall in preparation for a bolter, but before you hit the stops, the hook snags the wire, beating you to it.

Deceleration is impressive, and you rack to a stop in less than two seconds. Before you know it, you are rocking back, and someone is running out in front signalling you to pull the power back and retract the hook. Normally, the hook disengages the wire immediately, and the taxi director frantically signals for power and directs your plane across the foul line, clearing the landing area for the next aircraft. Operating squadrons look for 22 to 25 second intervals between arriving aircraft, and at that rate one out of ten will have to go around because of a fouled deck. Once in a while the hook will actually weld itself to the aresting cable, requiring a crewman to race out with a sledgehammer to pound them apart. Sometimes a combination of winds, left line-up, and weather will make taxiing so pre-carious that a nose-tiller bar will have to be installed and the aircraft guided clear of the landing area before the next aircraft can land.

After clearing the landing area, you are brought forward and spotted for the catapult or (should you need fuel) for the elevator. In a way, this is the most impressive time, because from this vantage point, out in the middle of the deck, you see that the ship is not a rock. The bow swings above and below the horizon, giving sequential views of whitecaps and scudding sky. Despite the heavy stabilization gear, the ship shoulders its way through the swells in ratcheting motion. An occasional maverick wave tosses the bow still higher and amidships the feeling is like being in an elevator.

During a CARQUAL period, waiting to be taxied forward to the catapult is about the only time you have to look the instruments over while you set the configuration for takeoff. In the F-9, this means flaps down and trim at 3 degrees nose-up. A tiller bar is attached to the nose gear to allow the launch crew to guide you onto the catapult, and the taxi-director signals for you to come ahead or stop. The pace is frenetic. The catapult is set to your aircraft's fuel weight, and then you are lashed down. The shuttle and bridle are the forward thrusting mechanisms, while the holdbacks secure the airplane to the deck. The minute you are tied on, the cat officer signals for run-up. From this moment on, you could be fired, so delay is discouraged. After a final check of the instruments, you figure that you're as ready as ever, so you snug your head all the way into the headrest, make sure that you've locked the throttle and catapult handle between your thumb and fingers, take your feet off the brakes (not that they would slow your progress off the front of a boat an iota), and looking straight ahead, signal your readiness with a salute to the cat officer.

You never know how long it will take for the launch instructions to get to the end of the line, but my experience has been that just about the time I am going to exhale my first big breath, that's when it comes. In the late-model boats with steam catapults, the feeling is one of inexorability. In the older ships with the hydraulic cats, it's more violent.

WHANGGG! Every nut and bolt in the airplane adds to the din as your eyeballs press into the back of your head, your feet lift off the rudder pedals, and the stick slams unbidden to its aft stop. In the next instant, you are forward against your shoulder straps, airborne and climbing away in a slight clearing turn, thankful that all those little details that go into a successful cat shot worked as advertised.

"Two Four Six, your signal is Bingo. Pigeons to homeplate two-six-five for sixty-two."

The rest is anticlimax. All that remains for the students is the Wings Ceremony, which is acutely embarrassing to all concerned except for the occasional parent who braves the south Texas weather in order to watch Dilbert get his due. There is far more relief than elation, and after a mercifully simple check-out exercise, the newly designated Naval Aviator is off to his first duty station.

After two and a half years of guarding switches and sweating sucked runs—a period unrivalled before or since for genuine satisfaction, during which I had the opportunity to fly with upwards of 300 flight students—I received orders in late 1968 to report to El Toro for refamiliarization training in the Phantom prior to reassignment overseas. It was by no means unexpected, but little did I suspect what surprises were in store for me when I arrived on the West Coast. The first came when I checked in and found that three of my own students were in the squadron. The second was that there were over fifteen first-tour pilots on the roster. The third was that they were getting minimum flight time for pay purposes (four hours per month) in the air group's Bugsmasher rather than in the Phantom. The answer was simple. All available flight time went to people who, like me, had orders to Vietnam (or to the squadron commanding officer who was about to retire, or to a young captain who was also about to get out but whose father was a general). The squadron was a far cry from any to which I had ever been attached, but in retrospect, I see that it merely reflected a larger malaise. The troops were far more interested in what was going on in downtown Tustin than in what they were doing at the base, so that when five o'clock rolled around they were out the gate even if it meant leaving a job unfinished. There were days when not one single airplane was in an up status.

It seemed incredible that the Marine Corps was actually letting the opportunity pass away to blood junior officer aviators while people like me went back overseas. "We need to develop more command experience," I was told. It sounded good, so I accepted it. The truth is that I was eager to get away from the emerging chaos here in America and back to the good flying in Vietnam. While I sympathized with the junior aviators, I was more concerned with my own opportunity than with theirs.

— 8 —
—— Wings of Death ——

My return to Vietnam was anything but triumphant. Rather, I had a sense of foreboding. Where before I had been imbued with purpose, now I felt a detachment that masked a deeper frustration at the polarization between the civilian world and that of the servicemen sent to fight half a world away.

In contrast with my previous departure with its thrill of expectancy, this one was subdued. I was driven to Norton Air Force Base in San Bernardino by friends. Shaking hands gravely at the entrance to the passenger terminal, I grabbed my bag of flight gear and skivvies and waved good-bye as they drove away bound for an afternoon of swimming with their children. I didn't feel jealous or cheated. I felt instead that I was being catapulted back into the past. Although I looked forward to seeing old acquaintances, I felt resignation at the prospect of playing a part in a war that seemed so long ago.

In the hypnotic whisper of 39,000-foot jet stream, I sat quietly watching the endless expanse of ocean unfold, conscious that I had changed. Before I had been essentially childlike in my love for flying; now I was a precision instrument of destruction to whom flying was an unquestioned but minor skill. I was the weapons system, with a twenty-five-ton monster

130

as an extension of my will. It was an odd sensation, but one that was less melodramatic than it sounds.

The first stop was Okinawa, which was the primary staging point for men and materiel bound for Vietnam. It had changed. Where in 1966 it had been wide open, anticipating what the next moment might bring in a tumultuous live-for-today atmosphere, now it seemed top-heavy and lethargic, full of bravado and idiocy. Instead of adventure, there was macho, and even the gentle natives showed the strain. Camp Butler at the north end of the island (the Marine Corps' Northern Training Area and wild animal cage) was packed to the rafters with troops in transit or in training. I dined next to a young second lieutenant fresh from Basic School, who told me that his burning desire was to leap on top of a hand grenade so he could get the Congressional Medal of Honor.

"That seems a little risky, doesn't it?"

"Oh no," he announced brightly, opening his utility jacket for me to see. "I bought a lightweight bulletproof vest to go under my flak jacket."

"Terrific."

Later, I walked into the bar during happy hour and stood around listening to stories about "wasting Charlie" and how "them mothers won't stop talking when they see you shove one of their buddies outta the chopper," and "just wait until you get to Nam." What really bothered me was that I couldn't blame these guys. Most were on their way to line outfits where all they'd have to look forward to for months on end was heat and mosquitoes and punji stakes and boredom. And rain and cold rations and mud and the mad-assed screaming terror of elephant grass alive with whizzing death. For all of this, in thirteen months they could go home to political turmoil and public ignorance. Sick as it seemed, the world there made more sense than back in the States.

"When do you want to go into country, Major?" asked the pimply-faced corporal at the manifest desk, indicating by his conspiratorial manner that he could delay the process as long as I wished.

"First plane you can get me on."

"Can't wait to be a hero, huh, Major?"

"Something like that. I'll be in my room at the BOQ or at the mess."

I was summoned from dinner and told that transportation would take me to the airfield at Futenma for a midnight flight. We stood in a torrential downpour for forty-five minutes while the plane was fuelled and when we got airborne, the crew informed us that the cabin heating system was inoperative. In the morning's harsh glare, my eyes were grainy and my sinuses throbbed. "Hell of a way to show up," I thought, still shivering despite the fact that the plane had descended to warmer air. Looking out through the skimpy porthole in the C-130's forward access door, I watched familiar landmarks slide by, details accented in the brilliance of the early morning sun. Da Nang fell behind us to the north and then we were banking to turn final at Chu Lai.

There was no one behind the desk at the Marlog shack, and it took several tries before I could find someone to point me in the direction of my new unit. The temperature had been reasonably comfortable when I started the three-quarter mile hike to the MAG-12 area, but by the time I arrived, it had risen to over a hundred degrees and I was a soggy mess. If things weren't bad enough, the group personnel officer had worse news.

"Welcome aboard, Major. I don't know what the hell we're going to do with you. You make the twenty-sixth major in the group and there just aren't any billets open."

"How about sending me down to a squadron?"

"Unh-uh. I've got a waiting list of twenty people—captains, majors, light colonels—all chomping on me to get to a squadron. Wing says lieutenants get first crack, only there aren't any lieutenants."

"Can I volunteer for lieutenant?"

"It's not a bad idea when you stop and think about it, but the way things are going, you'll be lucky to get into a squadron before they call this whole thing off."

Of course I thought "they" meant the North Vietnamese.

The personnel situation was absurd. Among the aviators, there were literally more field grade officers (major and above) than company grade (lieutenants and captains). There were lieutenant colonels walking around with nothing to do and some of them didn't even want to fly.

I was assigned to the group staff, where I was left to my own devices to accomplish more or less whatever I wanted with the help of two corporals and a staff sergeant, both of whom had short-timer attitudes. I spent most of my time begging flights from the different squadrons, admonishing my troops to keep from doing anything noteworthy, because noteworthy things generally caused the most problems for others. My official title was base development officer, which had a classy ring to it, but there was very little to do except explain to an exasperated squadron commander or two why this project or that was still not completed. My job was mostly one of liaison with the various construction and maintenance outfits on the base, each with a different charter. There was the Army Corps of Engineers, who worked primarily with the Americal Division, the Navy Seabees, who handled most of the facilities construction, RMK, who handled heavy airfield construction, and Philco Ford, who seemed to have overall cog over construction and maintenance.

"When are we going to get our hard-covered revetments?" I asked the Navy ROICC (resident officer in charge of construction) for the fortieth time in two weeks. It was our standing joke.

"About the time that we turn the base over to the commies lock stock and barrel, and haul tail," he'd say with suitable gravity. "What's your hurry?" That was the answer he gave to any of my inquiries, and as our list of priority projects ran to well over fifty, it got a lot of mileage. "Ever notice how the rockets never hit the flight line or anything of military value?" he'd ask when I'd show signs of exasperation. "They make damned sure they don't hurt anything now so that the base will be in top shape when they take over." Events would seem to have proved him right.

We were newly embarked on what was euphemistically referred to as the "Vietnamization Program," according to which anything the Vietnamese wanted, and that we were not using at the moment, was to be turned over to them—never mind what they intended to use it for. We were told that because the South Vietnamese had come so far so fast on the road to self-determination, they would soon be able to do with nothing from us but a little material help. What was actually going on was that the smart Vietnamese were grabbing and selling everything in sight so they could afford to get out of the country with some cash before we pulled the plug.

Many South Vietnamese simply wanted us, our money, and our war machinery out of their country—particularly the ci-

vilians up in I Corps. It wasn't a matter of politics: they understood all too well that whoever ran the show—be it Saigon,
Hue, or Hanoi—was going to steal them blind. It mattered not
what our motives were—whether or not we were committed
to self-determination and free elections. To them America meant
dismemberment and death, not prosperity and opportunity. They
watched us from the fence line in silence. In the depths of their
baleful stares was the knowledge that in time, American presence would amount to little more than the blood of its soldiers
left to fertilize the hills and paddies of a people who no longer
gave a damn who won.

Unlike Da Nang, the airfield at Chu Lai hadn't existed prior
to the war. In 1965, the Marines waded ashore and established
the base, laying aluminum matting on the sand for a makeshift
SATS runway. SATS stands for short airfield for tactical support, a concept for achieving an advanced close air support
(CAS) capability in a remote tactical location, the notion initiated and developed by the Marine Corps in the early sixties.
The idea was to carve out an airstrip and make it operational
for jet operations within twenty-four hours, using nothing but
air-deliverable equipment and supplies. The pilot project was
Bogue Field, located in the midst of the North Carolina coastal
forest.

Significantly, a SATS field resembles an aircraft carrier in
a number of ways. The 2,500-foot-long-by-fifty-foot-wide runway made of aluminum matting was able (at a price) to handle
even high wheel-loadings of F-4 Phantoms, which were beginning to enter the fleet. The trees were cut back enough to
allow KC-130 Hercules transports to land, but not enough so
that they could turn around. Instead they had to back up the
runway to offload and take off. The jets landed into the arresting
gear, designed to allow more runout than shipboard gear. We
tested a number of different arresting systems. A field catapult
(called a cataport) was installed and developed at the site. It
was the laughingstock of the operation at the time, but by the
time it was brought ashore in Chu Lai in 1965, it worked.

By strapping two rocket motors (mistakenly called JATO
units, for jet-assisted takeoff) on the side of the aircraft, the
newly arrived A-4 Skyhawks had access to an extra 7,000
pounds of thrust for takeoff—enough to get a normally loaded
aircraft off the ground in 2,500 feet. It's a dazzling sight (and

one that never fails to excite the audience at an airshow). The first squadrons at Chu Lai flew A-4 Skyhawks using JATO for takeoff much as we had at Bogue Field. The big difference was that at Bogue under controlled conditions and lighter loads, a JATO misfire could be uncomfortable but not disastrous. At Chu Lai, with the high ambient temperatures and heavy gross weights of the aircraft, a malfunction was almost certain to send the bird into the weeds. Even in 1969, with a 10,000 foot runway and 500 feet of prepared overrun on each end, planes still ended up in the weeds off the end.

Even as construction of the runway was in progress, a field cataport was installed to accommodate F-4s on the aluminum strip. A Phantom had arrived to test the system in late 1966 only to be destroyed as the shuttle exploded, tossing chunks of metal into the belly of the airplane. The pilot and RIO ejected successfully at ground level, but it was decided that until the new runway was complete, the Phantoms would stay where they were.

Over the next six months the field took shape with provisions for many of the permanent facilities included in the design. Even so, when the runway opened, the field continued to operate much as before with expeditionary equipment instead of heavy-duty stuff. Many Marines didn't consider it anything more than a way point.

Many of the pumps and generators and stoves that had been rushed ashore with the assault troops in 1965 were still in service in 1969. Aircraft refuelling was accomplished with tactical aircraft fuel-dispensing systems (TAFDS), in which small stationary engine-driven pumps were used to transfer fuel from large rubber bladders lying above ground in berms at the edge of the taxiway. To expedite aircraft turnaround, refuelling was accomplished with the aircraft still running, but the process was so painfully slow that with both engines idling (burning 1,200 pounds of fuel per hour apiece) the system could barely make headway. Even with one engine shut down, refuelling typically took upwards of twenty minutes, which would have been agonizing under any circumstances, but was doubly so in the boiling heat of the flight line. The answer lay in the installation of an automatic high-pressure refuelling system that had been delivered in pieces in 1968, but was not set up for nearly a year. Even then it took another six months to make it

operational—three months to get someone to come out from
the United States to get it to work and a like amount to train
an operator.

The mess hall which fed nearly 2,500 people at every meal,
was little more than a field kitchen as late as September 1969
and would have remained so had not one of the stoves disin-
tegrated of old age, seriously burning several of the messmen.
The new equipment made little difference in the quality of the
food and actually took more people to operate.

In 1968, infiltration by the NVA had grown so sharply, that
the Marines were seriously outnumbered. The majority of the
action still took place at An Khe and Khe Sanh near the DMZ,
but pressure was mounting at the south end of I Corps as well.
Army units were brought in to help stabilize the situation, and
before long they grew to be far larger in number than the
Marines they had come to augment.

Chu Lai became the seat of the Army build-up, and during
the early days, it seemed to the Marines at the base that their
arrival was a godsend. In they came with all of their equipment
and facilities. There had been a period just after the Army's
Americal Division arrived with their huge diesel generators that
the Marines had an excess of electrical power and all that that
implied, but the embarrassment of riches was short-lived. As
time passed, the load doubled—then tripled. The excessive
demand, coupled with wear, created a critical situation for all
of the base services that depended on electrical power for operation.

By the time that the Americal's base-wide water system got
to us, it was inadequate, so we used TAFDS units for our own
needs. The pumps ran around the clock, barely coping with
demand, but the real problem was the water itself. It was
potable, but hardly worth the effort. The water table was twelve
feet beneath very porous soil. In 1967 several aircraft had been
defuelled by the expedient of dumping the JP-5 directly onto
the ground, the only defueller available on the base having
become a casualty of overwork. Kerosene quickly percolated
into the water table, contaminating the entire area. Whatever
potability remained, the health people took care of with chlor-
ine. It was safe enough to drink, though you felt that you ought
to refrain from smoking for a while after imbibing the swill.

Chu Lai's physical plant was not the only thing that had
undergone a change since 1965. I was prepared for differences

in the attitudes of the troops, but I was totally unprepared for the magnitude of the change. From the moment I stepped off the transport, I sensed the mediocrity of the situation. It was as if our troops were wallowing in molasses. "Four-hundred days and a wakeup, baby" became the duty slogan for boots no more than hours off the plane. "Just make sure that there's cold beer at the club." Trucks and jeeps with lolling drivers from the Americal cruised the main service road in an endless stream as if it were Main Street on Saturday night. Hundreds of soldiers with long hair and seedy fatigues lounged around outside the Americal PX smoking dope in blatant defiance of their officers and NCOs. "Bust me, you sucker," their postures said, "and see what kind of grenade comes through the door to your hootch."

Part of the problem stemmed from the living conditions themselves. In Da Nang, we had lived and operated out of strongback tents, but in Chu Lai, we lived in Southeast Asia (SEA) huts. For certain they were vastly more comfortable than tents. Moreover they lent themselves to improvements of a radical nature. The problem was that they were permanent structures without the slightest pretense of being expeditionary. The central concept of the Marine Corps involves mobility and flexibility, yet here we were constructing a replica (low rent to be sure) of an American suburb. The incongruity of our living conditions and the war around us was a mistake.

As if to hammer home the incongruity, television had come to Vietnam, courtesy of the Armed Forces Radio and Television Network. For us, it was of minor concern because while ground operations were actually beginning to wind down (the highest level of U.S. involvement took place in mid-1969) the air war business was booming, keeping our maintenance personnel busy fourteen to eighteen hours a day. Yet television did have its effect. It brought home the widening gulf that existed between our concept of our role and that which was piped into living rooms back in the States. Most of it could be dismissed, but statements such as the one made by Gen. David Shoup (the recently retired Commandant of the Marine Corps), defining the war as an internal struggle between "Those crooks in Saigon" and Vietnamese Nationalists striving for a better life, took their toll in the morale and resolve of those whose lot it was to carry out his orders. If he and others like him really felt that, why didn't they do their moral duty and resign in protest?

Dope had become a major, perhaps *the* major, factor in unit performance in Vietnam and provided the backdrop for the polarization at home. It was popular to refer to that polarization as being one of age, but the real polarization was a matter of which side of the dope fence one sat on—age was only a reference point, and a very poor one at that. In the same way that a generation of young men got turned onto cigarettes in World War I (because the government passed them out for free), another generation had turned onto dope in Vietnam because it was cheap, ubiquitous and "better than twiddling your thumbs, booby." It was "Vietnam status," and it made the rounds quickly as the vets hit the streets back home. For different reasons, both combat and support units were easy marks for dope. For the former it was the roller coaster ride between terror and boredom, while for the latter it was boredom enhanced perhaps by a sense of shame. But whatever the cause, the results were the same. Only units thoroughly immersed in their work were reasonably immune to the siren call of cannabis rex.

Another factor affecting unit morale and performance was the rise of the black-power movement in the armed forces. Though they had been in existence far longer, 1968 saw the beginnings of cohesive and effective black-power cells overseas. By 1969, the Marine Corps line units were showing the effects. Dissension in the ranks in combat can be disastrous, so when a cell was discovered, its members would be split up. One of the primary destinations was the air wing because its units contained a miniscule number of blacks compared to line units. The prospect of injecting known troublemakers—most with little or no formal training in aviation skills—into such a technically demanding environment received something less than enthusiastic support from the majority of air wing personnel. Moreover, things had come to such a pass in the Americal Division that fraggings were becoming a routine affair, and Army personnel, black and white, were restricted from entering the Marine compound except on official business. The worry was that incoming troops from ground units would hook up with their counterparts in the Army, creating a volatile and potentially disastrous situation.

As it turned out, the fears were for the most part unfounded, a testament to the leadership qualities of the staff NCOs in the aviation units. Their task was not a simple one, because on them fell the responsibility for incorporating the newcomers into the mainstream of squadron activities, training them in aviation skills, and most importantly, inculcating in them a sense of pride and mission. It was all too tempting to set blacks to the necessary but menial tasks of mess duty and guard duty and the like, freeing trained technicians from these quotas. To have done so would have been justifiable but self-defeating. The minor trouble that it took to give blacks on-the-job training was well worth it in the long run, providing for an assimilation rate scarcely believable at the outset of the program.

Though not as visible as the black-power situation, a more fundamental problem to the Marine Corps in general, and the air wing in particular, was introduced in Vietnam. For the first time since World War II, the Corps had had to turn to the draft to fill its manpower quotas, removing one of its most effective arguments for discipline and order—"you volunteered for this." All at once we were inundated with people who hadn't volunteered, and the effects were profound. The air wing got a disproportionate number of the draftees. There were several reasons for this: in the first place, many of the draftees had more schooling than the Corps' typical volunteer; secondly, the infantry people in boot camp and ITR tended to shuttle the complainers out of their own pipeline, pointing them towards aviation fields; finally, troublemakers in line units were often sent to the air wing as a place where they couldn't get people killed. Most draftees made the effort and became assets, but there were the few whose attitudes and convictions were so foreign to the Corps that they succeeded in severely disrupting the morale and discipline of their units.

These were the surroundings I found myself in on my arrival, and they would in time have their effect on my thinking and being. But that was to evolve in due course. At the moment I was eager to get into the air.

My first flight upon my return was what is called a familiarization hop, where I was supposed to cruise around the area and look at the landmarks. As we climbed out northward staying east of the Assam Range, I began recalling missions of two and a half years before at Hoi An, An Khe, Elephant Valley, Hai Van Pass, the Rockpile and dozens of other places dredged from the dusty corridors of my memory. After we passed to the north and west of Da Nang, my eyes were drawn to the Ashau Valley by the broad swathes of red clay etched in the greenery.

"Looks as if we've really upgraded the base in Ashau," I remarked sagely, eager to impress the taciturn RIO assigned to show me the ropes that I was no tyro.

"Yeah," he said dryly, obviously appalled at my ignorance, "only we don't control it, they do." I was stunned, as it became increasingly apparent that the retreat was in full swing. Everywhere I looked, we were pulling back into enclaves—the ubiquitous fire support base network—leaving more and more of the coastal plain to the enemy.

As we approached the DMZ, I saw pockmarked hillsides whose fresh scars overlay craters I had made in 1966, and I wondered whether the villagers in the grassy plain below were steeped in stoicism or sustained by hatred, or whether indeed they cared at all anymore.

It was different in the hills where the Montagnards lived. They were racially distinct from the people on the coastal plain, and though little was said about it by our press, the Montagnards were the target of genocide by both the North and South Vietnamese regimes. It was popular to cast us in the role of the villain, but with all the trash that was heaped on them by the ARVN, NVA, and the Cong, to the Montagnards we provided a ray of hope.

From 15,000 feet, the forests looked peaceful and quiet, but it was an illusion. Beneath the towering 200-foot canopy, a bitter struggle raged. The infiltration routes increasingly encroached upon the domain of the mountain tribesmen, as the North Vietnamese continued to add to the network of roads and paths that made up the Ho Chi Minh Trail. If they failed in their attempts to recruit the Montagnards, the invaders resorted to butchery and worse to establish their will. Escaping tribesmen fared little better on the coastal plain, where the inhabitants practiced the same acts that forced the Montagnards into the mountains in the first place. Though this had been going on for decades, I had been unaware of it throughout my whole first tour. How many tribesmen remained in their mountain villages is hard to say, but their numbers had shrunk drastically over the last several years. For certain, many who remained did so as slaves, so that when we bombed the passes where the Trail wound through Montagnard territory, we were no doubt taking some of their lives. As if to underscore my point, a cloud of dingy smoke boiled out of the hills behind

Cam Duc, and a tiny dart sped away along a wall of boiling cumulonimbus.

The village of Cam Duc itself looked as if the war were a million miles away, yet less than three years before, I had taken part in a strike that had levelled it. A reconnaissance force in platoon strength had come under attack just east of the village and it quickly deployed to envelop the town. There was a high volume of fire coming out of the southeast corner of the ville, and the platoon was being eaten up by a heavy barrage of mortar fire. We were diverted by Joyride from another mission and had no trouble finding the area with all the smoke and confusion. We were quickly joined by a spotter plane whose pilot told us to hold clear while he took a look around to see if he could find the mortars. He found them all right, but his plane took a hit for his trouble.

"The mortars are in a line of bunkers about four hootches diagonally in from the northwest corner. I've got a rough runner and my spotter's taken a round in the chest. I'm heading for home." He never made it. No sooner had he unkeyed the mike than the Birddog burst into flames and plummeted into the trees behind the friendlies' lines.

My wingman was in position to make a run and his first hits appeared to be on the target. There was a fairly stiff wind on the ground, because by the time I reached the roll-in point, the dust and debris were already out of the way, giving me a clean shot at the target.

As I screamed across the bunkers at 200 feet, pulling the plane back into the sky after release, I was slammed from one side of the cockpit to the other by a gigantic pressure wave. Normally, you felt a slight nibble on the airframe as you released snakeyes and occasionally I could sense faintly the explosions behind me, but nothing like this.

Oh hell, I thought, envisioning us sitting on a torch, I've had a bomb go off right under the airplane. I wasn't thinking of the target anymore as I sheared off towards the coastline instead of back around again to the west.

"What was that, Captain?" asked Lieutenant Buckley in the back seat. I was scanning the instruments for the first indication of our troubles, but nothing moved. Everything was in the green, which seemed impossible.

Then over the radio came the answer from my wingman:

"Man, what a secondary, Dash One. There's nothing left of the whole end of the ville." It was true.

When I finally convinced myself that the plane was all right and returned to the target, I could see that the explosion had taken out more than a dozen hootches and that secondaries were still going off. We worked over the southeast corner where the firing had been coming from until we were out of bombs, but we could have saved the effort. The force of the explosion and the ensuing fire was so great that the defenders evacuated the village in all directions, allowing the disorganized elements to be taken piecemeal by the recon unit.

It was sobering to look down on the area now after all that time. It was as if Cam Duc had lived in peaceful isolation for centuries with nothing more threatening than a wandering mountain lion in search of food to spoil the dull routine. But the vividness of the memory brought me on-line with my mission, and in that moment I made the transition from peacetime aviator to fighter pilot.

We continued the tour to the DMZ, studying the terrain around Cam Lo, Dong Ha, and Khe Sanh before turning south for the flight home. What I saw—the indications of increased enemy activity—disturbed me, but when I caught sight of the base at Chu Lai, I felt better. With all the activity going on around the clock, the most notable thing about the base was the beauty of its setting—from on the ground or in the air. Chu Lai was a four-mile strip along the South China Sea, bounded on the north by a cresent-shaped bay. Once sand dunes and marshes, it was now laced with asphalt and smudged with red clay from the hills to the west. From the air, it was an arabesque of reds and blacks and greens, set on a background of undulating whites. The sea ranged from cobalt and slate during storms to sparkling azure and turquoise in the midday sun. Best of all was the vista to the west, where the leading edge of the Assam thrusted up from the coastal plain much as the Santa Ynez Range does in California. At set times of the year the mountains were transformed by the elements: sometimes early morning puffballs developed into gigantic thunderheads, holding court until long after the sun went down; at others a stratus mantle slipped over the brow of the mountains, spilling part way down the coastal face; then there were days on end when there was nothing but the sharp division between the deep green of the hills and the solid blue of sky; finally there were the days when the wind poured off the sea bringing torrents of rain to erase the hills completely, making them an ever-present menace to an off-course plane.

My assignment to the group staff wouldn't last forever—about six months before I finally got orders to a squadron—but it seemed as if the period of limbo would never end. As a member of the group staff I was assigned to fly with a squadron, but such arrangements were by far the hardest. There were too many staff officers, and the squadrons jealously guarded their good missions. It wasn't too tough getting TPQ flights—particularly the late night ones—or the BARCAPs, but I found that the surest way for me to get on someone's schedule was to volunteer for the night Steel Tigers. It was like 1966 all over again with the distinction that instead of a temporary shutdown of missions over the North, Alpha strikes had been out for over a year. The "out-of-country" action was in Laos, and places like Xepon and Ban Karai Pass were no more friendly than they had been during my first tour. The big difference lay in our tactics. Before, we had generally gone in four-plane flights, making six runs apiece over the top of illumination flares that lit up our undersides to a far greater degree than they did the targets. Now we went in two-plane flights, making a minimum number of runs at targets that were referenced to a pattern of ground-burning flares. "On a run-in heading of three-three-zero, the target is at four o'clock at 200 meters from the northernmost flare." It seems complicated, but more often than not, before we got around to crunching trucks, a gun position would open up, ending the mystery of where the target was.

The weeks dragged by interminably. Sometimes I'd get two flights; sometimes four in a seven-day period. The best I did was nine, but then it was discovered that I was flying with all three of the group's squadrons, so they kept better track of me after that. Mostly I flew the group's C-117—the Hummer—which ran people and equipment around all over I Corps by day and dropped flares at night. I started checking out in the bird the second week I was there, and after a month, they designated me as pilot-in-command, making me one of two in the group when my instructor left for home. Except for the fact that it wasn't a fighter, I was in staff pilot heaven. I could fly as much as I wanted, checking in with my office only occasionally to make sure that nobody had made off with my typewriter. Some days I'd spend eight hours jumping from one strip to the next, taking people and cargo back and forth to the various Marine Corps outposts in I Corps. Then, after a quick meal, I'd jump right back into the crusty old junker and drop flares in the boonies. Finally, orders came to go to a squadron— the same squadron with which I had deployed in the first place in 1965.

It was October, and the ink hadn't dried on my assignment paper before I had cleared out my desk at the group headquarters and headed for my new digs. I was at the squadron operations office before seven, eager to begin checking in, only to be asked if I wanted to stand the Hot Pad. Absolutely, because if anything interesting was going to happen, that's where it would be. Ten minutes after I arrived at the Hot Pad van, the duty officer's phone went off, and I was on my way. There was a reconnaissance patrol of fifteen men pinned down by two companies of NVA near Khe Sanh, so A Pad scrambled with Dan Martin on my wing and Skip Sines in my back seat. The weather was fine at Chu Lai, but north of Da Nang we picked up a cloud layer that thickened the farther we went, until it extended from a few hundred feet above the ground to more than 6,000 feet, obscuring not only the enemy positions but the surrounding mountains as well.

Although we couldn't talk directly with the men on the ground, we could relay messages back and forth through the leader of the rescue helicopter flight hovering in the clear, awaiting a chance to retract the patrol. The news was not good. The patrol had already taken heavy casualties with three dead and six wounded, three seriously. The NVA units were above them in prepared positions with fields of fire choking off escape by foot and preventing helicopter evacuation. The choppers couldn't go in until the patrol moved several hundred yards farther into the valley.

We let down underneath the overcast over the coastal plain, popping out at 500 feet near the entrance to the valley on a northwesterly heading. Some of the hills went up to 7,000 feet and there were smaller outcroppings that didn't register on the maps. Typical of the weather at that time of the year, the bases of the clouds were ragged along the hills, so that only in the center of the valley was there room to maneuver.

Leaving Dan over the flatland, I worked myself up to the end of the valley where the fighting was taking place. From the description the choppers had given, I could make out where the friendlies were, but we ran out of maneuvering room before we could find (much less drop on) the enemy positions. Reaching the end of the valley, I had to light the afterburners and climb straight up through the clouds to avoid the unseen hills— the ubiquitous "cumulo granite." It was frustrating to be in the area with the right ordnance just when it was really needed and not be able to do anything to help. I was about to call Joyride to see if they could arrange for naval gunfire support when the lead rescue chopper came on the line.

"Keep it up, Asp. Recce Six says that you came right over the top of the enemy position and got their attention. They stopped firing for nearly a minute."

"Relay to Recce that I didn't see a thing, but I'll keep making dummy runs to keep them down until the clouds lift."

During the next fifteen minutes, we made half a dozen passes, each time allowing the recon patrol to withdraw a few yards, but the clouds showed no signs of lifting. Fuel was beginning to be a concern, and Skip, who had arrived overseas just that week and had never been exposed to the madness of continually punching up and down through the clouds, was getting panicky. At first, his protestations were mildly irritating, but after a while he got to me. Why anyone would volunteer for the rear seat is a mystery, but once there, it was his job to stick it out. This was the first time that I had had a serious concern that an RIO might just punch out, and he was so out of control that I told him make sure that his ejection select switch was in the "rear seat only" position so that I wouldn't get lofted into the boonies if he followed through with his threats. Finally I'd had enough and ordered him to shut up, unplug his microphone, or go the hell on and punch out, whichever suited him best.

"Asp, Recce Six reports that the unfriendlies are moving out of their positions and readying for an attack." That was what I had been afraid of. We had made a bunch of runs and failed to drop, so it was only a matter of time before they got the idea that we were a paper tiger.

"You'd better ask Recce if things are bad enough that he's willing for me to drop over the top of him. Tell him to mark his farthest forward position with red smoke."

"Roger, Asp. Red smoke on its way. He says 'sock it to 'em.'"

Any run in the hills is hard enough, but in this case we were stuck with releasing horizontally, or perhaps even in a slight climb, in order to reach the enemy position on the hillside with the bombs. There just wasn't any gunsight setting for releasing snakeyes that took this into account, so it was going to be "wing it" time.

"OK, Dash Two, I'm setting up 210 mils for a level 450 knot delivery. Give me a forty-five second interval and if my hits are confirmed and if you have everybody's smoke, go on and drop. Otherwise abort it high and dry."

With a grim determination, I plunged once again through the clouds and into the valley, only to be greeted by an amazing sight. The clouds had lifted as if by magic, and I could see the plume of red fully five miles away. Rocketing by Asp Two, I reset my gunsight for a 10-degree delivery, selected *cluster*, *all*, nose and tail *arm*, and master arm *on*.

"Ask Recce how many meters forward of the smoke the gooners are. I'll be on target in thirty seconds."

"They're twelve o'clock for 100 meters in the open! Waste 'em!"

Rolling inverted with the belly of the airplane scrubbing the clouds, we ripped over the top of the recon team. Pulling the nose below the horizon, I planted my sight on a point a football field's length beyond the smoke and corkscrewed back to the upright, boring in until everything but the spot beneath the pipper was a blur. Just at the instant of release I saw a swirl of movement where the bombs were aimed, and then I was off into the clouds.

"Outstanding! OUTSTANDING! Right on the mark. Dash Two, put yours right on top of Dash One's smoke."

Another flight followed in behind us, but it wasn't necessary. The enemy had ceased firing, allowing the recon patrol to withdraw into the valley for pickup by the choppers.

"Cheer up, Skip, we've got two more hours on the pad when we get back." But he wasn't consumed with enthusiasm, opting instead to go to sick bay.

That night I got a phone call in my hootch.

"Hello, Asp, this is Recce Six. I just want you to know that we got out with eight troops. We had to leave seven, but we're going back tomorrow to bring their bodies out. I'll try to get a KBA on the dinks while we're up there. Come up to Quang Tri and we'll do the town."

I felt good to have done something of value—all the more

so because it hadn't been easy. I called Skip over to cheer him up, and Dan and his RIO, and after several toasts to the guts of the Force Recon people, I proposed that the first chance I got to fly the Hummer up to Quang Tri, we would go up there and accept their hospitality. We never got the chance. After the close call, you'd have thought Recce Six lived a charmed life, but luck no less than fame is an illusion. Though we didn't learn of it until several weeks later, he died the next day when the rappelling line parted as he dangled over the jungle at a hundred feet during helicopter retraction. At least he had the extra day, which may seem small for all the effort, but I'd still take the Hot Pad for lesser triumphs than that.

— 9 —
—— Scramble A Pad ——

At the flat buzz of the Hot Pad phone, conversation came to a stop. All eyes were on the squadron duty officer as he snatched the receiver from its cradle. The acey-deucy games stopped abruptly, hands poised to roll the dice. No Marine Corps or Navy ready room would be complete without a full complement of acey-deucy boards. The game is similar to backgammon but with a kicker. The roll of a one and a two allows the player to take a one and a two and any combination of doubles and roll again. An ace-deuce at the proper moment can radically alter the game, making it far more a matter of chance than backgammon. Aviators love it . . . and there was a reason for its existence in the alert van.

Hot Pad was five-minute alert, and it went on day and night around the clock. Hot Pad activity was an on-again off-again thing that went pretty much according to the weather. There were some days (and nights) where the pad wouldn't launch at all—others where it turned into a madhouse, and we ended up cancelling prescheduled flights to make the emergency sorties. On balance, though, the pad was a lot of waiting, where you sat around for hours until a call came in. Generally, it came during daylight hours to support a troop movement not anticipated in the daily flight schedule, or because a patrol had come under attack, or because a plane had been shot down and the area had to be sterilized before the rescue chopper could go in. Then, you might also find yourself launched at midnight into a rip-roaring thunderstorm to throw yourself at troops dug into well-concealed bunkers in the mountains. For this (and lesser missions as well) your mind had to be alert and ready to go. This was why we had acey-deucy boards, chessboards, and the "songbook," which was the written record of some 2,500 rotten jokes that had been catalogued over the years, attesting to the hours and hours of boredom that were an integral part of the program.

"OK, you turkeys," someone would come up with after two hours of total silence, "let's hear it for number 275." For a moment, there would be more silence as the assemblage sorted through the possibilities. Number 275 as it turned out was the one about the "Maid from Madras," and the response would be one of derision. "That's sexist" would come a voice from out of the perpetual gloom of the red-lit bunkroom at the rear of the van, and the pad would lapse back into silence until someone else decided to test the water, or until the phone rang.

A new arrival to the squadron—particularly one just in from the States—found himself a minor celebrity for a week or two, and he was the big cheese of the Alert Van until everyone knew his stories by heart. It was a letdown for the gregarious, but a downright levelling experience for big talkers, and many a neophyte found himself the object of heavy sarcasm for telling only slightly tall tales glorifying some aspect of himself. All in all, life in the Hot Pad van was a pain, and it was little wonder that the crews looked forward to a launch, even a night when there were all those funny noises coming from the airplane's innards, and there was (as everyone knew) no lift in the air.

Crew members for the first alert team would be fully dressed and ready to go, and given an extra two minutes, the second section could be out the door as well. Hot Pad duty rotated between squadrons on a weekly basis, and while some squadrons disliked it because it tied up a minimum of four airplanes while taking priority over all other flights, others (like mine) found in it not only the essence of why we were there but a source of extra sorties as well. Sorties were the measure by which squadrons compared themselves. The more sorties you had week after week, the better you were. What could be more obvious than that? The competition could be fierce, and the squadron with the Hot Pad had an advantage if it could come up with more aircraft than were needed to meet the schedule.

A normal day's flight schedule was for between thirty and forty flights from the twelve (or fewer) assigned aircraft and eighteen flight crews. The squadron with Hot Pad would be assigned something like three-fourths of the normally scheduled missions in anticipation that scrambles would balance things out. A good day on the pad might net an additional ten to twelve hops, and the record (to the best of my knowledge) was thirty-six, yielding a *seventy-sortie day*.

Sortie rate, tonnage delivered, total flight hours, and so on might seem like petty statistics, well beneath the dignity of such an august undertaking as smashing people's heads with bombs, but they were important. They were important not because they allowed the operations analysis people to figure out the rate at which we were winning the war, but because they were the only tangible record of the time and sweat that had been expended in what was a very intangible cause. Our maintenance people put in twelve and sixteen and even twenty hours a day, day after day, and mostly what they saw were the same problems with the same airplanes with the cycle broken only when one of the planes got trashed. There were no weekends, no holidays or rope-yarn Sundays. All there was was the satisfaction of being top dog. Our people were going to go back home after thirteen months of hardship and have to deal with people who either didn't understand or simply didn't care about what they'd done; so if they couldn't explain the reason behind it, they at least would be able to tell themselves they'd "been the best." That's why the petty statistics.

"A Pad!" barked the duty officer without turning his head. "Three-five-zero for twenty-one, Quang Tri. Troops in contact."

Todd Plank had just rolled an ace-deuce and was about to send several of my players back home. The duty officer continued to copy the scramble order, and long before the RIOs had made their way to the front of the Hot Pad van, Todd and I had piled out the door and were sprinting—if that's what you can call our careening plunge in all our gear—for the Hot Pad birds at the far end of the flight line. Todd outranked me (he was a lieutenant colonel), but because of his relative inexperience (this was only his fourth real combat hop in six months), I was the flight leader. Todd hadn't seen the inside of a fighter cockpit for the ten years he spent pushing papers around the various Washington puzzle palaces before receiving orders overseas. As an aviator, he was obliged to fly whatever he was assigned, but it was unrealistic to expect him to come up to speed in such a short time. Not only had the aircraft and tactics changed substantially, but he too had changed. Proficiency flying in staff or trainer-type aircraft may put a little gloss on the basic skills, but it is no help for the fact that over a period of time, one's priorities are bound to change. Unless you're at it day after day, the risks begin to outweigh the rewards, and what was once a part of your reason for living becomes a nightmare. Sometimes a pilot will turn in his wings, admitting that combat flying is better left to others. In Todd's position, that would have been acceptable and not necessarily disastrous to his career; it would have meant that he would not stand out among his staff peers. In the world of "up or out," the uncertainty of promotion often weighs as heavily as the dangers of flight, so Todd was there, hoping that by limiting his exposure by flying mostly TPQs, he would live to go home.

The A Pad birds were loaded with bombs, or bombs and Zuni rockets, whereas the B Pad aircraft carried bombs and napalm. Unlike napalm, bombs and rockets are reasonably accurate, especially the Zuni rockets, which go right where you point them. The ground troops loved for us to use napalm whenever there was safe stand-off distance, feeling it to be our most effective weapon. The truth is that it wasn't, but it was impossible to change their minds. There was no doubt that its fireball had a terrifying effect on those who saw it, but even a near miss was a total waste. Not only was it impossible to control precisely where napalm would hit, but the method of attack placed the delivery aircraft in grave jeopardy from ground fire because it had to be flown straight at the target in a stabilized wings-level glide. When we first started using napalm, the enemy troops would dive for cover as we made our attacks, but gradually they learned that with napalm they were in no greater danger if they stood and fired back; and with that recognition, our losses mounted. A 500-pound bomb could miss the target by a hundred feet and still produce combat ineffectives. And with the Snakeye fins (fins that pop open like speed brakes and retard the flight of the bomb) we could bore in so close that our hits were extremely accurate.

My bird was Victor Whiskey Eighteen, one of three super-bombers on the line. The way that an airplane became a super-bomber was by having some incurable malady with the external fuel transfer system. At first, this meant not only electrical or pressurization problems but, because they were at one time in short supply, damage to the drop tanks as well. Once the parts were in the supply system, it took some thoughtful planning to come up with an abstruse malady that would allow us to maintain a reasonable fleet of these beasts. Thankfully, our maintenance people were up to the task. While lacking fuel for strikes in the North, superbombers were extremely effective for in-country work. If it had been up to me, I'd have turned every airplane we owned into this configuration, telling Wing to give the out-of-country missions to someone else.

With its tanks removed, the superbomber had bomb racks slung from all five hardpoints. The plane could be configured in a number of different ways, starting with the way that Eighteen was loaded—twenty-four 500-pound bombs. Alternately, we could load it with twelve 500 pounders and seven napalm tanks, eighteen bombs and sixteen Zuni five-inch rockets, or ten CBU cluster bomblet containers and a gunpod. Any way you looked at it, the beast was formidable. The only real drawback to the superbomber was that it was a little squirrelly in flight—particularly slow flight—responding somewhat more abruptly to pitch command than its conventionally configured counterpart. This minor idiosyncrasy allowed us to place an arbitrary restriction on who flew them, holding them for our more experienced pilots. The fact was that superbombers were fun to fly and in the finest tradition of rank has its privileges (RHIP), I made sure that if there was one available, I got it.

When the Hot Pad was launched, everyone on the flight line pitched in. It was a matter of constant amazement that after so many days and weeks and months and years of this, a scramble was still a source of excitement to us all. The RIOs were still back in the van getting all the information they could. The scramble claxon was blaring above the background din, bringing troops on the run from the various maintenance shops to make certain that there were no delays in getting the birds going. In the early days of the previous tour, a scramble was a little like a Chinese fire drill with people going in every which way, but now it was down to a precisely choreographed stage review, generally going off like clockwork.

From the van to the aircraft was less than 200 yards, but before I was halfway there, I began to sag from the heat and the weight. I heard swift steps coming up behind me, and as Private Winston came abreast, he snaked my helmet and charts from me and drew easily ahead. The equipment was stowed long before I got there—oxygen block plugged into the seat receptacle; helmet poised on the ejection seat top; kneeboard and charts on top of the glare shield next to the gunsight— and Corporal Wilkins was perched on the canopy rail waiting to help me strap in. I heard the start cart beginning to wind up, and as I scaled the footholds, Private Grunewald slithered out of the left intake and dropped to the ground. We had to check the intakes for sabotage before each flight. It hadn't happened to our squadron yet, but the outfit next door had had a rash of destructive acts during the last month and they still hadn't caught the rat. Though one of his tricks was to reach up inside the aux air doors with a pair of sidecutters and snip a bundle or two of wires, his favorite thing was to tape a bolt to the back face of the inlet guide vanes. He liked to use duct tape (known around there as 500-mile-an-hour tape because it was often used to seal up little holes until the tin-benders from the metal shop got a chance to make a new panel) so the bolt would stay in place until the plane was banging and shimmying along on its takeoff roll. Then the bolt would work loose and be ingested by the engine. So far, three engines had been destroyed—two just as the airplane became airborne. Nobody had lost a plane yet, but it had been close. As a result, we were taking no chances. Access to our flight line was tightly controlled, and the area was constantly patrolled by maintenance personnel assigned to the task. If they or any of our flight line people came upon anyone they didn't know or who looked to be doing something out of the ordinary, they would check.

The flight line was a mess, with cement trucks and workmen all over the place putting in hard-covered revetments for the planes. It was about time because we were getting rocketed once or twice a week, and all it would have taken was just one round to hit the flight line and we could have lost six to ten planes and a lot of troops. But while the work was going on,

there was so much debris and traffic around the airplanes that it made for a real hazard—to the Seabees as well as to us and our planes. The revetments were forty-foot-diameter half-tubes made out of armco and covered with pumped and slip-formed concrete. Plans called for them to contain aircraft electrical and starting-air provisions, but at the rate things were going, it would be five years before anyone got around to installing the plumbing. The revetments were not an unmixed blessing, for while they did offer protection from rocket and mortar fire, they made maintenance more difficult, and more than that they proved to be a real hearing hazard. The Phantom is loud to begin with, but when the sound is contained it becomes unbearable, even when you wear both earplugs and Mickey Mouse (sound suppressor) ears. As a result, the birds had to be wheeled out of the revets prior to light-off, and this was not only extra work, but it meant that the taxiway was blocked for anywhere from five to ten minutes at a time. That is why we had to park the Hot Pad birds at the far end, so that they wouldn't get bottled in.

The right engine was already spinning up as Lieutenant Vanderloon (Loony to his friends) clambered aboard and began to strap in. As soon as Corporal Wilkins gave a thumbs-up, retreated down the footholds, and slammed them into their recesses, I switched air to the left engine and brought the right generator onto the line.

Loony switched to "hot mike" so that we could converse without having to depress the intercom button, which in the pilot's cockpit is on the side of the throttle. The RIO's button is on the radar control joy stick.

"It's the Quang Tri three-five-zero for twenty-one, right up at the DMZ. They've got a bunch of gooners pinned down in a ville and they want us to grease them."

The start cart was dragged quickly away, while a battery of linemen buttoned up the bottom of the plane and checked for obvious problems. The scope presentation blossomed and the ECM display was going through its start-up boogie even as Loony started down through his BITs. The scramble start procedure used an abbreviated checklist, cutting precious minutes from the time it usually took to commence taxi. Dust was rising behind Todd's airplane as I finished my checks, so he'd be with me in a matter of seconds.

"Asp Two up. I'll be ready in a minute. My scope can't

get his mask to stay plugged in. The plane captain's gone for a new one."

The flight equipment shop was supposed to have someone on the line for every launch—especially a scramble—with extra gear just to make sure that that kind of thing didn't happen. The oxygen block, which is part of the crew member's flight equipment, is a weak link, frequently refusing to stay plugged into the seat pan receptacle. Experience had shown that the best bet was to try a new one and let the flight equipment people repair the culprit back in the shop.

"OK, Asp Two is up and ready."

Although it was out of my field of vision, I knew what was going on behind me. Just the little amount of thrust required to get the aircraft moving had raised a pall of dust fifty feet in the air and it would be minutes before it would settle out enough for the Seabees to get back to work. As bad as the discomfort aspect was, the real problem lay in what the dust did to the aircraft and support equipment systems. Hydraulic actuators were devastated by the continual abrasion, while the deterioration of canopy pressurization seals prevented half the aircraft from achieving as much as 5,000 feet of cockpit pressurization differential. The canopies themselves were in continual need of blending, and the cockpits often filled with a cloud of fine grit during the takeoff roll when the air conditioning system came on the line. The people who designed the Phantom would have dissolved in tears if they'd ever seen how we abused their progeny.

"Chu Lai ground, Decorate Two Two taxi two, active scramble northbound."

"Roger, Decorate Two Two, taxi runway three-four. The winds are one-six-zero at eight knots. Altimeter three-zero point zero-one. Break. Whimpy Six Two, exit the taxiway at the next intersection. Give way to two Phantoms taxiing southbound on an active scramble."

Whimpy Six Two was a Navy COD (carrier onboard delivery) Grumman C-2 here to pick up supplies. Ground control sent him up a dead-end taxiway, so he'd have to shut down and get someone to push him back onto the main taxiway again. He was going to love us for that.

Out on the taxiway, Loony read the pretakeoff checklist while I touched the switches and confirmed settings. The post-start checks had been abbreviated to save time, but while I was taxiing, I had the chance to make up for some of it. Using the mirrors, I watched the control deflections. Monitoring the pneumatic and hydraulic gauges, I confirmed the operation of the RAT, speed brakes, and refuelling probe. Gunsight boresight calibration check, fuel quantity indicator check, and rudder pedal adjustment were done on the fly, and before we got to the end of the taxiway, the bird was set up for flight except for the final runway checks.

The arming crew was waiting for us at the head of the runway, ready to pull the bomb rack safing pins and check the bottomside of our planes one last time for leaks. They raced underneath, reappearing to pantomime the possession of the pins and their identification flags.

"Chu Lai Tower, Decorate Two Two, scramble two."

It had been five minutes since the Hot Pad phone rang, and there we were, ready to roll.

"Decorate Two Two is cleared for takeoff. Wind is zero-one-zero for eight." Had there been an aircraft on short final for landing (landing traffic usually has priority), he would have had to wave off. Hot Pad scrambles were taken very seriously by the airfield operations people.

For a moment I thought that Todd was having a problem, but finally his flaps came down, and after another painful delay, his head came up out of the cockpit, and he signalled that he was ready to go.

"Decorate Two Two is on the roll." As it had so many hundreds of times before, the Phantom changed its personality under the prod of the afterburners and came to hand like a fine horse about the time we passed the south morest cable.

"Asp Two airborne. Button five." Todd confirmed that he was airborne.

"Hello, Joyride, Decorate Two Two airborne at two-two with a flight of two Fox-fours carrying thirty-six Delta-fives. We're feet wet heading for angels one-five."

"Roger, Decorate Two Two, you'll be working with Smiley One Four on black. Proceed feet wet to rendezvous Quang Tri zero-niner-zero for twelve. Cleared to Panama."

"Panama was a Ground Control Intercept (GCI) site located at Da Nang, but because there was little threat of enemy air activity in South Vietnam, it spent the bulk of its time performing much the same mission as an air route traffic control center (ARTCC) does in the United States. What was signif-

icant was that for once, the equipment they had was state of
the art, equalling or exceeding anything in the hands of the
FAA at home. The radar controller was able to pinpoint not
merely our position over the ground but our absolute altitude
as well. Moreover, if interrogated, his system could provide
him with readouts of our true airspeed, and track, as well as
heading and how much time it would take us to intercept any
other aircraft on his scope.

"Decorate Two Two, I hold you twenty-five north of Chu
Lai, heading three-five-five, passing angels one-five. You have
opposite direction traffic in your one o'clock at eight miles,
descending through one-eight." Two smudges of black slightly
above the horizon established them as a pair of Phantoms probably returning to Chu Lai.

"Roger my position, tallyho the smokers." It was a beautiful
day, with inflight visibility greater than forty miles—the kind
of day you began to see in the early spring in the mid-coastal
area. We drifted feet wet to avoid the Da Nang area and then
turned northwest to intersect the coast between Hue and Quang
Tri.

"Decorate Two Two, contact Smiley One Four on black."
Panama's release shook me back to the present. More and more
I had been finding myself caught up in reverie. It went with
the territory the longer you flew there, and now that I knew I
was into the last month of my tour, that awareness seemed to
drive me deeper inside myself.

Smiley One Four was an Air Force FAC (forward air controller) flying around in a Cessna 337 Skymaster, a fore-and-
aft twin known more commonly as the "push-me-pull-you."
"Hello, Decorate Two Two. How about holding feet wet while
I find something for you to do."

There we were, folks, banged off the Hot Pad and told to
hang loose while they found some place for us to deposit thirty-
six 500-pound bombs. Don't get me wrong. I would rather
have been dropping bombs on a Ho Chi Minh tree farm in the
open than sitting back in the Hot Pad van playing acey-deucy,
but it seemed a little bit stupid when you thought about it. Here
we'd busted tail getting there, shoved some poor Navy trash-
hauler into the weeds, and used up a plane captain's aural half-
life, all so we could orbit over the water while the FAC found
us a bogus target.

"OK, Decorate Two Two, we've got a target for you. We've

been getting reports of ground fire from this treeline north of Cam Lo. Are you in position to see my smoke?"

"Roger, Smiley One Four. I have you in sight. We're at your four o'clock, high and dry at eight point five." What a crock. If there had ever been any military activity there it was long gone by then. I figured that the most we'd do was scare the hell out of a lot of farmers who had decided that the woods were safer than their homes. I was burning to say something over the air, but I didn't because I had nothing better to do with the ordnance and I sure didn't want to haul it back to Chu Lai or dump it out over the water.

Smiley rolled up quickly, letting his nose drop into a shallow dive to disgorge a "Willie Peter" (white phosphorus) spotting rocket. It streaked into a scrawny tree stand. Almost before it hit the ground, I rolled in for a look-see pass.

"Make your runs on a heading of 350, left pullout. The target is two o'clock for 200 meters."

"Roger, 350 with a left pull. Two hundred at two on the smoke. I have several hootches in the area."

"That's affirm, Decorate. That's where the fire's been coming from."

"Do you have the target, Dash Two?"

"Dash Two affirmative."

"Dash One in, dropping pairs." I figured that we might as well make this a good practice session. Todd needed the work. I decided to use the center hootch as the aim point and work outward from that.

The dust cloud from my bombs was already boiling through 500 feet as I bent the aircraft back around to the south in a 5-g turn.

"That's the spot, Dash Two. Put a couple more on top of the smoke." Todd's canopy flashed in the afternoon sun as he banked up to start his run, and the entire clearing was still obscured as Todd disappeared into the pall.

"Walk it on to the east, Decorate. Might as well beat up the bushes a little."

We had to be careful there because there was a village about a kilometer to the east, at the edge of the tree stand. I could imagine what the villagers were thinking at the moment with all the noise and smoke. Hopefully they'd go climb into a hole just in case there was some shrapnel. Todd was off, and I watched his bombs strike 200 meters short of the clearing.

"Probably using a 30-degree sight setting and making 20-degree runs," Loony observed from the back seat. In fact, I wasn't so sure that he had gotten that steep.

"Dash One in." This time I decided to aim for the eastern edge of the clearing, about fifty meters from my first hit.

The smoke from Todd's next drop was about halfway between his first hit and the clearing, and I prepared to roll in on my third run.

"Up to 25 degrees, Maj. Four more runs and he's liable to get it all the way up there." Todd had eight bombs left—I twenty—four more runs apiece with him dropping in pairs. Unless something came up, I'd ripple the whole load on the clearing on my last run.

"Smiley, this is Dash Two. I think I caught some small-arms fire from off to the left on my last run."

"Was that from the ville?"

"Affirmative. Small-arms fire from the ville. Am I cleared to hit it?"

"Roger, Dash Two, you're cleared."

"Dash One off. Hold on, Dash Two. Loosen up your turn and let me look you over for damage." His airframe was already in planform as he approached the dive path. "Negative damage, Dash One. . . . Dash Two in!"

The village was obscured from my sight in an eruption of dirt and flame. Todd has rafted his remaining eight bombs in one run. What could possibly have provoked those idiots into shooting at a couple of aircraft who were off bombing a bunch of trees? They were too far away to have hit us with anything smaller than 37mm stuff, so they had to be nuts . . . or it was all a crock. If we had been back on the deck, I'd have asked Todd just what it was that he saw. I'd *never* seen small-arms fire from the air in the Phantom. The truth is that even 37mm was hard enough to spot in the daytime unless you were looking right down the barrel and saw the flash. On a deflection shot (which anything coming from the village had to have been), the flash-hider would have blocked off the muzzle blast. I wanted to yell out "I don't believe it," but you don't do that kind of thing to your wingman. Not on the radio.

I pulled in tighter and commenced my roll-in closer aboard the target than normal to see what was going on. The clearing was still obscured in dust and smoke, making it impossible to tell what was still there, so I popped my nose up, rolling away

from the target to widen back out for separation, bending back
around to the in-run in an octaflugeron—one of a number of
nonstandard acrobatic gyrations that defy codification, but was
in this instance a modified turning split S. Todd had hit short,
so I let the pipper drop to the top of Todd's smoke and start
its track up to the center of where I knew the village to be.
*Well, what the hell. . . . Maybe he did get small-arms fire. . . .
Maybe the ville is a NVA stronghold. . . . Maybe . . . hogwash!*

It was not until the bottom of my dive that I saw movement
in the village—people heading for the treeline. If I had punched
the pickle, a stick of sixteen olive-drab, 500-pound mud-
thumpers would have fanned out to flatten the town, probably
killing every living soul not pressed into a deep foxhole. By
hitting short, Todd's bombs may have sprayed the village with
shrapnel, but they left most of the hootches intact. The NVA
wouldn't have run into the open like that. If they were there,
they'd have been in their bunkers where only a direct hit would
get to them. Regardless of what was in the ville, it was poor
peasants like those who ended up getting massacred. The NVA
and their commissars came out looking like the white hats, and
we the enemy.

"Dash One off, no drop." I felt stupid and relieved at the
same time. "What's the matter, Maj?" Loony sounded per-
plexed. "Your dive angle and airspeed were dead nuts on."

"I forgot the master arm, Loony. How do you feel about
that?" Already we were back up to 7,000 feet, banking steeply
around to the west. Loony came up again after a pause. "My
guess is that you're going to play dumpex on the first clearing."

"You've got it," which was what I proceeded to do.

"Decorate Two Two flight off target at four-one, winchester.
Dash Two say state?"

"Two, state six-four, coming up on your port side."

"Decorate flight, your BDA is four enemy hootches, unknown KBA. You're cleared to Joyride."

"Joyride, Decorate Two Two off target grid coordinates
charlie-bravo, zero-seven-five, eight-five-seven at four-one.
Thirty-six Delta fives, BDA four hootches."

Heading out over the water for the trip back to base, I kicked
the speed up to 500 knots to get the birds back as quickly as
possible so the ops people could badger Joyride for another
pad launch. Todd sat back at my seven-thirty position for a
quarter mile almost out of my sight, but we were over South

Vietnam, not the North, so I wasn't going to worry about it. The fact was, the whole thing made me sick. If he had tightened in on my wing, I'd have been tempted to roll hard into him and get him to wet his pants. Maybe he'd have some sense scared into him. Luckily, he couldn't bomb worth beans; otherwise, I'd have really raised hell. It was one of those days where everything seemed absurd. Below and to the left, a destroyer lay offshore pounding away with its five-inch batteries, while a flight of Navy A-7s swept in beneath us, inbound from a carrier at Yankee Station. Off to the right a cloud of debris boiled up from the edge of a rice paddy east of Hue, and a little speck clawed back to the perch for a second run. Helicopters—their rotors strobing in the brilliant sun—shuttled troops from Phu Bai to a clearing in the hills near Hai Van Pass where an Army convoy had been ambushed. A pall of black smoke from several burning vehicles rose in a flaccid column, anvilling at 10,000 feet where I punctured it just for drill. High above, a Japan Air Lines DC-8 pulled majestic contrails as it bisected the isthmus on its way to Bangkok. Another ho-hum day at the office.

I waggled my wings at ten miles out to signal Todd to tighten up for arrival at Chu Lai. Regardless of anything else, it's important to look good around the field if only for the sake of the troops. Nothing is worse for morale than to look up and see your squadron's airplanes straggling into the pattern. The wind had shifted to the south, so we would approach the break straight in, turning downwind over the beach and completing a 360-degree turn to touchdown.

"Chu Lai Tower, Decorate Two Two, five north for the break."

Vietnam was among the last places in the world where American fighter pilots were allowed to act like it. The break is a case in point. Nominally justified as a means of achieving a proper separation of aircraft in formation for landing, it is the fighter pilot's best way of saying "hi" to the people on the ground. Back in the States, they had all but regulated the break out of existence, but in Vietnam, it was still a "go-for-it" proposition. It was an outlet for the pilot's natural exuberance that got submerged in the day-in day-out necessity of avoiding mistakes that could cost others their lives.

To explode upon the field at 1,000 feet above the ground doing 500 knots is a chance to exhibit skill in front of an appreciative audience that knows the difference between mediocrity and finesse. With a pat on the top of my helmet, indicating to Todd that I was putting him on his own, I kissed off, reefing the Phantom into a 90-degree bank. The combination of g-force, power reduction, and speed brakes threw me forward into my straps, slowing the aircraft from 500 knots to 250 knots (gear down speed) by the time I rolled out on the downwind. From there, I dumped the flaps, checked my gauges, pumped the brakes, locked my seat, and continued in a smooth arc to touchdown. True perfection comes when you arrive on the glide slope and centerline at the proper speed without ever once having to touch the power, but it just wasn't going to be one of those days. Behind me, Todd had delayed his pitch for three seconds to allow for the correct separation at touchdown.

From the flight line, the sound of two Phantoms hitting the break is a bracing experience. At 500 knots, there is virtually no warning, just a shattering "whoomp" as the planes arrive overhead. At high speed and at a high g-loading, some of the air over the top of the wings becomes supersonic, creating a roll of dry thunder. Speed brakes bite the wind, adding to the din, as first the leader and then the wingman peel into knife-edged flight, arcing in decreasing radii turns to the downwind. Silver streamers of supersaturated air mark their courses. Then there is near silence as the planes slow on the downwind, coasting until power must be added. Boundary layer controls come alive, disgorging an unworldly series of pipe-organ shrieks and moans that rise and fall, seeming to come from all directions at once. The sight of the superbomber with its racks cleared of bombs, spindly legs sticking down amid the bristling hardware, seemed particularly menacing—the more so with its primordial silhouette pinned against a darkening backdrop as an afternoon thunderstorm bore down on the field from the north.

"Chu Lai Tower, Decorate Two Two turning base with gear and flaps."

"Decorate Two Two is cleared to land. The north and south morests are rigged."

— 10 —
Crowning a Hangar Queen

Waiting for me at the line shack when I landed was Sergeant Olsen, a look of real concern on his face. "It's a crummy day all around, Major. Thirteen just came in with a fragged stabilator. It's one of the new boron filament composites, so the tech rep is looking it over to see whether we can epoxy it here or send it to Da Nang."

"If it has to go to Da Nang, how long will it be tied up, do you think?"

"Be at least three weeks . . . maybe a month or more. They're backlogged to the hilt. Seven will be going back together tomorrow, so we might as well plan on Thirteen becoming our hangar queen. Seem reasonable to you?"

I was the squadron maintenance officer, which might sound important, but there was really not much for me to do except explain things to the commanding officer and pat people on the back. Sergeant Olsen humored me every once in a while by asking for a decision that we both knew he had already made, but at least he knew that I'd back him up, which was better than some maintenance officers I'd seen—and about the only thing I was good for. The troops had things under control, which was not only the way it should have been but the reason

why the squadron had always outflown the other units and
would continue to do so, regardless of how hard Wing tried to
even things out.

"When will Seven be ready for test?"

"It could be ready by late tomorrow afternoon if we get
lucky, but midmorning the day after is a better bet. You want
me to go with you?"

There was some history behind his question. I had taken
Sergeant Olsen flying during the previous week. It was highly
irregular to say the least—probably marginally illegal. The
occasion had been a mandatory test flight of a battle-damaged
aircraft that had been down for nearly two months awaiting the
arrival of a leading edge flap to replace the one that had lost
an argument to a tree during a bombing run. Because it was
obvious that the aircraft was going to be down for quite a while,
maintenance used it as the "hangar queen," which is to say that
any time we needed a part to get another aircraft "up," we
would rob it from good old Number Six to avoid waiting for
the material people to locate the part and provide it through
channels.

From the standpoint of availability, the spare parts situation
had improved dramatically from the early days, but in terms
of response time, the system was if anything worse. In 1965,
squadrons had been much more responsible for their own parts
procurement, and even when more Phantom squadrons arrived,
the supply effort reflected its initiation from the operating units
rather than (as later) its imposition from above. Before, you
could call over to Supply with a requirement, and even though
the letter of the law said that you had to turn in the old part
before Supply could pull and issue the new one, they would
respond in the knowledge that every delay could cause you to
bust your flight schedule. Now we played it according to the
book, and even where a part was in ready supply, the system
imposed a minimum delay of twenty-four hours.

As ridiculous as this was, we had learned to live with it by
the creation of "goody lockers" and hangar queens, providing
us with our own internal source of supply. Among the three
Phantom squadrons in Chu Lai, there were enough illegal spares
to totally circumvent the best efforts of the supply system to
put us out of business. In desperation, the group supply officer
went to the group commander and got him to issue an order
requiring us to get rid of our goody lockers and return all illegal

spares to Supply. The maintenance officers of the other two
squadrons balked at first, but finally they capitulated over my
pleas for resolve in the face of the enemy. The weak link was
the maintenance officer of our neighbor squadron, who told
me it was my solemn duty as an officer to obey orders and
turn in my spares. I told him that I knew nothing about spares.
Being literal about it, I told him that I "had not laid eyes on
the spare parts locker for several weeks"—which I hadn't because I had received warning that this was in the offing and
had ordered Sergeant Olsen to make sure that I would hence-
forth have no knowledge as to the existence or whereabouts of
the spares. Sergeant Olsen had the spares removed to the living
area so even he wouldn't know where they were.

For the first several days after they had turned in their spares,
the other two squadrons were able to manage because of their
hangar queens, but gradually they fell farther and farther behind
until they needed two queens instead of one, and then three.
Within a week they couldn't make their flight schedules and
we were beginning to pick up some of their Hot Pad launches.
Finally, the other maintenance chiefs came to Sergeant Olsen
asking for access to our spares.

"How do their bosses feel about this? Are they going to turn
us in for cheating?"

"They say 'to hell with them.' They'll pay us back and build
their own goody lockers back up without telling anyone." So
the crisis was over, but it still took them another six months
to get things back to normal.

In order to prevent the creation of hangar queens, there was
a maintenance directive which required (under the pain of court
martial) that any assigned aircraft *must* be flown at least once
every sixty calendar days. After fifty days, and with Number
Six's gizzards having spread to every airplane in the squadron,
we had to face the fact that we had a potential catastrophe on
our hands. The new leading edge flap had arrived and been
fitted, but there were at least 500 man-hours of labor staring
us in the face getting the airplane into any condition to fly. It
had already been decided that the aircraft was so badly damaged
that it would be barged to Japan for repair, but we needed to
get it to Da Nang, where it could be mothballed and embarked.
Right in the middle of all of this, another aircraft had come
back from a mission with a broken canopy, replacement of
which could take as much as six weeks. True to its present

mission, Six yielded up the required part, elevating the crisis
to an almost insurmountable level.

That night Sergeant Olsen and I met with all of the shop
chiefs to discuss the situation. We had nine days to virtually
rebuild the airplane, and even then it would be nothing more
than a shell. We could weld the flaps up and wire off the
boundary layer control; we could make an air dam for
the ejection seat mechanism for the front cockpit to prevent
the wind from firing the seat in the absence of the canopy; we
could add lead to replace the missing radar gear in the nose.
The thing that worried us the most was that in the race to put
an almost totally dismantled bird back together, some little facet
might be overlooked, leading to the needless loss of an aircraft
merely to meet a silly regulation. Still, we had no choice, but
it occurred to me that there might be a way to increase the
odds for a flyable airplane, so I gave it a try.

"How long have you been after me to take you for a ride,
Sergeant Olsen?" He lit up with a huge grin.

"Great. We'll weld the gear and flaps down and take it up
to Da Nang on the test hop. No sense making two flights out
of it."

As it turned out, the flight was a piece of cake. Every
maintenance man in the squadron came out to watch as we
fired up and went through our preflight checks. All the new
parts that had been requisitioned for Six had been put on other
aircraft, substituting them for "high-time" components to send
back to Japan. We exercised systems on the ground until the
shop chiefs were satisfied that everything we needed to get to
Da Nang was working and off we went. Stripped of every
single nonessential piece of gear to augment our goody locker,
and only partially fuelled to allow us to land immediately if
need be, Six thundered into the air in a 60-degree climb attitude
as we departed the pattern.

After we arrived at Da Nang, Sergeant Olsen borrowed a
crew from a resident Phantom squadron and removed every
part that he could get his hands on, going so far as to put on,
where missing components should have been, dummy covers
stencilled CLASSIFIED—NO ACCESS. When the Hummer
showed up to take us back, we had to bump all the other
passengers to make room for the parts. It isn't hard to imagine
the reaction of the people at Nippi, the rework facility for
F-4s at Atsugi, Japan, when this cannibalized piece of junk

rolled off the barge. They probably yelled and screamed for a month, but they'd get over it and go to work making it as good as new.

So here we were with Seven coming back together again after more than a month. Like its predecessor's, its innards had been in and out of it so many times to keep the others going, it was bound to have a few leaks and glitches, but hopefully nothing too serious. Thirteen was the obvious candidate to take its place, which was too bad, because she had always been one of the top performers. I was getting depressed just thinking about it. We never seemed to make any headway against the procession of ills that affected the airplanes. Besides, I needed to stretch my legs, so I suggested to Sergeant Olsen that we snoop around the area.

"Come on, Top, quit trying to snivel your way into another flight. Let's take a walk around the joint and see what's moving and shaking."

My domain was the middle hangar and flight line area at the north end of the field between two other F-4 squadrons. The hangar contained all but the flight line and ordnance shops and was able to accommodate three aircraft at a time. At the moment, Seven and Two were up on jacks with the engine bay doors hanging down, and Eleven was being rolled out following a hydraulic pump change. Once outside, it would sit on the apron while the various shops replaced the myriad pyrotechnic devices used for ejection and to ensure the destruction of classified pieces of equipment.

"She'll make the twenty-hundred Steel Tiger, Major," Sergeant Ross from the Maintenance Control branch reported, his tone showing pride in the rapid turnaround. "Seven will be out tomorrow afternoon sometime if the flap linkage pieces get here tonight like Supply promised." Frowning deeply, he consulted his clipboard for a moment. "Two's a mess. We fixed the leak in the number one fuel cell and buttoned her up, only to come up with another leak during the high-powered turnup. This one's a bitch." He started to say something, thought better of it, and slumped in resignation. "I don't know when it will be done." He mumbled, erasing and rewriting notes on his clipboard; then he brightened again. "Six is getting a compass swing, but she should be ready for an acceptance flight in another hour or two. It's been a total bitch sorting out the wiring, but the electricians think they have it whipped."

Maintenance Control was the nerve center of the effort and, next to morale, the key to our having a higher availability than our sister squadrons. Sergeant Olsen had instituted a system of close interval scheduling nearly a year before that revolved around the five-minute around-the-clock updates that allowed Sergeant Ross and his Maintenance Control people to shift men and materiel to where they could do the most good. Like most things, the maintenance manual for the F-4 had been written during peacetime for peacetime operations. It was aimed at the most cost-effective utilization of resources in accomplishing the job. All well and good for the boys back in Memphis (home of Naval Air Maintenance), but in Vietnam, our job was to turn around aircraft to fly missions. When time was of the essence (as it nearly always was), it was often imperative that we pull people from one job and set them on another, even when it meant that we had five people doing the job that the manual said took only two.

As soon as Eleven had its pyrotechnics reinstalled, it would be towed clear of the apron, and Five would be in to have its radar replaced. At the same time, we planned to put the comm-elect people on her to see if they could get the radios to work a little better. Braun, who was our best trouble-shooter, thought that there might be a bad connection behind the air-conditioning pack, so it made sense to give it a shot.

Outside the hangar, the scramble claxon blared. Long . . . short . . . long. It was the signal for the B Pad—napalm and snakeyes—so we trotted after the stream of troops who were heading out to add their assistance. Eight—still hot from her earlier flight—was already loaded and sitting in the middle of the flight line ready to fill one of the soon-to-be vacated Hot Pad spots. "She'll take Nine's spot on the A Pad, and Nine will go out on Colonel Jeffries' TPQ." This was a tacit acknowledgement of what everyone knew—that Nine was a dog, better suited to straight-and-level work than heaving around a bombing pattern.

The first pad bird pulled out of the chocks, swinging its tail around to face us. The exhaust blast was warm even at a distance of fifty yards, and the billowing dust was overwhelming. It's amazing that the equipment stayed together as well as it did, considering the conditions under which it was forced to perform. Messrs. McDonnell and Douglas would likely drop a pair of gourds were they to catch this act.

Choking from the dust, I yelled out to the world in general, "Damn, I'll be glad when the revets are finished and we can clean up the flight line." And then to Olsen, "Let's duck through here and talk to McDivitt."

McDivitt was the MAC tech rep attached to our squadron and the person most qualified to decide what was to happen to Thirteen. In the group, there were a dozen civilian tech reps providing us with technical assistance in various systems. There were people from Westinghouse (radar and fire control), Sanders (ECM), GE (engines), Hughes (gun pod), Raytheon (missiles), and half a dozen more. Without them, we would have been in deep trouble.

"No, I can't tell you about Thirteen until I hear back from St. Louis, and that won't be for another hour at least!" That was McDivitt's way. His office was a ten-by-twelve enclosure in the back of a partially collapsed SATS hangar that served as a none-too-effective shelter for flight line dunnage and supplies. In front of him on his desk there was a Xerox Telecopier and a telephone, which together pointed up some more of the ridiculousness of the situation. Chu Lai—in fact almost all of Vietnam—had a better telephone system than I had back home. McDivitt could direct-dial anywhere in the world from his rinky-dink little office; and with his telecopier, he could even send photographs or documents halfway around the world in real time. (Yet over in the American area there was this communications center with olive-drab boxes and antennae out the yin-yang that couldn't raise Saigon half the time, much less Washington. Their favorite reply to a transmission request was a five-minute spiel on sunspots, and even under the best circumstances, their turnaround time was something in the neighborhood of twenty-four hours.)

McDivitt started to say something else, but he was totally drowned out by the racket coming from the construction battalion crew, which made further conversation impossible. McD as he was known to the troops, waved his hand in disgust.

"Screw it," he yelled, and Olsen and I beat a hasty retreat back outside.

There were at the moment two concrete pumps at work on the revets, requiring the services of twice the number of cement trucks as normal. They were lined up single-file blocking the entrance to our hangar, preventing our line people from dragging Five inside. It would never do. "Let's go find Steve," I shouted to Sergeant Olsen through cupped hands, and we took off at a trot. Lieutenant Commander Stevens was the head of the Seabee detachment building the revets, and we found him fuming over one of the concrete pumps that was currently out of commission.

"Hey, Steve, we've got to do something about the trucks in front of the hangar."

"It sure would be easier if we could use the taxiway, John. We could lay some aluminum matting down there between the end of the runway and the main service road that would cut off a mile of driving for our trucks and keep them away from your hangar to boot." We'd been over this one a dozen times before. "Yeah, I know about the FOD," he continued, "but it would sure be easier." After a few more grumps, he signalled his resignation with a shrug. "Yeah, I'll pass the word to the drivers to keep the front of the hangar clear. I'll sure be happy when this job is over. We'll be finished by noon the day after tomorrow if nothing else breaks down, and then we can get started on the air wells and three-phase power."

"Steve, why don't you and your troops take about a month's vacation? That way, when you get back, Top and I will be long gone."

Sergeant Olsen and I poked our heads into the nooks and crannies of our domain for another half-hour, talking to people to get a feeling for how things were going. I have always been amazed by how good the morale was considering the circumstances. It was a real tribute to Sergeant Olsen and his NCOs.

Walking back to the hangar, we were intercepted by Sergeant Ross, who was brandishing his clipboard aloft like a trophy. You could always tell when Sergeant Ross had good news, because he'd barge right into the middle of anything and let fly. "Six is ready for test, Maj. You got anyone in mind?"

"Yep, me. Has anyone seen Lieutenant King around? I'd like him to go." Bud King was our senior flight test RIO and the person I generally took when I was doing the test hop myself.

"He's on his way down from Ops." There were five maintenance test pilots in the squadron, and I tried to see that everyone got about the same number of flights, but it was funny how people were able to anticipate me. I hadn't said anything to anyone about taking the hop myself, but on that afternoon, I felt the need to fly one. Our new Number Six had arrived two days before from Nippi, and the electricians had spent nearly 150 man-hours sorting out the weapons-select wiring. About the only thing they couldn't handle was when some squadron had made its own *field fix* without telling anyone or sending along a schematic. A previous F-4 squadron commander, looking to get more flexibility in bomb coverage, had buggered the electrical systems of his squadron's aircraft. All was well and good until after he was long gone and his modified aircraft began showing up from overhaul where an ASC had been incorporated to accomplish exactly what he had set out to do, but in a different manner. Nippi's job was to install the new wiring, which they did in a literal manner, attaching wire A to pin B and so forth without regard to what changes had been performed. The result was chaos, and it was up to the recipient squadron to sort out the mess that cost close to a hundred man-hours an airplane to get things right.

Then there had been the "great potting compound disaster." Potting compound is a polymer sealant used to isolate and protect from crosscurrent the individual pins of an electrical connector plug. The Phantom contains some 2,000 of these connectors known as cannon plugs, so when the potting compound began oozing and our all-weather airplanes began to go bonkers every time one ran into a cloud, everyone panicked. As it turned out, there was a spore residing in Southeast Asia that had an affinity for the coagulant in the sealant, so the fix was merely a matter of creative chemistry. But this shows what a profound effect seemingly insignificant things can have on the most sophisticated mechanical equipment, raising some doubt as to the level of confidence one ought to have in any machine.

Anyway, Six was now ready for its operational test flight, in which the plane would be put through all of its paces right up to the limits of its envelope. There were two theories in the air group as to how to go about an operational test. One group held that you should do everything in your power to get something to go wrong, and then fix it, while the other contended that you can always get something to go wrong, so why not wait and let it happen on a normal hop and fix it then. My own opinion held to the former tenet, though I was not altogether unsympathetic with the latter in certain cases. Operationally, there was no way that we were going to run our airplanes out to mach 2 so long as our primary mission remained bombing.

Even on BARCAPs, because we flew them with external tanks and because we were in a point-defense mode, it was highly unlikely that we would ever be called on to go much faster than mach 1.2. So even though the test procedure called for it, why subject the bird to the stress of high-mach flight? Why? Because it was fun. It got different kinds of juices flowing, and it was one of the "bennies" of being in the Maintenance Department rather than Operations.

You could recognize Six right off, even if it hadn't had a number painted on its nose. It was the only airplane on the line—perhaps the entire base—that had all of its paint. That was not about to last long, because the heat build-up at mach 2.1 would blister the paint off the leading edges and inlet ramps. In two days, Six would look as humble as all the rest of the planes on the flight line, but today, she was sleek, beautiful, a virgin... and all mine.

Aside from the high-speed portion of the flight, there were a number of other conventions that went along with test hops, geared to ensure the greatest amount of pleasure for the flight crew. Since the only parts of the flight that would not be performed over water were the takeoff and landing portions, and since those would be inside the base perimeter, I didn't bother to put on all the survival gear—in fact, I hauled out my pressure suit torso harness, which dispensed with all but the essential straps and was therefore vastly more comfortable. Bud and I both weighed twenty pounds less than we did for a normal hop as we headed out for preflight, and if it hadn't been for the heavy flight boots, I'd have flipped an entrechat for the fans.

While I did the "walk-around," Bud wormed his head and shoulders up inside the aux air doors to take careful stock of the fuel and hydraulic lines that traverse the engine bays. He was always meticulous in his inspection, so that when he finally emerged with a thumbs-up, I knew that everything was secure—which was why I invariably took him along on test hops. Though it was not absolutely required, I had the check crew unbutton various access panels to such things as the air-conditioning pack, LOX (liquid oxygen) converter, and pneumatic pump, as well as to a variety of fuel and hydraulic connection points. It was a fetish of mine—a holdover from my A-4 days where it was possible for a pilot to know all the systems and their rigging. The F-4 is far too complex, but I seized on certain items that had a history of misrigging. To a certain extent, it was showmanship, so it's possible that the check crew troops were secretly laughing up their sleeves, but even before I got to it, Corporal Grover found a missing safety wire on a fuel connector in the left rear trunnion-mount access panel area. No doubt there were others that wouldn't be found, but we were one up for the day.

Unlike normal combat flights, where time and fuel were of the essence, on test flights we went through the poststart and systems checks as if there were all the time in the world. To begin with, there are some 256 separate circuit breakers in the aircraft, seven of which are in the front cockpit. The rest reside on four panels in the rear under the control of the RIO. In most cases, if a circuit breaker pops and won't reset, the answer is to forget it and continue with the mission if the safety of the aircraft is not involved. There are, however, some systems in which a more complete knowledge of the circuits involved is important, and often a great amount of time and effort can be saved by the use of proper trouble-shooting procedures by the RIO. It is important that we exercise each circuit during the test, and if we are going to have problems, the place for it to happen is in the chocks rather than at 30,000 feet. Aside from the safety aspects of the test flight itself, we could head off a lot of other problems by catching them then and there. With everything clean, even a minute hydraulic leak can be quickly traced to its source. Small rigging defects can lead to greater problems down the road if they are not corrected early on.

At last Bud and I were satisfied that Six was ready for flight, and with a thumb jerk to pull the chocks, and a farewell salute to the ground crew, we were on our way. The sight of a clean bird, devoid of such impediments as racks, rails, pylons, and tanks could mean only one thing, and already there were troops from all three Phantom squadrons heading for the sandbag walls that lined the taxiway to get a grandstand seat for the upcoming extravaganza. As we rounded the head of the runway, Bud called for takeoff clearance.

"Chu Lai Tower, Volkswagen Six ready for takeoff, requesting unrestricted climb."

"Roger, Victor Whiskey Six, unrestricted climb approved. Cleared into position and hold." The rush of intake air subsided as the canopies came closed, and in the confines of the cockpit, the engine sounds were soft and distant. Even during run-up, as I brought each engine in turn to 100 percent, the predominant

sound was that of our own breathing on the ICS, broken by
an occasional comment as to the engines' temperatures and
pressures. It's funny how I was always more aware of this
during a test hop than on a normal mission.

"Beer cans down; seat pins pulled; handle down; visor down;
seat locked; ready to go in the back." I confirmed the trim
setting and fuel. "Victor Whiskey Six cleared for takeoff. Winds
three-five-zero for one-two. Unrestricted climb approved."

The BLCs screeched as I rammed the throttles to the stops,
and the unladen Phantom sprang forward as if unleashed. Almost at once the airspeed indicator was off the peg, and checking to see that the engine temperatures and pressures were
where they belonged, I scratched the throttles outboard and
forward to the afterburner stops. The airplane squirted forward
like a greased pig bent on running out from under me. Unlike
the more leisurely acceleration of a heavily loaded airplane,
there was barely time to recheck the engine gauges before it
was time to raise the nose to takeoff attitude. With the nose
pointed 12 degrees above the horizon, the main oleos extended
rapidly, and there was almost no hesitation in becoming airborne. Even in the leaden air, our twenty-ton beast had taken
less than 2,000 feet of ground roll. At the instant that the
shaking stopped, I rotated the gear handle up, simultaneously
lowering the nose to maintain my altitude at twenty feet above
the runway to remain in ground effect.

We were two-thirds of the way down the runway—abeam
our squadron area—when the airspeed needle passed 310 knots,
and I pulled into a 2.5-g right climbing arc, looking to lay the
airplane on its back in a 45-degree climb heading feet wet over
the coastline. It was hotdogging, but the troops loved it—and
even if they hadn't, I did. We were inverted, coming up on
400 knots as we rocketed past 2,000 feet, still looking straight
down on the flight line. *This* had been what the engineers at
McDonnell had in mind when they first put pencil to paper.
Despite the fact that it is grossly overused, the word is *awesome*. The latest airplanes are even hairier, but the differences
are a matter of degree, not kind. If you stop for a moment and
imagine the wildest, fire-breathingest, farthest-out thing in the
world, and then let your imagination out one more notch, you've
got it indexed. It was a healthy Phantom hauling buckets into
its element, and the only quicker thing around at that moment
was a Phantom coming off the catapult where it'd gone from

zero to one-eighty in two and a half seconds. That puts it in
dragster country.

Rolling to the upright at 5,000 feet with the airspeed at 450
knots, I lowered the nose to the horizon to allow the bird to
accelerate to 550 knots while checking my instruments for any
abnormalities. Once established at the new airspeed, I rotated
the nose nearly 30 degrees back into the vertical, watching the
altimeter going crazy trying to match the terrific climb rate of
nearly 40,000 feet per minute. By 18,000 feet, we had achieved
supersonic flight, and I repositioned the nose to maintain mach
1.2 until reaching 450 knots CAS. It was at this final calibrated
airspeed that we would continue our climb until attaining our
target of mach 2.1.

Once the Phantom achieves supersonic flight, it becomes
more stable, requiring increasingly larger longitudinal stick
deflections to bring about a given rate of nose response as the
mach number increases. It is a function of center-of-pressure
location, which moves farther and farther aft on the airfoil in
tandem with the shock wave. As we approached mach 2, Bud
and I were silent save for our breathing, looking for any inkling
of a problem. There was just the slightest hint of a gallop, but
other than that, we could have been sitting still in the chocks.
The inlet ramps had scheduled to their fully deployed position,
which placed the shock wave so as to maintain the duct airflow at subsonic speed. Though I couldn't see it happening,
the paint on the ramps and inlet cheeks was blistering and
in the process of flaking off. On an aluminum-skinned aircraft,
the range between the sound barrier and the "thermal thicket"
(the speed at which aerodynamic heating begins to weaken the
aircraft's skin) is small indeed, as Six was about to demonstrate.

Though its activation was silent, the illumination of the
master caution light acted like a flash of lightning, spiking my
adrenaline and sending my hand to the throttles. The windshield
high-temp telelight had come on, mandating that I abort the
run. I noted the second hand on the clock to record the duration
of the illumination and looked once more to the telelight panel
to make sure that nothing else was lit up as well. There was
nothing critical in the situation—in fact on an actual mission
I would have kept right on going—but if I were to have continued on this hop, it would have been senseless, as the high
temperature could have weakened the bulletproof portion of
glass in the forward windscreen, causing it to lose temper.

Thereafter, any sharp blow from some object (such as a bird) might shatter it, showering the pilot with a load of glass, which at high speed could have the same effect as a buckshot blast in the face at close range.

Reluctantly, I retarded the throttles slowly, first out of the afterburning range, and then to 80 percent. The deceleration from high mach with the throttles back was stunning, pressing me tightly forward into the seat straps and pinning my test checklist against the gunsight. Done without warning, I could have put Bud's helmet into his radar scope, and if I had not been braced for it myself, I could have bounced my own helmet off the gunsight as well. The windshield high-temp telelight went out as silently as it had come on, and I checked the clock again before logging its illumination period on my knee pad. Then I returned the throttles to their 100 percent position and reefed the plane into a 3.5-g turn to maintain the airspeed bleed-off.

In the early days, while we still had the artificial feel system incorporated into the longitudinal control network, pulling g's at supersonic speeds took a real gorilla on the control pole. The artificial feel was there because . . . well . . . that's the way it'd always been. Feel was a natural phenomenon when there were direct linkages between the controls and their respective surfaces—the faster you went, the heavier the pressures became—but at jet speeds, the pressures became too great to overcome by muscles alone. At first, the controls were boosted, allowing for a certain amount of feedback to the stick, but with the Phantom (as with most modern jets) the surfaces are fully powered, allowing for no natural feel. The Phantom originally employed bob weights, springs, and ram air bellows to provide feel, and that's the way things were until the Blue Angels got hold of the airplane and decided that the artificial feel got in the way. They disconnected the system and decided that it was a better idea. Finally, when no one was able to come up with a good reason to keep a system that the pilots didn't like—and one that was capable of causing problems—we too were allowed to dispense with it.

While the transition to supersonic flight is barely noticeable, slowing to subsonic flight is something else. The Phantom shudders slightly, like a puppy offloading a flea. If you happen to be pulling g's at the moment, the plane will notch instantaneously to a higher g-loading. The phenomenon is called g-jump, occurring in response to the disappearance of the shock wave. The center of pressure runs quickly forward, and there is just a moment of relative instability that feels like a slowing boat being swept up in its own wake. You're quickly through it, and the handling characteristics return to their subsonic norm. It's a situation you have to anticipate, because if you were already pulling the plane toward its structural limits, the additional loading could cause an overstress.

Overstress needs a little explanation. The Phantom's normal stress limit is 8.5 g, and if you exceed this, the airframe must be inspected for damage. The chances are that individual excursions in the range of 9 to 10 g will do little or no damage, but the problem is that after a while, these excesses begin to aggregate. Aluminum has a memory, and repeated cycles above a certain value will take their toll. There is, however, a point at which a single excursion will produce catastrophic failure—the point known as the ultimate or yield limit.

During the high-mach portion of the flight, we had burned down to 5,600 pounds of fuel, and it was time to get on with the rest of the test. From the fringe of mach-2 flight to the edge of flaps-up stall, the aircraft goes through nearly 30 degrees of pitch change on the attitude gyro, while subtending twenty-five arbitrary units angle of attack. Much of our flying—particularly as we approached the low-speed limits of the envelope—used angle of attack as a reference, rather than airspeed, because it is the true measure of the airfoil's lift/drag performance. Throughout the entire range, I had been relating angle of attack, airspeed, trim position, and pitch attitude to one another, while feeling out the airplane at various g-loadings. While the pilot can elect to maintain attitude by means of stick displacement alone, this is not only tiring but jerky as well. The patch to smooth coordinated flight is the continuous use of trim, accomplished through the electrical positioning of follow-up mechanisms in the various hydraulic-control-surface actuating systems. While I had been recording the different flight data, Bud was engaged in checking all of the communications and navigation systems. While I cycled the ram air turbine, air refuelling probe, gear, flaps, and tailhook, Bud tested out our ECM gear with the help of Panama. Finally, when the entire checklist was completed—all the systems checked and their anomalies noted—it was time to head for the barn—but not before one last series of aerobatics. Up we

went into a barrel roll, a graceful high-arcing 360-degree roll
about a point. It's a beautiful maneuver in the Phantom, requiring use of all the aircraft's controls. It is commenced by
pulling back on the stick to achieve 3 g's and initiating a
15-20 degree-per-second roll in either direction. After 90 degrees of roll, the plane should be poised in knife-edged flight,
45 degrees nose-high and 45 degrees from the initial heading.
You then continue the roll and pull, seeking to arrive wings-
level and inverted with the nose at the horizon pointing 90
degrees from the entry heading. The last half of the maneuver
is the mirror image of the first, with the nose below the horizon,
looking to finish at the original altitude, airspeed, and on the
entry heading. Following the barrel roll, I did a loop, another
barrel roll, an Immelmann, and finally a pair of split S's,
plummeting through 6,000 feet while pointed towards the field
with the speed increasing through 600 knots. The sensations
are in a category of their own. This string of maneuvers displaced fifty cubic miles of airspace, at loadings running between 0.5 and 8 g's, and took nearly two minutes to complete,
during which we had traversed more than 20,000 feet of altitude
in a continuum of physical sensations. What was unique was
not so much the number of g's but rather their duration—a
reflection of the high speeds involved. No wild tumbling orgy
of delight this; instead it was a stately saraband witnessed by
only the puffball clouds over the South China Sea.

"OK, Bud, let's go tower for landing."

"How about a 122 pass?" Bud was referring to the supersonic
field entry at the conclusion of a test hop by a pilot from a
neighboring squadron—122 refers both to the squadron's designation (VMFA-122) and to the diameter of the NVA's favorite
weapon (the 122mm rocket). So smoothly does the Phantom
transition to supersonic flight that without watching his mach
meter, the pilot really didn't know that he was doing in excess
of mach 1 when he hit the brake, but everyone on the base
did. The twin concussions of the shock waves sent people
diving for cover, while the attack alert sirens took up their
strident wail. It was nearly an hour before normalcy returned,
and supersonic passes on the flight line were officially banned.

"No, Bud, I think that we'll just coast this one in," an idea
that turned out to be lucky. No sooner had the gear started
down than a utility hydraulic system line to one of the gear
doors broke, expelling under 3,000 pounds of pressure the

system's several gallons of fluid into the airstream. It was really a disappointment after such a good flight, so I almost hated to tell Bud about it—except that I needed his help. "Oops, Bud. We've got a utility failure. Drag out the emergency checklist, will you please? I'll talk to tower."

"Chu Lai Tower, Victor Whiskey Six on a go-around with a utility hydraulic failure. I'd like to remain in the pattern while I set up and then make an arrested landing into the south morest."

"Cleared as requested, Victor Whiskey Six. The morest is set and ready. Say engagement weight." My fuel gauge showed 2,200 pounds, which, added to the aircraft's basic weight of 28,000 pounds, put me slightly above 30,000 pounds. "Victor Whiskey Six will be touching down at three-zero thousand."

Now Bud and I began the challenge and response as we went down the checklist.

"Below 250 knots, gear handle down."

"Roger, gear handle down."

"Gear breaker, pull."

"Gear breaker pulled."

"Gear handle, pull aft and hold."

"Roger, aft and hold." The landing gear had in fact already gone to the down position, but this procedure put 3,000 pounds of air pressure on the downlocks to prevent the gear from folding under the forces of landing.

"Gear position indicators, check."

The same litany of challenge and response accompanied the lowering of the flaps to their emergency (one-half) position, and after a final discussion on potential problems—the loss of lateral stability augmentation, the lack of wheel brake boost and nose wheel steering, as well as the high (160-knot) approach speed—we were ready to do it.

With half flaps, the nose position was slightly higher than for a normal full-flaps approach, but aside from a little dutch roll where the nose described 10-degree circles about a point, the aircraft was docile enough on final. The morest wire was a third of the way down the runway, which, if the chute worked, would allow us to slow to under 120 knots. Unless the brake lines had been damaged, I figured that I would have enough brake authority to maintain the centerline of the runway, and I'd hold the hook until about 500 feet before reaching the cable. If the hook skipped, I could still catch the north morest, and as a last resort, the brakes could be locked up with air pressure from the pneumatic system.

On-speed indexer . . . slightly low ball . . . wind a little from the right . . . just a scooch of power . . . hold the nose. . . .

THUMP. We touched down slightly to the left of centerline, directly abeam the mirror.

Chute out . . . get it up on the crown . . . good chute . . . throttles OFF . . . 2,000 feet to go.

With the chute out and the engines shut down, the plane decelerated smartly, so that by the time I dropped the hook, the airspeed was rapidly approaching the century mark. The nose wheels thudded over the cross-deck pendant, and then the hook grabbed . . . SWOOSH--SH. Just like that.

Fire trucks surrounded us as we secured all the switches, and even before I'd unstrapped, a helmeted crash crewman bounded up the steps and gave me a thumbs-up to tell me that there was no fire under the airplane. As I climbed down to the ground, ground crewmen were installing gear braces while a tow vehicle maneuvered a tiller bar into towing position on the nose gear. The runway was clear and the morest reset in less than five minutes from touchdown. The broken hydraulic line could be repaired in almost no time at all, but the utility pumps would have to be replaced and the system purged, a procedure that took something on the order of four hours. Our maintenance people had utility hydraulic failures almost down to routine. Despite the ending, the flight had been a good one, with Victor Whiskey Six showing herself to be a solid performer.

But there was always something to ruin your day. I had no sooner finished writing up the test report when Corporal Taylor stuck his head in the door with some bad news.

"They think the Hummer's crashed, sir. Group Ops wants you up there right away."

The Hummer—Gorgon 7284—held a personal interest for me. For the last month, Gregg Barnes and I had been the only command pilots in the group, sharing all the flying duties despite the fact that we were both in Phantom squadrons. We were working hard to qualify some other people. Joe Baldwin was the closest to completing his checkout, but he still had a long way to go. Gregg and Joe were both aboard at the time of the crash. Group was setting up an accident board, and obviously, I'd be on it. I hated sitting on accident boards. Occasionally, they turned up some kind of design or material defect, but usually they found human error—pilot error for the most part—and from there on out, things would be painful. On the way to Group Ops to listen to the radio tapes, I thought about Gregg and Joe, but most of all about Sergeant Mines, our senior flight engineer, the person responsible for keeping the Hummer in airworthy condition. He had flown with me during most of my checkout, sitting with me for hours on end and teaching me the systems and emergency procedures.

Though we would still have to convene an accident board to file an official report, I found out what happened, and the investigation and conclusions would be pretty much cut and dried. While I had been testing Victor Whiskey Six, 284 had been on a MARLOG flight from Chu Lai to Da Nang to Phu Bai to Quang Tri and back again. It was inbound to Chu Lai when approach control asked Gregg whether he would be willing to help them check out their radar in the sector to the west of the air base. Approach assigned 284 to maintain 5,500 feet on a vector of 235 degrees, a heading and altitude designed to keep him clear of the rising terrain. Along the coastal plain, he had been in and out of broken clouds, but now he was in solid overcast. The approach control transmission tapes told the story.

"Gorgon Seven Two Eight Four, turn further right to a heading of two-five-zero, vector to enter Sector Charlie at nine miles west of homeplate."

"Roger, right to two-five-zero at five point five. Are you sure this'll keep me out of the rocks?"

"Affirmative Two Eight Four, the highest elevation five miles either side of your course is forty-four hundred and sixty-eight feet, twelve o'clock for five miles."

"Roger, approach, we're popeye."

"Two Eight Four, I hold you two-six-zero at ten from the Chu Lai TACAN. Do you concur?"

"Roger, approach, concur. We're getting bounced around pretty badly. Can we climb?"

"Stand by, Two Eight Four, I'll see if I can get your clearance ... Two Eight Four, I'll have your clearance in three-zero seconds."

There was a pause of approximately twenty seconds while the controller coordinated with Panama for a clearance that would let 284 climb to 7,500 feet. When he returned to the screen the target was missing.

"Two Eight Four, I've lost your squawk. Recycle transponder mode three, code zero-four-two-two. . . . Two Eight Four, I've lost radar contact. Say your position. . . . Gorgon Seven Two Eight Four, if you read, attempt contact on button silver. Turn right to zero-nine-zero for vectors to the field. . . . Gorgon Seven Two Eight Four, Chu Lai approach on guard. If you read, turn right to zero-nine-zero. Attempt contact on button silver. I say again . . ."

It was futile. The weather in the area had lifted even before I had shut down from the test hop, and almost immediately a chopper spotted the wreckage and landed to search for survivors. The plane had hit the 4,468-foot mountain at the 5,500-foot level! It had struck the up-sloping rocks in an almost flat attitude, indicating that Gregg had broken out of the clouds far enough ahead of time to pull the nose up nearly 30 degrees. The maps were wrong. People had been flying around there for five years, and the Hummer had eaten a face full of rock because the maps were wrong. The mountain actually went up to 5,800 feet, but nobody had ever thought to check.

One would assume that death in the combat zone ought to be the result of hostile action, but all too often it wasn't. Sometimes, the tactics employed in going to and from the target area placed an aircraft in a tricky situation to begin with, so that when something else entered the picture, adding complexity, the margin for error would be just too small. All that it took to depart from flight and enter a low-altitude spin was a little inattention—perhaps concentrating too hard on the target to the exclusion of flying the airplane.

I wasn't in the cockpit, so I'll never know the answer for sure, but in another accident, when a newly arrived lieutenant augered in on the downwind leg of a bombing pattern with neither crew member ejecting, there was reason to suspect that he had spun in by mistake as opposed to taking a hit. Whether out of mortification at having lost control or because he honestly thought he could recover the bird, he and his RIO (also new) rode it in. In the absence of sure knowledge, the crash was ascribed to hostile action (as were most), and though I had no beef with that, it obscured the essential truth that little mistakes could kill you quicker than guns could.

Some accidents were so bizarre that even I am tempted to think it had to have been fate. A two-plane flight of our aircraft was refuelling on a tanker, getting ready to go over to Laos,

when another Phantom from our own air group, flown by a
new pilot on his area fam, bull's-eyed the tanker head on. His
airplane hit the C-130's cockpit on the left side, carrying on
through to sever the port wing at the root. The combined wreckage took out the Phantom on the port drogue so suddenly that
the crewmen on the starboard side (whose sight picture on the
hose kept them looking the other way) never saw a thing. Their
first realization that something was amiss came when they
found themselves closing on the crippled tanker with 50 knots
of excess airspeed. They smashed through the starboard wing
just as it began to rotate up around the mangled fuselage.
Luckily, they managed to eject just before the wreckage blew
apart, becoming the only survivors in an accident that snuffed
twelve lives and four airplanes in the space of two seconds.
With all the opportunity for getting dinged in combat, dying
in a simple midair collision was ridiculous—you could do that
back in the States.

The Hummer's crash demonstrated an entirely different category of accident that nobody but a madman could have anticipated. The waste was so senseless that it heightened the
ridiculousness of my earlier Hot Pad mission. It was almost as
if some demonic deity was exacting retribution for Todd's and
my vandalism except, instead of visiting it directly at Todd or
me, he dumped it on someone else so we could think about it
a little.

— 11 —
— Heroes One and All —

That night we were to hold a wake. The day before, Tom Monroe had died, and now it was Gregg Barnes, Joe Baldwin, and Sergeant Mines, so the air group had a stand down, with the aircrews mustering at the O Club as soon as the last flight was on the ground. The Hummer crew's death was truly one of those things for which there is no solace—no redeeming factor other than to say "they never knew what hit them," or some other such cop-out. Tom's was different. It was totally to purpose. He was killed trying to hold an enemy platoon at bay with his pistol after being shot down in Laos.

Nothing could be as frightening as the prospect of being shot down and captured. Two of our airplanes and crews disappeared without a trace the very first week we were there in 1966. "They must have crunched into a mountain trying to get below the soup," we decided. "They just bit the dust in some rock garden north of the DMZ." It was inconceivable that two aircraft could have been shot down with neither able to broadcast the situation to one of the airborne command-post aircraft maintaining radio surveillance over the North, but as it turned out, we were wrong. Word came back that they had been seen, humbled and gaunt, taunted by jeering crowds on their way to

187

the Hanoi Hilton. It was a real shock. We were forced to consider the very real possibility that it could happen to any of us.

Though there were no doubt exceptions, we had to assume that there were no friends in the countryside, and that no place was totally safe, North or South. Even though it was a physically riskier proposition, ejection over the water was the preferred mode—the farther offshore the better. If you lived long enough to get out of your parachute and inflate your flotation gear, you would almost certainly get picked up by a rescue helicopter. On land, you had to trust to God and hope the choppers spotted you before the natives did.

All aviators went through escape, evasion and survival training in which we were taught what to expect if we got shot down. The one message that came through loud and clear was DON'T GET TAKEN ALIVE. "You can serve your country even in captivity," we were told by people who then proceeded to demonstrate the insincerity of their words. It was the first time in my life—military or civilian—that I began to wonder about my safety. "Well maybe they can kill me, but they can't eat me," was my attitude in boot camp, so that even when one of the Smokey the Bear hatted DIs (drill instructors) was thumping me in the gut with his swagger stick, or I was about to drop from doing push-ups, I always knew that I would endure. Not so during EES.

Pickle Meadows, located in California's High Sierras at nearly 10,000 feet, doubles as the Marine Corps' cold weather training and EES School. Several of the thirty-odd staff had been POWs in Korea, so their knowledge of the methods and goals of the Communists was first-hand. A class consisted of approximately fifty people, made up of aviators (there were six in my group) and Force Reconnaissance troops in platoon strength. We had no sooner arrived when we were "captured" and marched up a mountain to the prison camp.

It was with an air of unreality that we wended our way to confinement, chatting easily in the chill autumn air, eager to see what surprises lay in store. Our casualness was due in part to the way in which our capture took place. After an evening spent unpacking and making new acquaintances, we'd mustered in the main classroom for a welcome-aboard briefing prior to going to morning chow. At the stroke of 0630, the base commander strode purposely through the door and addressed the class with his warmest smile and a cheery, "Good morning, men, consider yourselves prisoners of war."

That was that. We were herded outside and led amiably (it seemed) to our "new quarters." Cresting the hill, we saw what was to be our home for the next forty hours. There was a compound about the size of a baseball diamond encircled by a double fence, each line of which was topped with concertina. An observation tower with a cluster of floodlights overlooked the back fence, while the main interrogation hut sat fifty yards in front of the gatehouse. It looked benign.

"Good morning, comrades. Today is your first day of freedom from your capitalist oppressors. We welcome you as brothers into the new world order."

"Hell," I thought facetiously, "my dollar bills did that a long time ago." Luckily, I kept this bit of information to myself. The greeter was a ramrod picture-postcard Marine dressed in a People's Army outfit that would have looked outlandish under any circumstances. The whole situation had all the possibilities of becoming a grade B Hollywood war epic.

"Before we let you into our midst, you will first cleanse yourself of your capitalist filth. You will be allowed to take the first bath of your new life in the People's Pool. You may leave your clothes where you stand."

For several moments no one moved. It was below freezing, and the People's Pool was covered with a layer of ice. "It's not thick, comrades. Don't be afraid, but hurry, we've got much to accomplish today."

He made it seem like a lark. "Here," he seemed to be saying, "we'll play a few games—have some laughs together—and before long we'll get on with the rest of the program." So while the water was a numbing experience, our native enthusiasm and humor held fast.

"Don't worry about your clothes, comrades," we were told after we emerged from our bath and allowed to don our shorts, "they'll be returned after they've been purged of their capitalistic filth. Now, comrades, line up by rank!"

After we had thus arrayed ourselves, our host had us count off starting with the lowest ranking man and working up. Obviously, he thought that he would be able to invert the system, but we knew that deep down we would be able to maintain control.

"Remember your number, comrades. Any time you are

needed we will refer to your number. You no longer have a name." All the while he had been talking the "camp commandant," as he proclaimed himself, wove his way through the single-file line until he reached the end.

"Comrade Number One, you have the distinct honor of raising the flag over the People's Compound. Take it from that footlocker at the base of the flagpole and raise it!"

The young private looked around nervously, hoping to meet his platoon leader's eyes for guidance, but it was to no avail. His dilemma was severe, but when pressed again to raise the flag, he refused. Without the least hesitation, the camp commandant whirled, delivering in one fluid motion a straight right hand to the side of the hapless Comrade Number One's jaw. He dropped as if poleaxed. Without so much as a look at the fallen figure, the commandant turned to the next man and directed him to raise the flag. Number Two's situation was even more acute than his running mate's, but in due course, he too refused, bracing himself for the blow he knew to be forthcoming. Instead, he was felled by a knee to the groin, and even before he was on the ground, Comrade Three was on his way to the footlocker.

Surprisingly, the flag was Old Glory, which ground the message home more surely than could have anything else. The fallen "comrades" were removed from the camp and excused from further school activities. The seriousness of the situation was now apparent to one and all, and while nothing again happened of quite such consequence, the point was made. Different threats and techniques were employed on different people, some effective, others not. I spent a considerable amount of time in a small box in which there were stones to make things more unpleasant, but because it was warm, and I wasn't the least claustrophobic, I thought it a "good deal." In fact, after milking the situation by calling out occasionally that I could "feel the snakes," I made the mistake of going to sleep, which lost me my cozy situation.

Some people took part in far more uncomfortable "games"—one was being trussed tightly and dunked headfirst into a fifty-five-gallon drum of water—but none so terrible to justify the fact that two people actually signed confessions that they were guilty of using germ warfare against helpless civilian women and children. The fact that both broke down in the first hour was all the more amazing.

I came away with a pair of cracked ribs—souvenir of a kick when I feigned the inability to do more push-ups—and a deep appreciation for the men who had been forced to endure captivity. Mine had lasted less than two days, but it seemed an eternity.

What you would do if you were shot down was not something you talked about with others. Intentions like that are sacred. My sincere hope was that I would never be taken alive— that I would escape and evade or die in the attempt—but that was me talking over a hot cup of coffee. I'd like to think that I could have held to my convictions, but in the cold light of day, in a rice paddy ringed by armed men, that's where the tale would be told.

So early the day before, Tom Monroe had eaten some flak over the Ho Chi Minh Trail just south of Xepon and had ejected into the forest. His wingman was orbiting overhead, ready to provide assistance when Tom came up on his emergency radio to report that he was OK despite the fact that he was hung up in the trees, a hundred feet above the ground.

"I'm getting ready to rappel, so I'll call you when I'm on the deck," he reported before settling down to the task of getting out of the tree. Extracting the 200-foot bundle of parachute cord we all carried in one of the shin pockets of our g-suits, he tied one end securely to the riser from which he dangled. Looping the line twice through the lower torso-harness fitting and the helicopter retract D-ring, he let the free end of the line fall to the ground. When he was satisfied that the connections were correct and secure, he unhooked from the risers and began the slow and arduous descent. It took nearly ten minutes, and after taking stock of things on the ground, he radioed his improved situation to his "playmate."

"Roger, Lunar [Tom's call sign], I've got your chute in sight. Jolly Green's inbound with a one-five ETA. I've got another five minutes time on station, but Hotdog flight is inbound to relieve me. He should be up on freq any second."

"Hello, Lunar, this is Hotdog with a pair of Alpha-Fours overhead at angels ten. How're you hanging?"

"Pretty good until just now. I've got movers down below me, coming up from the base of the hill."

"OK, Lunar, I'm going to drop a single, and we'll go from there. Dash One is in hot."

The A-4 wheeled through the brilliant morning sky, a dagger

against the mounting cumulus capping the Assam. Flicking wings-level, it streaked for the ground, spawning a small pod that diverged at an astonishing rate as the plane arced sharply up and away.

"You're 200 meters short, Hotdog. They're halfway up the hill."

"Got your spot, Lunar, Dash Two's in with pairs."

"Still short, Hotdog, they're less than 100 meters below me. They're starting to fire!"

"Roger, Lunar, can you move farther up the hill?"

"Negative, Hotdog, I'd be in the open for fifty meters before the next treeline."

"I got you, Lunar. Get your head down, then. I'm going to make a run north to south and ripple the whole mess. As soon as the trash settles, haul ass for the next treeline. Dash Two, cut your interval to twenty seconds, copy?"

"Hotdog, this is Jolly Green, ETA zero-five. What's your status?"

"Keep it coming, Jolly Green. We've got troubles. Can you get us a relief flight? We'll be winchester except for twenty-mike-mike in two minutes."

"Roger, Hotdog, we've got a flight of Sandys heading in from NKP. They should be up any minute."

"They're down to fifty meters now. I count twenty, spread out north-south on a fifty-meter front."

"Get your head down, Dash One's in!" The A-4 was still just a speck in the sky.

"Thirty meters now. They see me! . . . By God, I got one of those little buggers! . . . I'm out of ammo . . . too late anyway . . . lay it on top of me!"

And several seconds later . . . "Semper Fi, guys."

The Sandys showed up and worked over the area, and then came two more flights. In all, twelve aircraft took part in the operation, and Jolly Green hung around for half an hour monitoring the emergency frequency, but Lunar never came up again. The Hot Pad flight returned from its futile launch, the crewmen bitter and discouraged that they had been unable to help. The day wore on forever, but nothing more was heard. A preliminary missing-in-action report was sent in the late afternoon, but everyone knew that barring a miracle, Tom's fate had already been sealed. All throughout the evening, a listening watch was kept on the area, but nothing turned up.

When nothing had been heard by noon the next day, a killed-in-action report was drafted and reluctantly released late in the afternoon in concert with those of the Hummer crew.

It was a somber bunch that hit the club to prove again that there was no solace, even in a bottle whose contents diminished at two bits a hit. Squadrons had their own tables, though no such official assignment had ever been made. It's just the way it'd always been, their locations reflecting the position each maintained in the sortie rate pecking order. Normally, you had to shout to be heard over the din, and hardly an hour passed that the bell above the bar didn't sound, signalling that someone had broken the rules and had to buy a round for the house. Infractions included such dastardly deeds as entering the bar "covered," or bearing a weapon (pistols were hung on pegs by the door), or jumping on the tables, or (as is a nightly occurrence) swinging from the rafters. The large room was more packed that evening than I had ever seen it, as if attendance were by command; yet for all the crowd, you could have heard something spoken in a normal voice halfway across the room. There had been other deaths in the air group, but Tom's was the kind that made you reflect on your own mortality, representing as it did the pinnacle of devotion to duty. The feeling about that kind of death was deep and personal. There was just no way to share it. You wanted to celebrate it, not mourn it, but for a group of pilots to come to grips with it was asking too much. Finally, the group commander mounted the stage.

"Tom's last words to us were 'Semper Fi, guys,' and that about says it all. It's what is in the back of all of our minds. It is more than our motto, it's the embodiment of our Corps— the thing that makes a Marine just a little bit different than the rest. It's a compact that says something like 'We may walk in the company of brave men, but some of us will have to pay the ultimate price for the privilege.' Tom's death didn't happen in some unknown instant. He knew exactly what was going on and that, just as certainly, he was one of the ones chosen to pick up the tab."

The door opened and several people came in. It was Hotdog Lead with some of his buddies up from the other end of the field to offer their condolences. Taking in the mood of the room, he turned to his cohorts and issued a challenge: "Last turkey to the end of the rafters buys two rounds," and to the audience at large, "At least they didn't take him alive."

There was no way to keep up with who owed for a round.
Within five minutes nearly everyone in the place had joined
Hotdog and his gang on the rafters, and had everyone paid off,
there would have been free drinks for a year. Finally, the group
commander stood on top of the bar and announced that the
drinks were on the house, and that everyone would be docked
pro rata "except for you A-4 toads who drink free."

For two hours, the wake held to that intensity level, until
the combination of fatigue, alcohol, and emotion took its toll.
A bench fell over, dumping half a dozen people to the floor.
A cheer went up, and several pitchers of beer went to douse
the wallowers. Here and there a glass would crash on the floor,
and finally, Tom's wingman climbed uncertainly on top of the
bar, and wavering back and forth—tears streaming down his
face—held up his glass in salute, and without a word, turned
and flung it against the wall behind the bandstand. For a moment, there was silence, and then the air was filled with flying
glasses. The wake was at an end.

Now, at nearly twenty-three hundred, I was finally able to
get the chance to stop off at S-2 and sign off the forms for the
Smiley One Four flight. Normally you did your debrief at the
end of the hop, but with so many things going on, I had asked
Todd to go by and give them the coordinates and results. With
all that had happened in the meantime, I barely remembered
the flight.

"Your wingman says that you had a good one off the pad.
Come on in and tell me about it." Sam Johnson was the group
intelligence officer, the person responsible for forwarding our
very important "hot dope" to the Seventh Air Force. He was
finally beginning to mellow, but he still took all of this a little
too seriously. When he first arrived, he'd seemed so personally
crushed by the fact that we had little or nothing to report—
"Gee, guys, if nothing significant happened, then OK, but it
sure makes my job a lot harder"—that we took to embellishing
things, talking about "livid secondaries," "walls of flak," and
"clouds of vaporized flesh welling up," all from the fifty meters
of trenchline awarded our effort by some FAC bored to tears
with drilling around the boonies in his OV-10. After a while,
Sam began to get the picture, but he was still a sucker for the
"DFC (Distinguished Flying Cross) hop" opening gambit.

In the old days, debriefing had been a matter of walking by
the command center and waving to the S-2 officer so that he

knew that you'd gotten back. If you had anything to say, it
was assumed that you'd come in and talk. Nowadays it was a
big deal with lots of forms to fill out—just like the Air Force.

The terminology had also changed; one of the curious developments of the war was the use of euphemistic offsets to
assess results. At the conclusion of every mission, the flight
leader or the controller made up a BDA expressed in quanti-
fiable terms. "Six meters of trenchline" and "twelve hootches"
and "twenty-five KBA" were typical of the hogwash we reported to the intelligence debriefers, who passed it up the line.
When an actual assessment was impossible, the BDA might
read "twelve Delta-fives" or "six CBUs," as if their mere use
equalled some level of success. These BDAs were of little value
to us, or more importantly to the ground-pounders in the field,
because they contained no subjective appraisal of a mission's
value. But to the planners in Saigon and Washington these
measurements seemed to contain everything you needed to
know to be able to assess how the war was going. The attitude
they seemed to have was that if you expended "X" amount of
ordnance over "Y" territory you would achieve "Z" results.
QED. Granted there was information in these reports, but a
dearth of understanding, so it was as if there were a wall
between the decision makers and the operating forces they
controlled. Maybe the truth of things was just too hard for the
boys back home to bear, or maybe they were privy to things
that we didn't know about; but whatever it was, aviators were
rarely asked for their subjective opinion on the effectiveness
of their raids.

You debriefed with one of the intelligence toads, and every
day it was the same old stuff—hootches or guns. There was
really a lot of variety. Sometimes it was hootches in the open;
sometimes hootches in the trees; sometimes there were guns
with people shooting. But open or in the trees, it was hootches
or guns or both, and an occasional trenchline waiting to get
disappeared by a wandering bunch of happy warriors who happened to be in the area. Along the North Vietnamese border,
or in Laos, it was different. There we bombed Ho Chi Minh
tree farms in the open, catering to someone's seemingly in-
satiable demand for toothpicks. Most often there was a gun
site hidden in the lumber, and then we got to come back and
report guns in the Ho Chi Minh tree farm in the open. Heck
of a deal.

I kiddingly explained to a new RIO why we seemed to fly so many missions against guns in the nowhere.

"You see, we have this contract with the Russians that if they will put a gun somewhere out in the boonies, we'll send flights out there to bomb it." It was meant as a joke, but by then, the humor had paled.

"Didn't Colonel Plank give you the debrief already?" I said to Sam Johnson. I wanted to get this over as quickly as possible.

"Just the bare bones. He said you'd be along to fill in the pieces and sign it off as flight leader."

I almost gagged at the "bare bones" he had written.

"You didn't tell me John Wayne was on the flight. He's right, this must have been one hell of a mission."

"Aren't you going to fill in the details? . . . Well, at least sign it? . . . Hey, your name isn't Hemingway. . . . Hey, wait. Where're you going?"

I was seething at what Todd had written as I walked back to my hootch, and for a moment I was tempted to go tell him how I felt about it. As I slogged through the sand, my anger eased, and I told myself "what the hell, it isn't worth it," but when I got to my door, I found a note from Todd, asking me to drop by his hootch for a drink. That ripped it.

"That was really a good mission today, don't you think?" was his greeting, and he gestured for me to pour myself a drink from the line of bottles on the counter.

Uh-huh. Here it comes. I'd been this route before. This was the pencil pusher's idea of the bottom line of flying missions—the DFC hop. The Distinguished Flying Cross is the nation's sixth highest decoration, awarded for intrepidity and excellence. It's not the Holy Grail but an aviator who wants to make bird colonel better have one. Air Medals are nice, Bronze Stars OK, but the DFC is where it's at. There was sort of a routine that people like Todd had developed to lead into this. It would be interesting to see how closely he followed the script. Hostile fire? Reduced visibility? Rugged terrain? Quick response to a fleeting situation? He'd be sure to use three out of four.

"I called Smiley One Four at Da Nang and told him we were putting him in for a DFC for today's mission. How's that strike you?" Now there was an approach I'd never heard. Todd bore watching.

"Why not, Colonel?" I answered. "Being a FAC is a thankless task. Anyone who puts up with a push-me pull-you deserves something for his trouble."

"I thought that we ought to say something about his courage in taking his unarmed airplane close to the target to pinpoint the ground fire and his skill in marking the spot for us. Then we can talk about his decisiveness in sizing up the situation and clearing us onto the enemy base camp."

"Oh, well, by all means, but let's not forget to cite him for finding his way home without getting lost."

"I don't think that you're taking this all that seriously, John."

"Darned right I'm not. All that turkey did was find us a free drop zone and miss marking it by a grid square. If you want to go around awarding medals, start with yourself. You're the one who found the ground fire," I spat out bitterly, realizing that I was going too far.

"Well, yes, but it will get through a lot quicker if we have the Air Force working on it too. Besides, it'll look better for you as well."

"Hey, Colonel, let's be blunt. This wasn't a DFC mission. I went along with the two points [Strike/Flight Air Medals were awarded on the basis of "points"—one point for in-country flight, two if fired upon or in Laos and North Vietnam] because I really don't know that we *weren't* fired at, but face it, it was a waste of time."

"Are you telling me that you won't help me out on this?"

"If you want to write yourself and Smiley One Four up for a DFC, it's all right with me, only don't ask me to be a party to it. I'll keep my mouth shut, but keep me out of it."

"Look, it's easy for you because bombing and all that stuff are your *thing*. Me, I've been stuck behind a desk for almost ten years flying Sneebs for flight pay. I didn't ask to be sent to Phantoms—I even tried to get the orders changed to transports—but it didn't work. Mostly I fly TPQs, but there's no DFC in them. I've got another two months here, and I might never get another chance like today. All I'm asking for is a little help. You don't need to perjure yourself—just use a few words like *intrepid* and *skillful* and leave the politicking to me."

All of us had written the war off, but it didn't go away as easily. Presumably there was an enemy out there for us to hit and people who depended on us who would be better off if we did a good job, but who was to know? Todd needed a DFC so he could go back to his staff friends with a one-up on them. With a DFC, Todd would get promoted because he would stand out from the rest of the staffers; without it he would just have to take his chances with the rest, and that was a rough road if you'd been out of sight in Vietnam for a while. Well, what the hell, at least he was honest about it, and unlike most of his kind, he didn't find some way to stay out of the combat zone.

"OK, Todd. Sure, why not? Intrepid might not have been the first word that came to mind, but using it in this context seems to fit."

Inside Todd's hootch, I had felt superior to him, but now on the way back to my own I was flooded with a sense of the idiocy of my feelings. Until a moment before, I'd felt I had the right to judge his actions by my supposedly better standards, blind to the fact that in truth, mine were worse. Where he was fighting to further his career, I had already decided to chuck mine. Where he was doing everything in his power to keep his life, I was ambivalent towards mine, choosing to immerse myself in the flying rather than to think about what I was trying to be. Flying had become an addiction rather than a commitment. I was bored and skeptical and I missed the comforts of life back home, but there was the flying, which in Vietnam was unbeatable. Sure, there were the stupid Rules of Engagement, which had hounded us right from the start (although at last undergoing an almost constant relaxation), but on the other hand there weren't all the air traffic control rules foisted upon us by the "Smilin' Jacks" with a union who seemed committed to taking the joy out of flying back home. In Vietnam we could do canopy rolls if we felt like it, jump the Air Force any time we wished, bounce the VNAV with our vortices when we caught them unawares, and rub bellies with a thunderhead returning from a raid into Laos. We could scream down a desolate stretch of beach, raising a rooster tail to mark our passing, or trail sonic booms all the way back from a BARCAP if we had the fuel. It was the end of an era, not that there wouldn't be months—indeed years—more of fighting there, but they were for a new breed of fighter pilots. Those of us there (and many who were gone) represented a cult that was becoming as extinct as the dodo . . . and we knew it.

It was the patent absurdity of all of this that harried me with a nagging doubt. All this madness had become routine. It be-

longed, even if I didn't. It was like an old shoe. I flew missions
to the DMZ; I flew missions in Laos; I flew BARCAPs off the
North Vietnamese coast; I flew flare missions; I flew test hops
and trash-hauling flights and boondoggles and anything else I
could hustle up. I flew as much as I could—more than most—
but the trouble was that I found myself in my "auto mode"
more and more often. I looked at the new pilots, and some of
them were really good, natively better than I was, lacking only
the years of experience to blow me away. I could see in them
a lot of the same things I used to feel. I used to worry that for
so much of any flight I seemed to be "... just along for the
ride."

Then one day it came to me that so long as I was trying to
do things in the literal here and now, using my primary physical
sensors, I was bound to remain a slave to my own limitations.
It was a shockeroo. "You mean that that's the way it is for
everyone?" I marvelled, and "You mean that not everyone who
hit a target, or got the plane back safely on the ground, did it
in full awareness of what was going on?" Plateaus in the learning curve occur when you are married to a perspective that
allows you no growth. Accepting the fact that pushing a twenty-
ton behemoth through uncertain skies at gut-wrenching speeds
required both brute force and finesse at the same time was an
eye-opener. Balancing the two is the trick. You don't get there
all at once.

It gets easier when you begin to realize that physical limits
are truly there (for instance, you can't see what you can't see),
and that the only way around them is through use of the imagination. The fact that you can't see the edge of the flight envelope doesn't mean that it isn't there, but if you try to find it
rationally, you'll screw it up nine out of ten times. It's when
you look inside yourself that you find it, because intuition,
attuned to the threshold whispers of all the receptors, is your
supreme evaluator. The problem is that intuition itself has limits, and occasionally I found myself exploring it for its ragged
edge.

Intuition could take a freaky tack. A few weeks before,
we'd been finishing up a "nothing" mission—a Ho Chi Minh
tree farm look-around below the Ban Karai Pass. It was late
afternoon, and we were working with a TA-4 FAC bird out of
Da Nang, pooping and snooping along the Trail, looking for
activity. The scooter spent long periods yo-yoing up and down,

while it see-sawed back and forth across the Trail trying to scurry up a little activity, while I held high cover ready to pounce, keeping him in sight and looking for ground fire. We had been on station for nearly two hours, refuelling twice to increase our loiter time. Finally our relief flight came up on frequency, so it was time to go home. It had been a total shutout (the Trail was a sea of mud after a straight week of rain), but there was no sense lugging bombs back just so we could jettison them into the South China Sea. I asked Snoopy to lay down a spot in a likely area.

"Roger, Asp, Snoopy in with a raft of Willie Peter." The scooter's belly flashed as he rolled inverted to salvo a pair of five-inch Zuni rocket pods with white phosphorus warheads. A column of silver smoke boiled out of a copse between two strands of roadway.

"Hit my smoke, Asp. I'll be high and dry to the northeast."

"Roger. I'll make one run heading three-zero-zero with a right pull. I'm on downwind."

My switches were set to cluster all, so that the entire load of twelve 500 pounders would pump off the racks in something less than half a second. The target was off my left shoulder for a couple of miles, and all at once I had this weird feeling that I could hit the target with my eyes closed. One part of me was saying, "This is dumb, you idiot," but a deeper urge said, "What the hell, what difference does it make? There's nothing out there anyway." Finally, my warring parties agreed to a compromise. "We'll keep our eyes shut until we roll wings-level in the dive. Then we'll see what we've got." I continued on for another five seconds, burning the scene into my imagination, and after a final check of the switches and the target, I closed my eyes.

"Asp in hot."

It was kinesthesia for the most part—a knowledge of how the airplane should feel in carving a particular pattern in the sky. *Rap the stick against the right knee to break into a roll, and hold it there until . . . NOW . . . recenter to lock the 85-degree angle of bank in. Pull the stick back until the g-suit just begins to squeeze.*

Ten, twenty, thirty degrees of turn ripped by. *Pull it a little more into the buffet . . . sixty . . . seventy-five . . . OK, 90 degrees completed . . . another ninety to go. To the right knee again . . . hold . . . recenter and . . . PULL.*

*One ... two ... three ... stop the pull. Hold it ... left stick
to the peg ... right rudder ... center the controls. Open the
eyes and find the smoke.*

"... 450 stand by ..."

I was lost. I opened my eyes expecting to see smoke, but
the pipper was pointing at dirt. Then I realized I was still in a
30-degree bank to the right. As I flicked the stick to bring the
bird back to wings-level, the pipper arced back and to the left,
and *there was the smoke.* Not bull's-eye mind you, but close.

"... STAND BY ... MARK."

The hits were eleven o'clock for a hundred meters from the
smoke—terrible for visual bombing to be sure, but not bad
under the circumstances.

Snoopy wasn't so charitable. "I've seen better TPQs, Asp.
Let's go button orange."

In those later days, I had begun to experience a foreboding—
like Gotterdammerung. I saw all that I had worked for melting
away to nothing. It seemed so short a time before that every
flight held a lifetime's worth of fascination. My learning curve
had been straight up, and I felt the ache of growing pains at
the end of every mission. Now, ten, thirty, sometimes a hundred
missions strung together. What I did, I did well enough—why
shouldn't I with all my experience?—but I knew in my bones
that my talents were already out of step with the future. Soon
there would be smart weapons delivered by systems managers
enveloped in some kind of electronic cocoon. The life of the
fighter pilot is ephemeral—not merely the individual, but the
breed as well. In the winking of an eye, our day had come and
gone, and already we were on our way out. The cycle runs
about ten years, so I figured that one should start looking for
the chrysalis in the early eighties—long after I'd gone over
the hill, swapping war stories with an acuity equal to my weak-
ening eyesight. "Yeah, booby, there I was at forty thou, and ..."
but it wouldn't hold a candle to some hotshot in his Millennium
Series Super Mach-Buster. "Hold it, grandpop. All you have
to do to hit the speed of heat with this here XF-squared is *think*
it."

As I noted earlier, a pilot's most dangerous time was his
first and last week of flying, but for my part, I'd been dangerous
for a long time ... and known it. It was partly that after all that
had happened, you began to think that you could live forever.
A year before, I wouldn't have thought about making multiple

runs against antiaircraft defenses unless it was absolutely necessary, but several weeks back, I had made six runs against guns at the mouth of the Mu Gia Pass.

It had started out routinely enough. Our flight rendezvoused with an Air Force C-130 configured with night spotting gear with the appropriate call sign of Blind Bat. He was in the midst of detailing a target for us when a gun opened up on him.

"Blind Bat, you're taking ground fire from a gun that appears to be about five clicks northeast of the northern flare."

"We've got him Manual Forty-Five. He's located next to a treeline half a mile off the road."

"Have you got him, Dash Two?"

"That's affirm."

"Manual Forty-Five, make your runs heading three-three-zero with a left pull. I'll be off to your right. You're cleared for attack."

The gun was quiet for a bit, so I had to guess at its location.

"I don't have the gun in sight, Bat, but I'd like to lay a bomb in the area and get a reference from that."

"Go ahead, Dash One, I've still got him with the night scope."

"OK, Dash One is in."

My RIO that evening, Jay Bullard, began his recitation of altitudes and airspeeds as I punched over and established my glide to the vicinity of the gun position. The full moon should have been a help, but because of a deep haze, it proved to be disorienting, creating a milky effect that wiped out any distinction between ground and sky.

"Four thousand, five knots slow . . . thirty-five hundred, on-speed . . . stand by . . . MARK!"

Immediately after release, I checked my attitude gyro and found that I had released in a 10-degree left wingdown attitude, which meant that the bomb would fall short of my aim point by perhaps fifty meters. As the gyro showed my nose 50 degrees above the horizon, I overbanked and unloaded the airplane to coast back to pattern altitude and at the same time watch my hit.

"Oh, hell!" Even before the twinkle of bomblet explosions rippled through the tree sand, the gun opened up again from at least 500 feet farther east of my hit.

"He's firing, Dash One, keep your pull going. I'm fifteen seconds from roll-in."

"Jay, go ahead and pop a flare out in about ten seconds. It may take their attention away from Two." The flares were developed to attract heat-seeking missiles, but they were useful at night against guns because they distracted the gun crews.

"Two in."

Again there was no activity from the guns until just about time for Two to commence his pullout. Then all hell broke loose. Not just one gun position, but a second as well about half a mile to the south of the first.

As briefed, Two dropped all of his CBUs on the one pass, heading high and dry above the target. Though closer than mine, his explosions were short of the target.

I made five more runs, alternating between the two guns. On the next-to-last run there was a sharp secondary explosion that silenced the battery. On the final pass, the remaining gun stayed quiet, allowing me to withdraw without a snort.

Jay was silent all through the debrief with intelligence, but he stopped me on the way out.

"If you see my name next to yours on the flight schedule, Major, go find another dummy for the back seat. I'm not looking to get wasted over here because you want to play your loony games with the guns. It's your deal if you want to go home on your shield, but don't ask to send mine with it."

Somewhere, I'd crossed a line I'd suspected was there but hadn't seen. There is something in war that drives so deeply into you that death ceases to be the enemy, merely another participant in a game you don't wish to end. In a sense, it showed how well we'd been programmed that we were more given to dying for our country than going home to it. I did Jay the courtesy of honoring his wish, scheduling myself with the old-timers like Bud who had been with me the tour before.

As strange as it seems, despite the heat and stink and rotten water and dust and rain and lousy USO shows put on by no-talents with large guitars and humongous amplifiers, it was comfortable there. Everyone around was part of the same act, so you didn't have to try to explain anything to anyone except for the new people, and they got the hang of it quickly anyway. I was ambivalent about returning home, where, in order to fit in, I'd have to forget that any of this ever existed. It was not only the thought that this might prove to have been a waste, but that to some extent I might become a symbol of that waste.

Approaching the end of my first tour, I had doubted that I

belonged there, recognizing the States as being my real world. This time it was different, and I'd gone that one step over the edge to where the world in Vietnam made more sense than that other. So while I could look at a flight like Todd's and know that it was worthless and probably worse, there was always the promise that tomorrow held the great mission—the one that was always just behind the next row of clouds.

Epilogue

Strictly speaking, Vietnam took two and a half years of my life, and if you consider it to have been my contribution in return for the roughly $70,000 I received during my eleven years of service, the country probably got what it paid for. On the positive side of the ledger, I did fly a lot of missions, and some of them no doubt made it possible for troops to live to fight another day. To my uncertain knowledge, I did no harm to the friendlies, and on at least several occasions, I am tempted to think that I caused the enemy a modicum of heartburn. Had we won the war, it would be a lot easier to evaluate my contribution if only by resort to such specious reasoning as "well, the details aren't really important. . . . I contributed to the overall effort, and that's really what matters." The trouble is that we didn't win, so there's no solace there.

On a cost-effectiveness basis, the outcome is less clear. Though I never kept track of any statistics, in a broad-brush sort of reconstruction, I would guess that the ledger would look something like this:

	INPUT	
Fuel	$0.12/gal	$ 87,500
Ordnance	$1.00/pound	3,600,000
Maintenance	$500/flt hr	350,000
Pay and allowances		25,000
Total		$ 4,062,500

This does not include cost of capital equipment, base construction, staff and controlling agency overhead, training and schooling, achieving and maintaining proficiency, governmental strategy formulation, or a multitude of other activities and agencies too voluminous to imagine much less enumerate. On the other side, we might find:

	RETURN	
Enemy aircraft	$1,000,000 ea	$ -0
Enemy trucks	$5,000 ea	250,000
Trenchline	$1.00/meter	5,000
Hootches	$50 ea	5,000
Trees	no charge	-0
Bridges	$500,000 ea	100,000
AA sites	$5,000 ea	100,000
SAMs (wasted)	$100,000 ea	300,000
Barges/Trains/Ships	$50,000,000 ea	-0
Road repair	$100/crater	50,000
Miscellaneous	$10 ea	190,000
Total		$ 1,000,000

Of course this does not take into account costs to the NVA for training and equipping targets, capital expenditures for military facilities, bureaucratic costs, debt service to friends, etc. Nor do I know how others might evaluate the various categories, but I suspect that the overall totals are in about the right scale of values. This is the problem that most people returning from Vietnam faced. They were left with no clear-cut way to balance the books on their experience. The overwhelming majority returned home eager to resume their previous lives, and it is probably fair to say that most of them made whatever adjustments were necessary without serious difficulty. The trouble is that we were in such a hurry to close the books on the whole affair that, not content to betray an ally, we stripped the veterans not so much of honor as their right to self-respect.

But what about the others—the angry ones who returned only to find themselves ignored by a community that no longer shared their concerns? Most had gone to Vietnam angered by the thought that they had been caught in a numbers game, only to be told on their return that the "real heroes" were those who went to Canada. What do they put down on the ledger sheet?

The dead are dead—many (if not most) of their names inscribed in our nation's capital on a memorial that one hopes will stand as a warning to those who would ever again vote to fund uncertain action—but the slate is still not clean. Now and again, the subject of MIAs rises to the public notice, but our government's policy has been to quash the issue in a spate of denials, and then lapse into silence. This has left a bad enough taste in the mouths of those who have had a friend or loved one consigned to this Southeast Asian limbo, but it is hardly better for those who may once again have to lay it on the line for God and country over enemy territory. If I had one certainty going for me, it was that the United States government would *never* cease in its efforts to rescue me were I shot down. The extent to which this belief has been weakened will make it more difficult for today's fighter pilot to do his job.

Glossary

Afterburner

Common method of thrust augmentation for a turbojet engine in which raw fuel is injected into the jet exhaust to increase the engine's mass flow. While it is a less fuel-efficient way to increase thrust compared to such methods as increasing the compression ratio, bypass ratio, or the temperature of the exhaust gas, the penalty is a matter of fuel usage rather than engine size, weight, or lifespan. The J-79-GE-8 develops 10,500 pounds of thrust in basic engine while burning roughly 11,000 pounds of fuel per hour. In afterburner, the engine develops 17,800 pounds of thrust while burning nearly 40,000 pounds per hour. Unlike earlier afterburners, the Phantom's may be modulated through four different stages, so that thrust can be controlled fairly precisely.

Airspeeds

IAS: Indicated Airspeed—aircraft velocity displayed to the pilot without regard to sensor or instrument error. Depending on factors such as temperature, altitude, velocity, angle of attack, and aircraft configuration, the Phantom's Indicated Airspeed can be in error by as much as 100 knots.

CAS: Calibrated Airspeed—raw airspeed data that reflects instrument and sensor error. In the Phantom, CAS is provided through the CADC (Central Air Data Computer), and in the event that it fails, the pilot will be presented with IAS, which he will then have to modify according to a chart in his *Emergency Procedures* book.

TAS: True Airspeed—calibrated airspeed corrected for density and altitude factors. For a given CAS, TAS will increase with an increase in density altitude. In other words, for a given CAS, an increase in either the free air temperature or in the aircraft's altitude will give rise to a higher TAS, which is the velocity at which the aircraft is passing through the air.

GS: Ground Speed—the aircraft's velocity over the ground. The summation of TAS and wind components along the aircraft's flight path.

IMN: Indicated Mach Number—the relationship of the aircraft's speed to the speed of sound without adjustment for sensor or instrument error.

Angels

Altitude in thousands of feet. Thus "angels two zero" is 20,000 feet.

AOA

Angle of Attack—the angle between the airfoil and the relative wind. In general, an increase in the angle of attack will result in an increase in lift coefficient for the airfoil until the critical (stalling) angle of attack is achieved. It is also worthwhile to note that in swept-wing aircraft an increase in AOA does not necessarily lead to an increase in the overall lift production of the airfoil, even when the wing is below the critical angle. One of the characteristics of the swept wing is that at higher angles of attack, the airflow tends more and more towards *spanwise* flow beginning at the wingtips and working progressively inward as AOA is increased. Because spanwise flow contributes nothing to lift, the effective lifting area of the wing decreases and even while the coefficient of lift might increase, the overall lifting capacity of the wing could decrease.

ARVN

Army of the Republic of Vietnam, the South Vietnam Army, known as the "hometown VC."

BARCAP

Barrier Combat Air Patrol—sector air cover mission, most often to protect the naval vessels in the area. To maintain the assigned patrol station just off the mouth of Haiphong Harbor, Marine units out of Da Nang and Chu Lai had to have tanker support. Control came from picket ships off Yankee Station.

Barrel roll

An aircraft maneuver that exhibits motion in elevation, azimuth, and aircraft aspect to the horizon. The classic air combat maneuver for achieving angle-off from an attacker or for closing on a prey. Also, in the context of Vietnam, a class of missions in support of Royal Laotian Forces against the Pathet Lao in northern Laos.

Basketball

Call sign for VMGR-152 KC-130F air refuelling tankers.

BDA

Bomb Damage Assessment—the results-of-a-strike estimate at the end of each flight by the controlling agency (FAC, TACA, or flight leader).

BIT

Built-In Test—a series of fault-checking routines in the Phantom's radar that allow the RIO to trouble shoot and (perhaps) overcome system defects.

BLC

Boundary Layer Control—any of several techniques for controlling the energy and airflow in the surface next to the airflow. The Phantom employs a combination of movable leading edge flap and compressor bleed-air to add energy to the boundary layer at low speed, allowing minimum approach speeds for carrier landing. Because compressor bleed-air is pumped into the airstream through holes in the leading edge bleed-air ducts, it is known as a "blown" system. By contrast, there are installations in which the stagnant boundary layer is "sucked" from a surface to decrease drag and/or control airflow patterns.

Break
(1) A hard-as-possible, pulled-to-the-ragged-edge, last-ditch evasive maneuver performed to spoil the attack of an enemy who has reached the "saddle" position. (2) The act of breaking up a formation (usually incident to landing) initiated by a kiss-off signal (the leader pantomimes blowing a kiss). (3) A communications term indicating that the next transmission is intended for a different recipient. "Dash One, turn port 30 degrees. Break. Dash Two, turn starboard 30 degrees for separation."

Brief
Preflight intelligence and planning session. Depending on the type of mission and amount of coordination required, briefing sessions can take from five minutes (for routine strikes) to an hour or more for interservice gaggles over the North. Typically, flight members arrive at the briefing tent a few minutes before the published brief time to copy down frequencies and study the maps. At the specified time, the briefing officer outlines the purpose of the mission, gives a synopsis of expected threats, and goes over codes, squawks (IFF codes), and lost-comm procedures. The flight leader then takes over and details routes, formations, communications, delivery, and emergency procedures.

CADC
Central Air Data Computer—provides calibrated outputs to aircraft flight instruments, Aircraft Flight Control System (AFCS), artificial feel systems, inlet ramps, and the Aircraft Missile Fire Control System (AMCS).

CAS
Close Air Support—weapons delivery done in direct support of ground troops.

CBU
Canisterized (Cluster) Bomblet Unit—any of a variety of air deliverable weapons containing and dispensing a larger number of smaller bomblets. A typical package might contain

more than a hundred shotput-sized bomblets made up of ball bearings or flechettes imbedded in explosive. The CBU-24 container is released and free-falls to a predetermined height above the ground, at which time it detonates to disperse the bomblets that continue to themselves detonate on impact with any solid object. Although CBUs are generally thought to be "antipersonnel" in character, the ball bearings are capable of cleaving an automobile engine from as far away as fifty meters.

Click
    Radio slang for kilometer.

COD
    Carrier Onboard Delivery—an aircraft configured to take people, parts, and supplies from a shore-based depot to the ship.

Concertina
    Circular barbed wire that can be quickly and easily strung without posts.

DFC
    Distinguished Flying Cross—the nation's highest aviation award, seventh highest of all combat decorations.

DME
    Distance Measuring Equipment—part of the Navy's TA-CAN system, supplying the pilot with a readout of distance from a known point. That, in conjunction with the system's other attribute—azimuth—provides the pilot with his position relative to the radiating facility. When the onboard receiver receives a pulse, it transponds a discrete pulse back to the transmitter. The transmitter then transmits a coded pulse of its own back to the airplane, allowing the receiver to measure the time differential.

DMZ
    Demilitarized Zone—a fifteen-mile-wide buffer between North and South Vietnam astride the Seventeenth Parallel, established by the United Nations in 1954.

Dogbone

Weapon select panel in the F-4 cockpit, so named for its shape.

Drag

That force opposed by thrust in flight dynamics. In general, there are two types of drag: *induced*, which is a function of lift production, and *parasite*, deriving from all other factors, including frontal area, roughness, planform, and mach affects. The former is greatest at the slow end of the flight regime, whereas the latter increases as a function of the square of the aircraft's velocity.

ECM

Electronic Counter Measures—any of a number of techniques employed for the purpose of jamming or spoofing enemy search or fire control radar. The simplest form of ECM involves the use of "chaff"; more sophisticated techniques involve the use of timed return pulses capable of "stealing" the enemy's range gate or angle track, presenting him with an erroneous target location. Early ECM gear required continual monitoring and activation by the operator, but more and more, "little black boxes" are being tapped for the job.

EGT

Exhaust Gas Temperature—one of the primary parameters for thrust development in a turbojet engine. All other things being equal, an increase in EGT will result in an increase in thrust. In general, an increase in fuel will give rise to an increase in EGT unless the amount of airflow is increased. Whereas fuel is often used to cool the temperatures in a reciprocal engine, airflow provides that function in a turbojet.

ELINT

Electronic Intelligence—for air missions in Vietnam and Laos, it involved ferreting out of various radar signatures characteristic of search and fire control radars associated with SAM and AA batteries. ELINT differs from ECM in that the former is normally passive.

FAC

Forward Air Controller—airborne or with ground troops, the FAC has authority to designate targets and call in strikes.

Forest penetrator

A helicopter personnel retraction device that folds up to prevent snagging in trees and opens into a seat that helps to protect the passenger during retraction. The idea is that it snakes down through the trees in the folded position, and after it has landed, the person to be retracted deploys its legs, sits on them, and snaps onto the cable to keep from being snatched off by limbs and branches on the way up.

Formations

Section: Two-plane element comprising a leader and wingman—the basic unit for tactics.

Division: A flight made up of two or more sections, that, while still adhering to section integrity doctrine, work as mutually supporting elements.

Parade: A dress formation used for close maneuvering at night, in the clouds, around the field, and for showing off. The position varies from airplane to airplane, unit to unit, and even as to purpose. In the Phantom, we lined up the intake ramp with the leader's helmet, maintained a three-foot wingtip-to-wingtip separation and a three-foot stepdown.

Cruise: Essentially, a loosened parade formation, used to facilitate close-quarter maneuvering en route in a nonhostile environment. Here, the wingman drops back to a 45-degree bearing and loosens out to allow for nose-to-tail separation. Thus, if the leader wishes to take evasive action, he can do so without inordinate fear of being eaten up by his wingman.

Recce: Close combat spread, with supporting units elements maintaining position within a 45-60-degree cone aft of the lead. In recce, mutual support is sacrificed for maneuverability and massed firepower.

Spread: The basic fighting position where supporting units or elements maintain a position abeam the leader, stepped up or down as fits the situation and at a distance that approximates two-thirds the level turning radius of the aircraft at cruise. Maneuvering involves the use of both the horizontal and vertical planes, the mix reflecting the severity of the situation.

Free drop zones

Areas designated for indiscriminate bombing, the theory being that anyone or anything within the area is an enemy. Early in the war, most free drop zones were in the North, but as time went on, targets in the North came under tighter control and free drop zones were more apt to appear in the South.

G

Acceleration of gravity. Under 1 g of acceleration, one pound of mass weighs one pound. As an aircraft is displaced in pitch about its lateral axis so as to deflect its flight path about a point in space other than the center of the earth, the g loading will increase (in either a positive or negative direction depending on the locus of the center). At 8.5 g's, the lift required to sustain flight is eight and one-half times that required for straight and level flight, and the apparent weight of a 150-pound pilot is a whopping 1,275 pounds. Even the two-plus-pound flight helmet weighs nearly twenty pounds, making the simple act of turning the head a grim chore. The Phantom's 1-g stall speed in its bombing configuration is in the neighborhood of 160 knots (flight below 170 knots is a bitch), so that at 8.5 g's, stall occurs around 450 knots with pronounced buffet commencing almost a hundred knots above that.

G-suit

A pneumatically inflatable corset that delays blood-pooling in the abdomen and lower limbs during acceleration by exerting pressure on the thorax, calves, and thighs. Engine bleed air is piped to the cockpit as part of the pressurization system and directed to the suit in a proportional amount via the g-suit controller in response to an increase in the aircraft load factor. The g-suit adds 2–3 g's to the pilot's tolerance.

GCA

Ground Controlled Approach—an all-weather landing assistance system used primarily by the Navy, in which a ground-based controller relays azimuth and elevation information to the pilot. Since Air Force and commercial aircraft are generally equipped with ILS (Instrument Landing System) equipment that provides a cockpit display to the pilot, their use of GCA is as a "second opinion."

GCI

Ground Controlled Intercept—a ground-based radar system for controlling and vectoring friendly aircraft to engage hostile forces. The GCI controller selects aircraft from either a CAP (Combat Air Patrol) station or Hot Pad and directs them to a point from which they can acquire the raid visually or on aircraft radar and initiate their own attacks.

GMT

Greenwich Mean Time (Zulu)—the world aeronautical standard time. The world is divided into twenty-four 15-degree time grids based on the prime meridian passing through the observatory at Greenwich, England.

Ground effect

An aerodynamic phenomenon occurring close to the ground (nominally two-thirds the aircraft wingspan or less), where induced drag is reduced because of a reduction in the downwash angle of the airflow from the tailing edge of the wing. In ground effect, this angle is mechanically reduced by the underlying surface, reducing the drag without curtailing lift. It is a "free" benefit, allowing the aircraft greater acceleration within its domain.

Grunt

The Mud Marine—the guy who ultimately makes it all happen, and the one for whom the "zoomies" work.

Guard

An emergency communications channel in either the UHF (243.0 mhz) or VHF (121.5 mhz) frequency band. Military aircraft religiously monitor Guard except when someone starts talking on the frequency or when an emergency locator beacon goes off, destroying ears for miles around. (It's a good idea, but most aviators would eat gopher berries before using Guard. The tale is told about the American pilot returning with a damaged aircraft from a raid over the North who came up on Guard to describe his predicament. After several minutes of play-by-play by the stricken aviator, an Australian voice cut in to suggest, "Shut up, Yank, and die like a man.")

Horse collar
Helicopter personnel retraction device optimized for water pickup. The downed crewman need only get his torso and arms through the ring (facing the pickup line), and his own weight will hold him in place during retraction.

ICS
Inter-Communications System—between crew members. The normal ICS mode in the Phantom is "hot mike," where both parties can communicate between cockpits without having to depress a microphone key. The microphone itself is located in the oxygen mask, so that along with verbal communications, the crew member's breathing is transmitted. Since the oxygen system maintains a positive pressure in the mask of two to three inches of water pressure, the pressure-breather must work to exhale, which hampers speaking.

IFF
Identification Friend or Foe—a radar pulse transponded in response to a received interrogation signal from a friendly radar, allowing for a basic identification of the target while presenting an enhanced return image to the radar operator. An additional feature associated with IFF is SIF (Selective Identification Feature, in which various modes allow for the positive identification of a particular aircraft, mission, or intent.

JATO
Jet Assisted Take Off—used to cut the takeoff roll or to provide obstacle clearance after takeoff. A number of different units are available, but the most common is that used by the A-4s in Vietnam, which develops 3,500 pounds of thrust each (two per aircraft) for seven seconds.

Jolly Green

SAR (Search and Rescue) unit responsible for the recovery of hundreds of aviators in both the North and the South—no doubt the most universally respected group of airmen in the war. If there's a fighter pilot in the house, a Jolly Green should never be found with anything less than a full glass.

JP-5

Jet fuel—kerosene. There are several grades of jet fuel, the most prevalent being JP-4 and JP-5, whose difference is mostly a matter of weight and flashpoint. JP-5 was developed for shipboard use where fire is always a hazard. In raising its flashpoint, its weight was increased by roughly 7 percent (7.0 pounds per gallon versus 6.5 for JP-4). While relighting a flamed-out engine was made somewhat more difficult, the increased weight actually permitted an increase to an aircraft's range, because a jet engine derives its thrust from the *weight* of the fuel burned, not the volume. Thus one does not refer to range in terms of miles per gallon, but miles per pound.

KBA

Killed by Air—the body count after an air attack. The systems analysts seemed to have been extremely fond of this statistic.

LOX

Liquid oxygen. Normal breathing oxygen is supplied to the crew members from a five-liter LOX converter located in the aircraft fuselage. LOX is simpler to store and dispense than gaseous oxygen, and the full system is smaller and lighter than a gaseous system of equivalent duration.

MABS

Marine Air Base Squadron—repository of an air group's non-tactical support elements such as Motor Pool, Base Services, Heavy Equipment, Guard Detachment, etc. Traditionally, MABS is the catch basin for unskilled personnel.

Mach

Named for Austrian physicist Ernst Mach, it is a unit of velocity relating to the speed of sound in a particular medium. Thus mach 1 in air is 661.5 knots at sea level on a Standard

Day (15 degrees Centigrade). As the speed of sound in air is a function of temperature, and as temperature generally decreases as altitude increases, the speed of sound is less at high altitude.

MAG

Marine Air Group—a command composed of a Headquarters and Maintenance Squadron (HAMS), Marine Air Base Squadron (MABS), and several operating squadrons (VMA = attack; VMF = fighter; VMFA = fighter/attack; VMH = helicopter; VMGR = transport/refueller; etc.). MAG-12 at Chu Lai contained three VMFAs flying Phantoms and, counting Headquarters, Maintenance, Supply, Ordnance, Motor Pool, Heavy Equipment, and Base Service personnel, ran to more than 2,500 men—all to put out some 100 flights per day.

MARLOG

Marine Logistics Flights—to shuttle men and supplies from out-of-country staging areas, and between in-country operating areas.

Mayday

The international distress call, which is to be avoided at all costs by an aviator. It is better to die in silence than to display the bad form of alerting the world to your predicament.

MER

Multiple Ejector Rack—a six-station weapons carriage and deployment station carried on any or all of the F-4's three hardpoints designed to accept the load. The rack consists of six pairs of sway braces that fasten ordnance aboard, ejector feet that explosively open the braces and kick the weapons clear of the slipstream, and the arming catches that provide for the release of armed or dud weapons at the pilot's option.

Mil

An angular measurement amounting to 1/6400 of a circumference, or nearly one-eighteenth of a degree. Gunsight settings are in mils, allowing the pilot to offset the aircraft's flight path to account for a weapon's ballistic drop. With forward-firing ordnance, such as rockets or cannon, the mil lead is generally quite small. Bombs, particularly when retarded or when released at a large slant-range, require relatively large mil leads.

Nape

Napalm—the gooey, gelatinous mess made of fuel and soapsuds, delivered in tanks designed to tumble when released to increase the spread. It is tricky to employ because of its extreme range error potential, and risky to the deliverer as well, as he must bore well into the lethal range of small arms fire.

NFO

Naval Flight Officer—a school-trained nonaviator. He may be an RIO (Radar Intercept Officer), such as would be found in a Phantom squadron, or a B/N (Bombardier/Navigator), who occupies the right seat of the A-6 Intruder.

No joy

Radio communication indicating a lack of success. "I do not have the stranger (Bogie, Intruder, etc.) in sight."

Nordo

An aircraft with no radio. Also someone with less than adequate communicative skills.

NVA

North Vietnamese Army—the regular troops from the North who constituted the majority of the enemy elements faced by U.S. and ARVN troops in I Corps.

Pathet Lao

Laotian communist troops led by North Vietnamese advisors, operating throughout Laos but more generally in northern Laos or near the Plaines des Jarres.

PAVN

People's Army of North Vietnam—equivalent to the NVA, but operating primarily in Laos.

Pigeons

The vector to a specific point such as a destination, as in "Your pigeons to Homeplate are three-five-zero for forty-six miles."

PIO

(1) Pilot Induced Oscillation—an excursion about any or all of the aircraft's three axes (lateral = pitch; longitudinal = roll; vertical = yaw) aggravated by pilot input. The Phantom's stability augmentation system goes a long way towards relieving the pilot from the spectre of PIO. (2) Public Information Officer who creates and presents "plausible explanations" to the press and the public whenever something hits the public notice.

Pipper

The gunsight aim dot projected onto a combining screen in the pilot's forward field of vision. The dot subtends five mils and is itself contained within a 100-mil ring. The display can be raised (lower mil lead) or depressed through approximately 250 mils by a setting wheel on the side of the gunsight.

Pitch

Displacement of the aircraft about its lateral axis—nose-up or -down.

PLF

People's Liberation Force—the unfriendly Cong.

Popeye

A radio transmission informing the recipient that the flight is in the clouds and unable to see the ground or other aircraft.

Puzzle palace

Any headquarters or staff area, from bottom to top. "P-squares" are instituted for the sole purpose of confusing the issue and screwing up the works.

Ramps

Movable intake walls that regulate the position of the supersonic shock wave to control inlet airflow to the engines. The ramps, which sit on the inboard sides of the inlets, begin to schedule at 1.1 mach, reaching their fully extended position at 1.6 mach. Ramp scheduling is controlled by the central air data computer (CADC) and operated by utility hydraulic pressure. If the ramps fail to operate, the airflow disturbance in the intakes will preclude high supersonic speeds.

RAT

Ram Air Turbine—an air-driven generator and hydraulic pump that is deployed into the airstream in an emergency to provide essential electrical and hydraulic power.

RIO

Radar Intercept Officer—the "guy in the back seat," who is responsible for the use of the radar and the conduct of an intercept.

Roll

Displacement of the aircraft about its longitudinal axis—bank left or right.

Rolling Thunder

Strikes of a preplanned, on-call, or target of opportunity nature into North Vietnam.

Route package

Any of six areas in North Vietnam specified for flight leader-controlled strikes against targets of opportunity. Designated in November 1965 as part of Rolling Thunder, the areas were numbered RP-1 through RP-VI going from south to north from the DMZ.

Saddle

The final attack position with the attacker in range and drawing lead, as in "Check your six, sucker, I'm in the saddle."

SATS

Short Airfield for Tactical Support—a land-based aircraft carrier. The SATS concept calls for the air transport deployment of all elements of the airfield that is to be erected and made operational within a 24- to 48-hour period, able to launch and recover fighter-type aircraft on an around-the-clock basis.

Scissors

The basic air-combat-maneuvering tactic, where an attacker tries to close on a defender and cut down on the angle-off by cutting inside of his radius of turn through the use of the vertical. The defender employs the same tactic to hold the attacker at bay, except that in his case, he attempts to work the attacker out of phase (when his nose is up, yours should be down, etc.), and in so doing increase separation and crossing angle.

Scope
Nickname for the RIO. Also refers to the radar display unit.

Sidewinder
Any of several generations of heat-seeking (infrared) missiles developed by the U.S. Navy at its China Lake Weapons Facility. The 'Winder is the most successful family of air-to-air missiles ever built, designed primarily as a rear-quadrant weapon, though the latest variants provide for a limited head-on capability.

SIF
Selective Identification Feature—companion to the IFF, which allows positive identification by use of any of 4,096 discrete responses to interrogation.

SLAR
Side Looking Radar—high-resolution radar imaging for target discrimination. It is especially useful in locating camouflaged targets.

Slick
A Huey helicopter configured for troop transport or medevac duty, as opposed to a gunship. Also a Mark-80-series low-drag bomb.

Snakeye
A fin-retarded low-drag bomb. The fin assembly is mounted on the rear of what would otherwise be a slick and is designed to let the attacker release as close as possible to the target. Upon release from the rack, the tail-arming wire is withdrawn, allowing the fins to pop open like a parachute, thus retarding the bomb to give the delivery aircraft separation from the bomb blast.

SNB
Sneeb—the ubiquitous Twin Beech, designated the C-45 by the Air Force, used by the Navy and Marine Corps for staff

and proficiency flying, and in service with Air America because of its rough field capability. Also known as the Bugsmasher.

Sparrow

AIM-7 semiactive air-to-air missile carried by the F-4 in Vietnam, and capable of prosecuting a long-range forward hemisphere attack against an unseen enemy aircraft. Most of our present fighters are able to deliver Sparrow.

Stability augmentation

System for providing sensor-generated response input to the aircraft flight controls to counter adverse aircraft flight characteristics, thus easing the pilot's cockpit workload. While the Phantom exhibits positive static and dynamic stability about all three axes, it is subject to tiresome and sometimes uncomfortable excursions in a variety of flight regimes. Without stability augmentation, particularly about the vertical axis (yaw), the airplane can be a handful.

Steel Tiger

Interdiction strikes into Laos along the Ho Chi Minh Trail. Though they generally concentrated on the main bottlenecks (Mu Gia and Ban Karai passes) and crossroads (Xepon), Steel Tigers were often known to work against individual trucks as they snaked through the jungle.

TACA

Tactical Air Control Airborne—an aircraft designated to control flights operating against a particular target. A TACA could be a specially configured aircraft or the leader of the strike flight, but it would be his responsibility to designate the target and assess the damage.

TACC

Tactical Air Control Center—the command center for all air activity within a specified sector. Joyride was I Corps' TACC.

Tallyho

(1) Interdiction strikes into the southern portion of North Vietnam. (2) In communications, it means "I have the target [not necessarily hostile] in sight."

TER

Triple Ejector Rack—the running mate to the MER, able to be hung from any of the five hardpoints but usually found on the inner wing attachments, which cannot accept MERs.

TPQ

Ground-controlled radar bombing. A remotely located radar site controls the aircraft (verbally or by datalink) to a target, integrating the aircraft vector and altitude to determine the release point.

Tracer

Business end of a round of ammunition that is ignited at launch, creating a visible streak through the sky as it heads for the target. Banded among other types of warheads (we used one per dozen, or thereabouts), tracers aid the pilot in putting his ordnance on target.

Willie Peter

White phosphorus—(WP)—a highly flammable element used for creating fire and smoke, particularly for providing a spotting mark for easy recognition from the air. FACs universally carried Willie Peter rockets, and weapons platoons that valued life would likely be well stocked with WP mortar rounds.

Winchester

Standard radio communication meaning "I am out of ammunition."

Yaw

Displacement of the aircraft about its vertical axis—nose left or right.

ZPU (Zip-u)

A small-caliber (14.5mm), belt-fed, rapidfiring weapon that could be very lethal to low-altitude aircraft.

Zuni

Five-inch air-to-ground rocket. Combining a high degree of accuracy with high velocity, the Zuni is a good choice against small hard targets.

Aircraft

BOMBERS

A-1

SKYRAIDER (Spad, "Sandys"): Douglas carrier-based, piston-engined attack plane used by both the Air Force and Navy primarily for RESCAP and FAC work in Vietnam, and in support of Royalist Forces in Laos. It was also used by the VNAF, the South Vietnamese Air Force. As a quick and dirty recognition gauge, one has merely to envision a pair of stubby wings and a jaunty tail held together by a gigantic engine, the R-3350, which puts out nearly 3,000 horsepower. The superiorities of the Spad are its loiter time, heavy armament, and the ability to go low and slow to help spot downed crewmen. The latter is also the Spad's main drawback: its lack of speed makes it extremely vulnerable to enemy antiaircrft defenses.

A-4C/E/F

SKYHAWK (Scooter, Tinkertoy, Heinemann's Hotrod): McDonnell Douglas light attack plane initially developed as an expendable carrier-based nuclear bomber. The Scooter is like a warm puppy—a personnel-sized bomber that you strap on rather than into. It is a nimble performer with no real vices as long as you stay out of someone else's vorteces. Even though they keep throwing more and more little black boxes into the Scoot (they've given it a turtleback to make room for extra goodies), it is still a simple airplane whose innate ruggedness reflects both its small size and design philosophy, initiated by Ed Heinemann in the early fifties and maintained by two generations of designers who know a good thing when they see it.

F-100

SUPER SABRE (Lead Sled): North American Aviation fighter-turned-bomber that saw service early in the war, often in (as in the case of the two-seated F-100F model) the Wild Weasel mode.

F-105

THUNDERCHIEF (Thud): Republic Aircraft medium attack aircraft. The Thud was the Air Force workhorse throughout the early part of the war, flying 75 percent of all strikes into the North during the Rolling Thunder days of 1965 to 1968. Fast and rugged, the Thud is the largest single seater in our inventory. If it has a fault, it is the design of the hydraulic system in which the lines for the separate and redundant systems run along in tandem so that a single hit could take out both systems, leaving the pilot with no option but to eject.

F-111

AARDVARK (TFX, Edsel): General Dynamics swing-wing multipurpose aircraft configured for all-weather attack. Operating out of Thailand, the TFX crews worked diligently to brighten the less than lustrous image that dogged the airplane from its earliest days. it is probably fair to say that it was an aircraft conceived and built before its time, but whatever success these planes enjoyed in Vietnam was a testament to the bravery of the men who flew them.

A-6

INTRUDER: Grumman Aircraft carrier-based, all-weather, medium attack plane. It is capable of carrying up to thirty 500-pound bombs, making it number two on the ordnance hit parade, second only to the B-52. The Intruder is the Navy's most sophisticated attack aircraft, whose DIANE (Digital Inertial Airborne Navigation System) is capable of taking the bird from its base on ship or shore (better the former), proceeding to a preset target, performing a strike, and returning to base all on its own. It has a crew of two consisting of a pilot and B/N (bombardier/navigator).

A-7

CORSAIR II (SLUF—Short Little Ugly Feller): Ling-Temco-Vought light attack aircraft initially developed for the Navy but adopted by the Air Force. The Navy A-7 has replaced shipboard A-4s, and remains a workhorse in both services.

A-3

SKYWARRIOR: Douglas carrier-based heavy attack bomber used only in the early days of Vietnam. Originally designed as a long-range shipboard strategic bomber, it was more often employed as an air refuelling tanker and reconnaissance airplane in Vietnam.

B-66/EB-66

Air Force version of the A-3 used in the early days of the war for ELINT and ECM.

B-57

CANBERRA: Martin straight-winged two-place bomber designed in Britain before the flood. Used in the Vietnamese war as a bomber, its age and lack of speed brought it to an early retirement. Nonetheless, the crews that flew them were known for their accuracy.

B-52

STRATOFORTRESS: Boeing Aircraft strategic bomber developed as a nuclear weapons delivery vehicle but used in Vietnam to carpet-bomb the various supply corridors in Laos and finally in North Vietnam itself.

FIGHTER-BOMBERS

F-4

PHANTOM: McDonnell/Douglas mach-2 fighter/bomber. The most versatile aircraft of the war. Developed for the Navy but adopted by the Air Force, it combined speed, agility, range, ruggedness, adaptability, and prodigious firepower to an extent not rivalled until the advent of the F-14 and subsequent post-Vietnam-era aircraft.

F-5
FREEDOM FIGHTER (Scoshie Tiger): Northrop Aircraft lightweight fighter/bomber variant of the T-38 Talon trainer. Developed for the Air Force but given to the VNAF. It must be considered one of the most successful designs in aircraft history, considering the variants that exist and the numbers sold to friendly nations. Not surprisingly, the VNAF's F-5s fell into the hands of the North Vietnamese at the end of hostilities.

FIGHTERS

F-8
CRUSADER: Ling-Temco-Vought carrier-based fighter used briefly by the Marine Corps and Navy during the early days of the war. It was the first mach-2 shipboard fighter in the world and is best known for its sharklike appearance and funny wing. Because the fuselage is so long, subjecting the tailpipe to the danger of striking the ground at high angles of attack, the wing actually cranks up, allowing the fuselage to remain flat during takeoff and landing.

F-101
VOODOO: McDonnell Aviation. The interceptor variant was used primarily for air-to-air strip alert until replaced by F-4s, while the reconnaissance version was employed in North and South Vietnam as well as Laos.

F-102
DELTA DART: General Dynamics delta-platform interceptor used on strip alert until replaced by F-4s.

F-106
DELTA DAGGER: General Dynamics follow-up to the 102. Originally designed to be part of the SAGE system for air defense developed in the fifties but never finished, the 106 sported a larger power plant than its predecessor. Because there

was little threat of North Vietnamese air strikes into the South, it too was replaced by the Phantom.

RECONNAISSANCE

F-3D (aka F-10)
SKYKNIGHT (Whale): Douglas Aircraft two-seat fighter used during the early days of the war by the Marine Corps for ELINT and ECM.

RF-4
Photo version of the Phantom used by Air Force and Marines.

RF-8
Photo version of the Crusader used by Navy and Marines.

OV-1B
MOHAWK: Grumman twin turboprop sensor aircraft equipped with sniffers (a troop detection device), SLAR (Side Looking Airborne Radar) pod, IR (Infrared), and other imagers designed for tactical battlefield support. Used exclusively by the Army.

SR-71
BLACKBIRD (Habu): Lockheed "Skunk Works" special. Certainly the world's fastest, highest flying air-breather and likely to retain that title forever.

COMBAT SUPPORT AND GUNSHIPS

O-1
BIRDDOG: Cessna single-engine high-winged tail-dragger, whose ability to get low and slow made it the optimum spotter airplane in the war. Unfortunately, these characteristics made them meat on the table to enemy gunners. The intrepidity of their aircrews was without parallel in fixed-wing aviation during the Vietnamese war.

O-2
SUPER SKYMASTER (Push-me, Pull-you; Mixmaster): Cessna twin-engined FAC aircraft. Used by Air Force FACs in

South Vietnam and Laos. Although they enjoyed twin-engine reliability and excellent downward visibility, their mission was a hard and dangerous one.

OV-10

BRONCO: North American twin turbopro counterinsurgency aircraft built under LARA (Light Armed Reconnaissance Aircraft) funding and initially slated for the Marine Corps. Both the Air Force and the Marines made use of the plane for forward air control missions, and while it was faster and more rugged than the O-2, it was still in jeopardy in heavily defended areas.

TA-4

The two-seater version of the scooter, which was used by Marine FACs to work the Ho Chi Minh Trail during daylight hours in search of trucks or other activity.

C-47

SKYTRAIN (Puff the Magic Dragon): Douglas DC-3 equipped with miniguns and used for night close air support and flare drops.

C-117

(Hummer): Stretched version of the C-47 used by Marines for transport (MARLOG) and flare missions.

C-119

FLYING BOX CAR (Two A-1s flying wing on a Dempster Dumpster): Convair twin-boomed cargo plane equipped with miniguns and flares for night troop-support missions.

C-123

PROVIDER: Fairchild medium-haul cargo aircraft designed to operate out of small and unprepared strips, it earned the reputation as a "go anywhere-do-anything" workhorse.

CV-2

CARIBOU: DeHavilland (Canadian) light transport with exceptional short- and soft-field capabilities. With a little wind down the runway, it could take off in less than the distance of the runway's throat—a matter of not more than 250 feet.

CV-7

BUFFALO: DeHavilland big brother to the CV-2, capable of hauling up to forty-one combat-laden troops.

C-130

HERCULES (Herky Bird): Lockheed medium transport used by the Air Force and Marine Corps for supply and the latter for air refuelling. Sporting the same power plants as the Lockheed P-3 Orion (Electra in its civil guise), the C-130 was the premier trash hauler of the war, flying into strips that would make you shudder at the thought. A marvelous bird.

EC-121

CONSTELLATION: Military version of Lockheed's successful piston-driven airliner, configured with a monstrous radar sail on its back. These provided much of the airborne command and control of fighter aircraft over the North and in Laos.

KC-135

STRATOTANKER: Boeing's precursor to its civil 707, used by the Air Force for air refuelling. Refuelling is accomplished by the boom operator, who directs a "stinger" into the refuelling recess of the recipient, who flies a position below and slightly aft of the KC-135. The recent upgrade to turbofans will allow the KC-135 to remain in service into the next century. Not bad for America's first jet airliner.

C-141

STARLIFTER: Lockheed intercontinental medium jet transport. Although the aircraft saw less tactical duty in Vietnam than the C-130, it has emerged as the Air Force's first-line trash-hauler.

HELICOPTERS

OH-6

LOCH (Sperm): Hughes light observation helicopter capable of carrying a crew of two and four combat-laden troops in the aft cargo area. The 101st Airborne had a bunch of these, which they used for beating up the elephant grass. Light, fast, and nimble, they'd zip back and forth looking for enemy troops, and when they'd find some, they'd sit on them while calling in artillery or air.

UH-1

IROQUOIS (Huey; Huey Slick; Huey Gunship): Bell assault support helicopter used for nearly every mission you can imagine: transport, cargo, troop carrying, medevac, spotting, and, most ferocious of all, blasting away with miniguns and rocket pods.

CH-46

SEA KNIGHT: Boeing twin-boomed medium transport helicopter, capable of moving 4,000 pounds of men and/or supplies 100 miles at 150 miles per hour.

CH-53

SEA STALLION: Sikorsky heavy hauler used by the Marines for transporting troops and materiel.